GLOBAL DEBATES, LOCAL DILEMMAS

Sex-selective Abortion in Contemporary Viet Nam

GLOBAL DEBATES, LOCAL DILEMMAS

Sex-selective Abortion in Contemporary Viet Nam

TRAN MINH HANG

Australian
National
University

PRESS

VIETNAM SERIES

In memory of my father and for my family

ANU PRESS

Published by ANU Press
The Australian National University
Acton ACT 2601, Australia
Email: anupress@anu.edu.au

Available to download for free at press.anu.edu.au

ISBN (print): 9781760462420
ISBN (online): 9781760462437

WorldCat (print): 1079011471
WorldCat (online): 1079011443

DOI: 10.22459/GDLD.2018

Cover design and layout by ANU Press

Contents

Acknowledgements

There is a Vietnamese saying: '*Uống nước nhớ nguồn* [When drinking water, remember its source]'. This book would not have been possible without the contribution of numerous people and institutions.

I owe a profound debt of gratitude to the study participants for contributing their valuable time and for sharing with me the intimate details of their lives. This book is dedicated to advocates for women's reproductive health in Việt Nam.

This research was supported by the Harvard–Yenching Institute. I am thankful for the kind assistance of the institute's staff, especially Professor Tu Weiming, Professor Elizabeth Perry, Dr Nguyễn Nam and Mrs Susan Alpert. This book is based on my PhD thesis, which was completed at The Australian National University. The book was made possible by a generous grant from the 2015 ANU Vietnam Writing Fellowship and the 2017 ANU Publication Subsidy Fund. I would like to thank Professor Ken George, Melissa Orr and Anthony Chan for their great support, and Dr Carolyn Brewer, Jan Borrie, Emily Hazlewood, Teresa Prowse and staff of ANU Press for their assistance in editing and preparing this book for publication.

I am most deeply indebted to Professor Philip Taylor, who provided me with unflagging support throughout my studies and helpful advice on all the steps in writing this book. I benefited a great deal from the expert advice provided by members of my supervisory panel: Professors Philip Taylor, Tine Gammeltoft, Kathryn Robinson and Terence Hull, and Associate Professor Christine Phillips. I am indebted to Professor Annika Johansson, Professor Monique Skidmore and Dr Jennifer Alexander for their intellectual support. I am grateful to my colleagues at The Australian National University. My heartfelt thanks also go to Professor Kent Andersen and Professor Alan Rumsey, as well as Stephen Meatheringham, Fay Castles, Jo Bushby and Pen Judd for their generous support in smoothing out administrative issues.

In Hà Nội, I benefited from the cooperation and friendship of Dr Nguyễn Quốc Anh, Dr Nguyễn Duy Khê, Nguyễn Huy Bạo, Nguyễn Văn Minh, Phạm Ngọc Bỉnh, Vũ Thị Vân, Hoàng Tú Anh and Nguyễn Song Hà. I am also thankful for the assistance provided by the following institutions and organisations: the General Office for Population and Family Planning, the Department of Maternal and Child Health of the Ministry of Health, the health promotion consultancy group CIHP, and the hospitals and clinics where I conducted this research.

I wish to express my gratitude to all staff of the Institute of Anthropology in Hà Nội, with particular thanks to Associate Professors Phạm Quang Hoan, Vương Xuân Tình, Nguyễn Ngọc Thanh and Nguyễn Văn Minh for encouraging me and giving me leave of absence to go abroad for further study.

I am particularly indebted to my parents, my sisters and my brothers. I can never fully express my gratitude to my husband, Đỗ Văn Dũng, and my children, Đỗ Minh Quân and Đỗ Minh Hiếu, for providing me with continuous encouragement and emotional support.

Abbreviations

CVS	chorionic villus sampling
D&E	dilatation and evacuation
GOPFP	General Office for Population and Family Planning
ICPD	International Conference on Population and Development
IPAS	International Projects Assistance Services
IUD	intrauterine contraceptive device
LH	luteinising hormone
MOH	Ministry of Health
NSGs	National Standards and Guidelines for Reproductive Health Services
SRB	sex ratio at birth
UN	United Nations
UNFPA	United Nations Population Fund
US$	United States dollar
VND	Vietnamese dong
WHO	World Health Organization

Glossary

Bà cô	Spirit of unmarried female lineage member
Bất hiếu	Filial impiety
Cảnh giới	Specific realm
Canh trứng	Detecting ovulation
Cắt tử cung cả khối	Total hysterectomy
Cầu tự	Praying for a child
Chết oan	Unnatural death
Có thờ có thiêng; có kiêng có lành	To worship is to have sanctity; to abstain is to have goodness
Đàn lễ giải nghiệp	Incarnation-freeing ritual
Đầu thai của khác	Reincarnated into another family
Đổi Mới	Renovation
Lễ cầu siêu	Requiem ritual
Lễ cầu siêu cho thai	Requiem ritual for foetus
Phá thai to	Late-term abortion
Ruộng sâu, trâu nái, không bằng con gái đầu lòng	Having a piece of fertile land and a fertile buffalo is not as valuable as having a daughter as your first child
Tam nam bất phú, tứ nữ bất bần	With three sons, one will not be rich; with four girls, one will not be poor
Thừa tự	Male heir
Tổ tiên	Ancestor spirits
Trời sinh voi; Trời sinh cỏ	God gives elephants; God gives grass

Introduction

On a rainy day in the summer of 2003, I met Hương[1] and her husband in an obstetrics and gynaecology hospital in Hà Nội sitting on a bench outside the ultrasound room. I was in the hospital undertaking a research project on prenatal screening in Việt Nam.[2] The couple looked anxious as they waited for a three-dimensional ultrasound scan. Hương borrowed my pen to fill in her medical admissions form. I took this opportunity to ask her about her pregnancy. I learnt that the couple were doctors who worked for a provincial hospital about 100 kilometres from Hà Nội. They already had one daughter and Hương was 14 weeks pregnant. 'I will only fulfil my obligations to my husband's family if I have a son,' she said. 'If I have no son, my husband's lineage will be considered extinct.' The couple's worries began when a two-dimensional ultrasound scan at the provincial hospital where they worked revealed Hương's foetus was female. If they proceeded with this pregnancy and then later tried for a son, they would violate the country's two-child policy. So, they had come to Hà Nội for a three-dimensional scan[3] to obtain a more accurate diagnosis of the sex of the foetus. Hương confided to me tearfully that she would have an abortion if the ultrasound showed conclusively that she was carrying a female baby.

---

1   All personal names given in this book are pseudonyms.
2   Funded by the Danish International Development Agency, the project's title was 'Population, Development and New Reproductive Health Technology: Pre-natal screening in Việt Nam'.
3   Prenatal ultrasonography is the use of high-frequency soundwaves, which pass through the abdomen with the aid of a transducer to generate a video or image of the foetus. Three-dimensional ultrasonography is equivalent to two-dimensional ultrasound, but it also releases soundwaves from different directions and consequently makes a life-like image that plainly shows the characteristics of the foetus.

My conversation with Hương has stayed with me to this day. She was just one among a number of women I met in that hospital who were using ultrasonography to diagnose the sex of their foetus. Her story offered a glimpse into how new reproductive technologies were being utilised in Việt Nam, and it was my first evidence that some women were using them to prepare the way for, and obtain, a sex-selective abortion. Meeting Hương made me eager to learn more about such contemporary forms of reproductive agency and to better understand the motives, circumstances and experiences of women who use technology to change their reproductive destiny.

In the early 2000s, there was a dispute about whether the sex ratio at birth (SRB)—the ratio of males to females at birth—was increasing in Việt Nam. Hospital data on the SRB suggested that some Vietnamese families might have been resorting to sex-selective abortion. Data collected on all births at two major hospitals in 2001—one in Hà Nội (9,924 cases) and the other in Hồ Chí Minh City (29,437 cases)—indicated that mothers who were government employees tended to have a higher SRB for third-born or higher birth order children (Bélanger et al. 2003). The National Census of Population and Housing in 1999, however, recorded Việt Nam's SRB as 107, which was not far above the global standard (105 boys to 100 girls),[4] and demographers had no evidence on the use of sex-selective abortion in the country (Bélanger et al. 2003; UNFPA 2007). In a discussion of the issue, Danièle Bélanger and Khuat Thi Hai Oanh (2009) concluded that it remained an open question whether or not sex selection was occurring in Việt Nam.

Despite mounting evidence of an imbalanced SRB in Việt Nam (Guilmoto et al. 2009; UNFPA 2012, 2015), whether or not sex-selective abortions are occurring is in dispute. When I began research for this book in 2009, I believed an ethnographic study could provide a definitive answer to this question, while also offering insights into the circumstances of those involved in sex-selection practices and the meaning sex-selective abortion held for them. The research was driven by several questions: What factors drive sex-selective abortions? How have such abortions been able to take place? What do women feel about their abortions? And how does society respond to this phenomenon?

---

4   The average value of the SRB in human populations is 105. An SRB of between 104 and 107 is still considered a normal/balanced ratio.

While undertaking research in a hospital in Hà Nội between January 2009 and February 2010, I had the opportunity to meet 35 women who were in the process of having a sex-selective abortion. Thanks to the rapport I built with these women, I was able to explore their experiences in depth and gain insights into the circumstances and decision-making processes that led them to seek an abortion. I learnt about the methods used to determine the sex of the foetus and how the women elicited the assistance of doctors and other health professionals to procure an abortion. I came to understand the difficult emotional experiences that all parties to these procedures went through—before, during and after the abortion—and gained increased awareness of the complexities of the social response to such abortions.

As the first ethnographic study of sex-selective abortion in Việt Nam, this research sheds light on the social, cultural, institutional and personal contexts in which sex-selective abortion takes place. Focusing on the experiences of women who had sex-selective abortions and describing the role of abortion providers and others involved in these practices, the study illuminates the relationships and processes that enable these abortions to occur. Adopting an approach to ethnographic analysis inspired by phenomenological anthropology, the research provides insights into the lived experiences of those involved in sex-selective abortion. By locating women at the centre of this study and situating their actions within social and political contexts, the research examines why and how women undertake sex-selective abortions, and what they feel about their involvement in this practice. By exploring how regulations have impacted on the practice in both the public and the private sectors, I reveal how sex-selective abortion has been perceived, portrayed and acted on by significant state, quasi-state and civil society entities. Through an in-depth and multistranded analysis of sex-selective abortion in Việt Nam, the study contributes to the global and local debates about the factors that shape the phenomenon of sex selection.

To set the stage for my findings, I discuss recent research in a number of key areas that provides a preliminary basis for this investigation.

The context of sex-selective abortion in Việt Nam

The imbalance in the SRB appeared later in Việt Nam than in some other Asian countries, such as South Korea, India and China. Within a short period, however, Việt Nam's SRB rose from an estimated 106 male births per 100 female births in the year 2000, to 110.5 in 2009 and 112.6 in 2013. The SRB imbalance has increased in both rural and urban areas, but the rise has been most dramatic in the latter (UNFPA 2015). My ethnographic study was conducted in Hà Nội and the surrounding provinces. The registered population of Việt Nam's capital is approximately 7 million, but in fact is much greater because of a large number of unregistered migrants. Hà Nội is located in the centre of the Red River Delta, the most heavily populated region in Việt Nam, with a total population of 19,577,944 persons. The Red River Delta has recorded the highest SRB in the country—115.3 in 2009 and 122.4 in 2011. The high SRB and number of sex-selective abortions in Hà Nội and the Red River Delta occurred in the context of the transformation in the country's healthcare system and the provision of abortion services—changes discussed in the sections below.

In the 1980s, the government launched reforms that were highly successful at rejuvenating the economy. This process, known as *Đổi Mới* ('Renovation'), formally began in 1986. At the time of my research, Việt Nam's healthcare system—along with all other sectors of the economy—was in the midst of a dramatic transformation. This transformation has significantly affected people's lives nationwide, and especially in big cities such as Hà Nội. After the beginning of *Đổi Mới*, the implementation of a series of neoliberal health policy reform measures in 1989 affected the delivery and financing of Việt Nam's healthcare services. Private sector provision was first officially approved by the government in 1989, although it had undoubtedly existed before this. Private health services were often provided by traditional healers and government health workers operating after hours. The reforms have brought about a rapid commercialisation of health services. The private sector has evolved rapidly, particularly in urban areas. Private health clinics may have poorer equipment and higher fees than public ones, but they are usually more conveniently located, more flexible and offer a better care environment for their clients (Tipping et al. 1994).

Together with the economic and healthcare reforms, policies on population and abortion were reinforced. Although the Vietnamese Government's one-or-two–child policy was launched in the 1960s, after *Đổi Mới* the government began actively promoting a small-family norm of one or two children for each couple. In the 1990s, Việt Nam's one-or-two–child policy strongly focused on limiting family size through the provision of family planning services, including abortion (Johansson et al. 1998). Abortion has been legal in Việt Nam since 1954. Abortions were rare until the beginning of the 1980s, when they began to increase—first slowly and then rapidly during the late 1980s—at the same time as the reinforcement of the two-child policy (Johansson et al. 1998). Việt Nam has one of the highest abortion rates in the world (more than 1 million each year), with many women undergoing multiple abortions in their lifetime (WHO 1999). There were 37.5 abortions per 100 live births in 2004 and 35 in 2005 (MOH 2005, 2006).

In 2003, the Ministry of Health (MOH) published the National Standards and Guidelines for Reproductive Health Services (NSGs), which included a chapter on safe abortion. The NSGs stated that trained obstetricians, assistant doctors in obstetrics, paediatric specialists or trained midwives could legally perform abortions and that abortion services could be provided at three administrative levels of the health system: 1) abortion at six to 22 weeks gestation at central and provincial hospitals; 2) abortion at six to 12 weeks gestation at district health stations; and 3) abortion up to six weeks gestation at communal health centres. Private clinics were allowed to perform abortions up to six weeks gestation if they met criteria set out by the provincial health services. The revised guidelines in 2009 permitted medical abortion using a combination of mifepristone and misoprostol for gestation up to 63 days (gestation was limited at the district level to 49 days; the provincial level, 56 days; and central level, 63 days), and second-trimester abortion using a combination of mifepristone and misoprostol or misoprostol only for gestation of 13–22 weeks. According to the guidelines, first-trimester abortion by manual vacuum aspiration could be provided at central, provincial and district levels and communal health centres, while medical abortion was to be provided only at central and provincial levels. Dilatation and evacuation (D&E) have been introduced at two central and seven provincial hospitals. The cost of abortion services varies according to the period of gestation, the abortion method and the provider. In 2009, in public hospitals, a manual vacuum aspiration cost approximately US$4–7, a medication-induced abortion cost US$20–25 and D&E cost US$80–100. The cost of abortion services in the private sector also differed according to the gestation period and individual clinics, ranging from US$18 to US$100.

Việt Nam's transition from a planned to a market economy in the *Đổi Mới* process somewhat unexpectedly brought a renewed emphasis on the family in socioeconomic life and an expectation that households would take responsibility for their own socioeconomic wellbeing (van Praag et al. 2003; Nguyễn 2008). Culturally, the reforms ushered in a restoration of patrilineage and the reinvention of ancestor worship as part of the religious revival that swept the country. Such unexpected 're-traditionalising' has been documented by anthropologists (Werner and Bélanger 2002; Luong 2003; Taylor 2007). It is possible that such political, social and cultural changes create conditions that shape the sex-selective abortion phenomenon in the country.

The factors that shape the sex-selective abortion phenomenon

To situate the issue of sex-selective abortion in context, it is useful to think about the factors that shape such practices. Demographers and health researchers have used demographic data to speculate that the imbalanced SRB results from a number of factors, including the traditional preference for sons, the policy emphasis on small family size and the availability of new reproductive technologies (Bélanger 2002; Guilmoto 2007a, 2009; Phạm et al. 2008). However, it is necessary to find out more about the factors behind this trend and the experiences of those engaged in these practices. Microlevel ethnographic studies, therefore, are needed for a closer understanding of this complex issue and to situate the phenomenon within the context of people's everyday lives. In this section, I review research into the factors believed to be behind sex-selective abortion, highlighting calls to rethink the interaction of such factors in a multidimensional context.

Son preference

Preference for sons is considered one of the main causes leading to sex-selection practices (Croll 2000; Bélanger 2002; van Balen and Inhorn 2003). Son preference tends to be strongest in patrilineal and patrilocal societies (Goodkind 1999a), in which kinship, residence and customary inheritance practices, backed by religious and legal norms and institutional biases, accord men a central place in cultural, ritual and political roles, while devaluing or minimising the cultural, social and economic contributions of women (Ortner and Whitehead 1981; Croll 2000; Das 2007). In studying Vietnamese families, some authors have noted that son preference is a salient feature of the culture (Johansson et al. 1998; Phạm Văn Bích 1999). The main drivers of son preference are a need for familial labour, the value placed on the maintenance of patrilineages, regulations on the inheritance of family property and residence after marriage and social norms about the roles of sons and daughters in supporting their parents. In Việt Nam's traditional agricultural society, labour was at a premium. Farming families needed males for heavy work in their fields, and sons were considered necessary to maintain and extend the lineage. Worship of the ancestors was very important and only men could perform these rituals. If a man died without a son, his lineage was considered broken.[5] In their old age, parents lived with their oldest son; therefore, the son inherited the family property. In return, the son supported his elderly parents. In contrast, a daughter would be married early and live in her husband's house after marriage. She henceforth would provide little or no support for her original family; hence, any 'investment' in a daughter would be lost to the family. Daughters were considered 'flying ducks' because they were lost to their parents after marriage (Johansson et al. 1998; Phạm Văn Bích 1999; Tran 1999).

Such traditional values may no longer be relevant in the contemporary era. For instance, urban households have no need for labour for heavy agricultural work. Cadres who obtain the old-age pension do not need to depend on their children economically. Socialist reforms and, more recently, globalisation have led to a reevaluation of traditions and the

---

5   The minimum requirement for the observation of patrilineal ancestor worship is that a family must have at least one son, who is required to perform the rites. This suggests the priority accorded to sons in ancestor worship should be described as a 'son requirement' rather than a 'son preference'.

introduction of new norms and values. One may therefore wonder what role traditional norms and the value of son preference play in contemporary Việt Nam, and whether there has been a change in the value placed on sons.

Population policy and low fertility rates

Contemporary manifestations of son preference are also activated in part by the modern phenomenon of declining family size (Goodkind 1999a). Demographers assert that rapid fertility decline has created a new demographic environment and a demand for proactive sex selection (Löfstedt et al. 2004; Guilmoto 2009). However, some researchers emphasise that prenatal sex selection is rooted not simply in son preference and/or low levels of fertility; they argue that prenatal discrimination against daughters is also augmented by population policies. Under government pressure, parents' reproductive options are constrained, leading many to try to ensure they have at least one son among the limited number of children they are allowed (Goodkind 1999a; Jing-Bao 2010). The impact of changing policy on population outcomes, including on the SRB, has been discussed by international organisations, policymakers and social scientists. Daniel Goodkind (1999a) and others argue that contemporary manifestations of son preference are accentuated in the modern context of small families because the fewer children parents have, the lower is their probability of having a son (Das Gupta 1987; Gu and Roy 1995; Das Gupta and Bhat 1997). Analysing the SRB in Việt Nam, Christophe Guilmoto (2009) believes the rapid decline in fertility has undoubtedly created a new demographic environment for sex selection. Although demographers have hypothesised that low fertility encourages people to seek sex-selective abortion instead of having additional births, they often have no empirical evidence to support this argument. Moreover, our understanding of how the decline in fertility or in the allowable number of children in Việt Nam is perceived by parents and articulated in their reproductive decision-making and behaviour is still very limited.

The available evidence suggests that the interaction between population policy and what might be termed traditional reproductive preferences is quite complex. Annika Johansson et al. (1998) indicate that the need for sons is still strongly felt in North Vietnamese culture. In addition, they note, the one-or-two–child policy created potentially contradictory pressures on women. On the one hand, women who had not had a son were distressed about not producing a male heir. On the other hand, they felt pressure from local authorities to stay within the two-child limit (Johansson et al. 1998). What remains to be ascertained is whether this combination of factors is inducing parents in Việt Nam to seek sex-selective abortion. Also crucial is shedding light on the interaction between these different factors and how they are weighed by individuals as they make their reproductive decisions.

Availability of new reproductive technologies

In its guideline note on prenatal sex selection, the United Nations Population Fund (UNFPA) enumerates the various stages and strategies of sex selection: preconception (for instance, sperm sorting); reimplantation (for instance, in-vitro preimplantation genetic diagnosis, followed by implantation of an embryo of the desired sex); sex selection during pregnancy (for instance, using ultrasound, followed by sex-selective abortion); and postnatal methods (for instance, feticide, infanticide or neglect—with respect to nutrition, vaccination, curative care, abandonment and so on) (UNFPA 2009b). The new prenatal diagnostic techniques involve the use of two main technologies, amniocentesis and ultrasound. New reproductive technologies, especially ultrasound, are often considered one of the main causes for the rise in the SRB. Sex-determination tests became big business shortly after being introduced in India in the 1970s. As the number of clinics providing tests grew, competition pushed down the price of these services, making them more affordable to the lower middle class. In China, starting in the 1980s, ultrasound machines became widely available throughout the country for checking intrauterine contraceptive devices (IUDs) and access was free as part of the country's family planning program. New reproductive technologies for sex selection are now widely available in many countries.

Demographers suggest the rise in the SRB is closely linked to the increase of sex-selective abortion and the introduction of ultrasound and amniocentesis in the late 1970s (Hull 1990; Guilmoto 2007b). For instance, Terry Hull (1990: 74) notes the possible use of ultrasound to determine the sex of a foetus, leading to subsequent abortion if it is of the unwanted sex:

> Ultrasound technology for monitoring foetal development can also be used to determine the gender of a foetus … Despite the technical difficulties of the procedure and the regulations against its use for the purpose under discussion, the growing availability of ultrasound technology makes it easier for women to determine the gender of second and higher parity births and to obtain gender-specific abortions.

Ultrasound is one of the most common new reproductive technologies in Việt Nam.[6] Most district health centres and provincial and central-level hospitals have ultrasound machines and, in urban areas, most private clinics have a machine. At present, the price for a two-dimensional ultrasound scan is VND50,000–100,000 (US$2.5–5),[7] and for a three-dimensional ultrasound scan, VND200,000–300,000 (US$10–15). These prices are reasonable for most urban women, although they are prohibitive for the rural poor. Recent studies in Việt Nam have found that ultrasound is routinely being overused in pregnancy. One study found that, on average, women undergo six to seven scans during each pregnancy (Gammeltoft and Nguyễn 2007). In most European countries, it is national policy to conduct one or two scans during pregnancy (Marinac-Dabic et al. 2002). The World Health Organization (WHO 2002) has noted that the use of ultrasonography in pregnancy is not warranted in developing countries.

The practice of sex determination raises a number of ethical questions. Studying new reproductive technologies in China, Lisa Handwerker (2002) concluded that sex determination through prenatal diagnosis followed by abortion of a female foetus became widespread in that country, resulting in millions of girls never being born. She warns of the serious bioethical issues related to the use of new reproductive technologies such as the right to life, the right of free choice and equality of rights for male and female children (Handwerker 2002). Despite the disturbing ethical questions raised by these uses of technology, some believe these technologies could benefit women and their foetuses. Medical professionals consider ultrasonography a revolution for obstetrics. New reproductive technologies have the capacity to not

---

6   When I refer to new reproductive technologies used in sex selection in Việt Nam, I focus on ultrasonography in particular. Other new technologies such as amniocentesis, chorionic villus sampling (CVS) and in-vitro fertilisation (IVF) are rarely used because of their high cost and the high level of technical skill needed to administer them.

7   The exchange rate for Vietnamese Dong (VND) to United States Dollar (USD) is around VND20,000 to US$1.

only subordinate women, but also give them control over their own bodies (Sedlenieks 1999). Others argue that the availability of new technologies for sex selection, including abortion, could replace older and less 'humane' methods of sex selection, including infanticide and infant neglect (van Balen and Inhorn 2003). The ethics of sex selection and the use of ultrasound have been intensely debated by scholars, but often absent from these debates are the voices of the people who are undertaking these practices.

New reproductive technologies, especially ultrasonography, are often considered to be among the main causes for the rise in the SRB (Patel 2007; Hvistendahl 2011). Demographers suggest the rise in the SRB is closely linked to sex-selective abortion and the development of ultrasonography and amniocentesis in the late 1970s (Hull 1990; Guilmoto 2007b). These technologies were introduced to Việt Nam in the late 1980s and have become widespread in provincial hospitals since the mid-1990s. The use of ultrasonography in obstetrics and gynaecology is booming in Việt Nam; however, very little is known about how women use such scanning and how this technology is involved in the decision to have a sex-selective abortion.

In the global context, the role of reproductive technologies in sex selection has been widely debated. Some authors suppose that the rapid progress of SRB imbalances in Asia is most commonly related to the progress of ultrasound technology (Guilmoto 2007b; Patel 2007; Hvistendahl 2011). For example, Mara Hvistendahl's (2011) insistence on the global context of sex selection and the responsibilities of those supplying the ultrasound technology that facilitates it adds a vital contribution to this debate. However, she pays less attention to the local or 'demand-side' dimensions of the proliferation of new reproductive technologies in the countries where sex selection is occurring. Many questions remain unanswered. What are the responsibilities of the various governments, healthcare managers, private businesses, clinics and sonographers involved in utilising these imported technologies? In postsocialist countries such as Việt Nam, how does the rapid adoption of technology relate to the decline of the state's once central role in economic and social management, and to the devolution to households of the responsibility for their material wellbeing and their own reproductive decision-making? How does this modern technology fit within a preexisting spectrum of traditional techniques and practices for achieving desired reproductive outcomes, and do they coexist? My study examines one use of ultrasonography as part of a new reproductive trend: sex selection. Studying the role of ultrasonography in sex determination and sex-selective abortion, my case studies contribute to an understanding of the impacts of the transfer of new medical technologies to developing countries.

The experience of sex-selective abortion

Understanding sex-selective abortion in Việt Nam involves asking not only why they are occurring, but also how they are practised, and what such practices mean to those who engage in them. Addressing these aspects of the problem entails identifying the people who engage in sex selection and their social characteristics—what motivates them, what procedures they follow and how the practice of sex selection impacts on them physically, psychologically and socially. It also involves an exploration of the social and cultural contexts in which sex-selective abortion takes place and of the health system that both supplies and ostensibly regulates such practices.

Sex-selective abortion is an illicit practice in Việt Nam—and is widely seen as violating ethical and spiritual precepts and engendering considerable emotional turmoil in its participants. One central puzzle this book seeks to solve, therefore, is how a practice that is so heavily proscribed and controversial on so many levels can even occur. One answer to the riddle is compartmentalisation. There is no single actor or set of relationships that can be held solely responsible for sex-selective abortion and no single point at which a sex-selective abortion takes place. Instead, sex-selective abortion can be conceptualised as a set of procedures that unfolds over a number of stages, in different places, using a variety of different technologies and involving a series of discrete decisions taken by a range of actors. I suggest therefore that it is illuminating to adopt a processual approach to analysing sex-selective abortion. Conceptualising sex-selective abortion as a process that unfolds over several distinct stages is useful, I contend, as it has the potential to shed light on how such troubling acts take place, as well as illuminating the circumstances, relationships, experiences and reactions of the key actors involved.

By tracking the experiences of women undergoing sex-selective abortion, I discovered that the process could be divided into four stages: sex determination, decision-making, the abortion procedure and postabortion consequences and care. In the following pages, I discuss each of the phases to situate the case studies that make up the core of this book.

Sex determination

New reproductive technologies such as ultrasonography, amniocentesis and chorionic villus sampling (CVS) have been embraced throughout the world and are appreciated for their many positive applications in reproductive health. However, they have also been deployed in unforeseen ways, including for sex selection on a massive scale in some Asian societies. With its advantages of a high accuracy rate, low expense compared with other methods and ease of access, ultrasonography has become a popular method for determining the sex of a foetus (Hull 1990; Croll 2000; Guilmoto 2007a). A number of studies report that ultrasound machines are being used primarily for sex determination (Das Gupta 1987; Johansson and Nygren 1991; van Balen and Inhorn 2003). According to one survey, one of the main reasons for using ultrasound scanning in Việt Nam is to identify the sex of a foetus (Nguyễn et al. 2005).

One of the salient local factors in the domestication of this 'global' technology is its entrenchment in the Vietnamese public health system. Ultrasonography has become an indispensable technology in all matters relating to maternal and child health. In previous studies, Tine Gammeltoft and her colleagues looked at the use of ultrasonography for checking foetal anomalies (Gammeltoft and Nguyễn 2007; Gammeltoft 2008; Gammeltoft et al. 2008). These studies contend that a shift has occurred in Việt Nam's population health policies, from concerns about the size of the population to an increasing focus on population quality. This shift is informed by concerns about the potential strains on the public health system and on individual families incurred by the birth of excessive numbers of disabled or unhealthy children. Ultrasonography is being used extensively to detect foetal anomalies, and foetuses deemed abnormal are in most cases aborted on the recommendation of medical staff, broadly in keeping with national population health priorities. In short, the technology is being widely used to prosecute

Việt Nam's population health agenda. Considering the technology is already being used in the crafting of a demographically 'high-quality' population, I ask whether its use for sex selection represents a personalisation and privatisation of that public health agenda, as individuals and families seize the initiative and use the technology to craft their desired reproductive outcomes.

Ultrasonography represents an accurate and effective technique for identifying the sex of a foetus, and it is likely that the enthusiastic embrace of it in Việt Nam is in large part related to its perceived efficacy in facilitating desired reproductive outcomes. A survey of preconception and prenatal sex-determination practices, however, reveals that demand for 'traditional' practices has not dimmed, suggesting the new technology has not entirely supplanted traditional methods of sex selection. How are we to account for the existence of a vibrant and pluralistic market for traditional and modern sex-determination techniques? How does ultrasonography interact with preexisting methods to affect birth outcomes? What does this reveal about how women experience sex determination and the local expectations they bring to the new technologies? This research draws a portrait of patterns of sex determination and situates the use of ultrasonography in the context of the lives of the women who use it and other sex-selection practices. In Chapter 1, 'Chasing the gender dream', I explore the 'traditional' and 'modern' methods of sex determination that are being utilised in Việt Nam. In particular, I describe the motivations, circumstances and experiences of those seeking to determine the sex of their foetus. The chapter explores the application of new 'global' reproductive technologies such as ultrasonography to sex determination in Việt Nam.

Sex-selective abortion decision-making

Autonomy is a key concept when looking at decision-making. A number of factors influence women's autonomy in making reproductive choices, including ideology, national and international population policies, the availability of means for fertility regulation, new reproductive technologies and social barriers (Gupta 1996). The differences between women such as ethnicity, class or socioeconomic position and accessibility to resources, including knowledge, contribute to the differences in their levels of autonomy. Els Postel-Coster

(1991) supposes women's reproductive choices take place in, and are dependent on, their social context. Women's choice depends on their specific socioeconomic relations, political environment and culturally determined ideas about women and motherhood. As Jyotsna Gupta (1996: 7) points out, 'to study autonomy means studying ideas and structures of society which have a bearing on the measure of autonomy an individual can exercise'. These insights build on those raised by critical feminist researchers who have analysed how interlocking factors of power, class and ideology delimit the idealised notion of women's autonomy (Petchesky 1987; Rapp 2000; Mitchell 2001).

While feminists argue about the individual 'choices' and 'rights' assumed by Western liberal thought, this framework has found little favour in Asian cultural contexts (Lock and Nguyen 2010). One might ask whether the notion of individual autonomy assumed in feminist discourses on the 'right to choose' is appropriate for the cultural setting in Việt Nam. Looking at social shaping of abortion choices among Vietnamese women who had an abortion because their foetus were malformed, Gammeltoft (2014) argues that such choices were less a question of what an individual preferred to do than a matter of with whom they belonged, and a question of what demands were placed on them. She concludes by linking abortion choice to social belonging—belonging as state discourse, belonging as social practices and belonging as loss (Gammeltoft 2014). I wonder whether these findings hold true in the case of sex-selective abortion. In this research, I try to explore the social circumstances of individual women who are undergoing the process of sex-selective abortion decision-making to understand how these factors affect them. I also attempt to understand how women balance the different expectations and advice they receive when deciding to abort a female foetus. The structural factors—such as the distribution of economic, political and institutional resources—that are fundamental to the level of control women have over their decision-making and how cultural processes shape the contexts and meanings of their reproductive decisions are considered in Chapter 2, 'Sex-selective abortion decision-making: Beyond "a woman's right to choose"'.

Abortion procedures

Sex-selective abortion is usually conducted in the second trimester of pregnancy. Globally, there are often greater restrictions on abortion in the second trimester than on those in the first. Women confront a number of barriers to accessing such abortions—for instance, laws and regulations, lack of services and trained providers, high cost and extensive time demands (Comendant and Berer 2008). Hoàng Tuyết et al. (2008) indicate other barriers to Vietnamese women accessing second-trimester abortions, such as complicated administrative procedures and unfriendly abortion providers. I assume that women having a sex-selective abortion meet even more barriers in light of the fact that such a procedure is illegal. These suppositions are verified by this research.

Also, in terms of personal ethics, many abortion providers believe that sex-selective abortions are unethical. There are psychological consequences of terminating a pregnancy that are seldom reported, relating to the conflicting feelings experienced by abortion rights advocates and by healthcare practitioners themselves. This research gives an ethnographic account of how sex-selective abortion is conducted, and how its providers balance their potentially conflicting position as suppliers of medical care, as cultural consociates of abortion-seeking women and as professionals and citizens bound by the regulations prohibiting sex-selective abortion. The moral dilemmas of abortion are understood through the abortion practitioners' views, as well as by considering the limitations that their rights, duties and obligations impose on the receipt of healthcare services and sex-selective abortion procedures. This book covers interactions with the spectrum of social actors and health institutions implicated in sex-selective abortion. Chapter 3, 'Sex-selective abortion: Dilemmas in the silence', helps us understand the dilemmas faced by women having sex-selective abortion and the other people involved, and points us towards deeply grounded sociocultural tensions within contemporary Việt Nam.

Postabortion consequences and care

Understanding how personhood is conceived in Việt Nam's specific cultural circumstances is a precondition for unravelling and understanding the moral conflicts that infuse the process of sex-selective abortion in the country. Gammeltoft (2010) has demonstrated that abortion in Việt Nam is constructed as a sin and that it often poses intense moral quandaries for parents, many of whom address their feelings of guilt by making ritual offerings of forgiveness to the aborted foetus. Sex-selective abortion is potentially even more morally fraught, pitting acts conducted in deference to Confucian concepts of filial piety and state family planning guidelines against Buddhist conceptions of such acts as sinful. What cultural or religious ideologies exist in Việt Nam to frame or constrain the practice of sex-selective abortion? In what ways might women who undertake such abortions negotiate the social sanctions and moral proscriptions against such practices? Also relevant is an exploration of Vietnamese notions of foetal personhood, agency and identity. What relationships with and obligations to the foetus are engaged or violated by the practice of sex-selective abortion? Is a mother's relationship with the foetus influenced by traditional Vietnamese spiritual beliefs that construe that relationship as ongoing—or indeed that accord posthumous agency to the aborted foetus?

In keeping with its emphasis on the processual and experiential dimensions of sex-selective abortion, and its methodological focus on women as reproductive agents, this research is concerned with the effects on the mother of undergoing a sex-selective abortion. In addition to the moral dilemmas potentially thrown up by such procedures, the emotional complications are likely to be acute. Relevant to this question are several studies that discuss the emotional impacts of undergoing an abortion. For instance, Joanne Angelo (1994) found that grief after abortion was often hidden and remained undiagnosed for years. The psychological consequences seem more serious for women having an abortion in situations where abortion is considered sinful or is illegal. For example, women in Thailand who abort a pregnancy are considered to have committed a sin that is difficult to cleanse oneself of and that has consequences for their current life and future reincarnation. They are stigmatised and can never really cancel out such a serious sin (Whittaker 2004). In keeping with these findings and considering the illicit nature of sex-selective abortion, some of the additional potential consequences I anticipated encountering in this study were stigmatisation, loneliness and private suffering.

Research indicates that women's experiences of abortion are situationally specific. Several studies have addressed the relationship between experiences of abortion and social, cultural and political factors (McIntyre et al. 2001; Whittaker 2002; Andrews and Boyle 2003). Henry David (1992) finds the incidence of abortion-related mental problems is negligible in countries where abortion is legal and available. Mary Boyle and Jane McEvoy (1998) conclude that women's perceptions of abortion and their ways of coping with stigma and guilt are affected by the anti-abortion climate around them. Jean Peterman (1996), in a qualitative narrative analysis, demonstrates that women's abortion experiences are affected by their support systems, religious beliefs, desire for motherhood, opportunities and financial situation. Andrea Whittaker (2004) argues that the religious and institutional proscriptions against abortion in Thailand and the clash between biomedical and religious world views combine to make the experience of abortion in that country particularly traumatic and stigmatising.

Another consideration is whether late-term abortion is potentially more conflict-ridden and/or traumatic than others. In medical journals, abortions after the first 12 weeks of pregnancy are often described as late term. From a medical point of view, it is generally agreed that early abortions are preferable to late abortions, for, as the weeks go by, abortion becomes a riskier and more traumatic business for all concerned. Janet Hadley (1996) argues that late-term abortions require more soul-searching than those performed early in pregnancy. A number of studies have investigated women's emotions after late-term abortion (Rapp 2000; Gross 1999; Mitchell 2001; Gammeltoft 2002; Gammeltoft et al. 2008) and find that women and their partners have various emotional reactions to the procedure, including negative feelings typically associated with general psychological trauma, such as anxiety, grief, anger, loneliness, hopelessness, prostration and guilt. Looking at Vietnamese women's experiences after late-term abortion for foetal anomaly, Gammeltoft et al. (2008) observed that the women usually felt very sad, cried a lot and thought constantly about the child they had lost. They had doubts about their way of life, their reproductive capacity, their worth as wives and mothers, and their present and future positions in their kin group.

In short, existing research provides valuable insights into the moral dilemmas, psychological conflicts and social tensions experienced by women who undergo an abortion. It also addresses the effects on women's abortion experiences of prevailing ideological, institutional and cultural structures. As yet, women's feelings after a sex-selective abortion and the ways they cope remain largely unknown. In Việt

Nam, what political, moral, cultural and religious frameworks shape sex-selective abortion? What moral and emotional dilemmas do women experience? To what extent do they experience shame, stigma, loneliness and other forms of social suffering? How do women cope with these tensions and what forms of support are available to them? In addressing these questions, this research provides the first account of women's experiences of the consequences of sex-selective abortion. Chapter 4, 'After the abortion: Suffering, silence and spiritual relief', describes the range of emotions women experience during their journey through sex-selective abortion and provides a comprehensive understanding of women's experiences in dealing with physical and psychological recovery.

Social and political implications of sex-selective abortion

The issue of sex ratio imbalance and sex selection has received increasing attention from international and social organisations and governments. The UNFPA has been addressing this issue with its *Programme of Action Adopted at the International Conference on Population and Development* (UNFPA 1994), urging governments to prohibit female genital mutilation and prevent infanticide, sex-selective abortion and prenatal sex selection.

The politics of abortion are very controversial and focus largely on either a woman's right to choose or a child's right to life, and raise questions about rights to individual privacy. The principal controversy revolves around questions of who makes the decision concerning abortion—the individual or the state—and under what circumstances it may be done. Some believe the government has taken away the unalienable rights of the child by questioning at what point a foetus actually becomes a person and by recognising the rights of the mother over those of the unborn child.

Induced abortion is officially sanctioned in Việt Nam as a reproductive health service and an element of the government's efforts to provide reproductive choice and secure women's reproductive rights (MOH 2003). The Vietnamese Government's population policy aims to normalise abortion as a family planning measure. However, sex-selective abortion has been prohibited to reduce the imbalance of the SRB. Việt Nam has instituted a number of regulations on sex selection—for example, Decree No. 114, released in 2006, forbidding prebirth sex selection and the MOH's Decision No. 3698, also from 2006, forbidding prebirth sex selection using ultrasonography and abortion. While legalising abortion but prohibiting sex-selective abortion, the government faces a dilemma in striking the balance between women's rights, reproductive rights and customary rights. It must also balance making safe abortion accessible by enforcing stricter regulations on the procedure. In this book, I gather detailed information regarding the strengths and weaknesses of current policies and explore how regulations have impacted on the practice in both the public and the private sectors.

The experience of successful efforts to eliminate sex-selective abortion indicates that broad, integrated and systematic approaches need to be taken. Such approaches should involve governmental actors, social organisations and advocates to ensure that the social norms and structural issues underlying gender discrimination are addressed using the mass media and other social measures to encourage behavioural change (WHO 2011). Therefore, more research is needed to determine the drivers of sex selection and which policies and interventions work best in specific contexts.

The effects of sex selection are already considered a serious problem in some countries, such as China and India. Some experts—pointing to the association between an imbalanced sex ratio and violence—theorise that increasing numbers of poor, single men may lead to a rise in crime and social unrest (Gilles and Feldman-Jacobs 2012). My interest in this research is whether those involved in sex-selective abortion are concerned about the implications of these practices. I also address wider societal responses to these practices, discussing how sex-selective abortion has been perceived, portrayed and acted on by a number of quasi-state and civil society entities. Chapter 5, 'Social responses to sex-selective abortion', examines the social and political dilemmas surrounding sex-selective abortion and builds a profile of sex-selective abortion in Việt Nam, as a resource to enable governments, professionals and social organisations to establish policies, interventions and support services and contribute to the ongoing debate on sex-selective abortion.

Fieldwork

When I chose this topic for my doctoral research project in 2008, a number of my colleagues in Việt Nam advised me that sex-selective abortion was a sensitive issue. In other words, it would not be easy to conduct this research given the issue was not openly discussed and was illegal. Before starting this study in a Vietnamese hospital, I met the hospital manager to get his approval for my research proposal. After reading my application, he seemed anxious and stayed silent for a few moments. He told me the issue was a very sensitive one and studying abortion was never easy. I reassured him by telling him about the necessity of studying sex-selective abortion and my commitment to confidentiality. I had conducted previous research projects in this hospital and had some years of experience working with this manager; he trusted me, and I had always seen him as open-minded. At the end of the meeting, he signed my application, but reminded me of the sensitivity of this research. My research certainly is sensitive, considering that sex-selective abortion is a legally and morally transgressive practice, psychologically upsetting for those involved and fraught with public policy dilemmas.

The account presented in this book is based mainly on my ethnographic fieldwork in a hospital in Hà Nội from January 2009 to February 2010. It is based on interviews with 35 women who had a sex-selective abortion in this hospital and with the people around them. The ethnographic sample was developed gradually by following women I met in the hospital who identified themselves as seeking or having had a sex-selective abortion.

The most difficult obstacle to this research was how to approach these women and others involved in sex-selective abortion. I spent the first days of my fieldwork learning about the hospital's administrative procedures for abortion. I discovered the counselling room was a good starting point for connecting with women seeking an abortion (my core cases). In this room, women went through the preparatory administrative procedures, received abortion counselling and gave their written consent. The main data of this research are based on my observations and conversations with the women who identified themselves as having a sex-selective abortion and with their relatives when I accompanied them during their procedures in the hospital and made home visits. In September 2010, I spent two weeks following up with the women in my core cases. Together with the above activities, I accompanied relatives, colleagues and my core respondents when they used reproductive health services in private clinics. I took advantage of these visits to find out about the foetal sex determination and abortion services provided by private clinics. My understanding and knowledge have been gained from routine and repeated observations. I learned my way around the clinics and the homes of pregnant women, their families and other people around them. I adopted a proactive approach to participant observation by spending as much time with my core cases as possible to learn more about their decision-making, as well as their experiences after the abortion. Through my conversations with women's family members, I gained insights into how the social environment and kinship relations influenced the ways in which women exerted their agency in making reproductive decisions.

Other important components of this research were my observations of medical practitioners in public and private health facilities and formal and informal interviews with medical practitioners involved in sex-selective abortion. I also conducted interviews with doctors, nurses and sonographers working for the public hospital. I had frequent conversations with nurses in the counselling room and doctors in the Department of Family Planning, where abortions were performed. The purpose of working with these interlocutors was to gain insights into the experiences and perspectives of this group of key actors. I sought to ascertain their awareness of what they were involved in and to understand their motives.

In search of wider social perceptions of and responses to sex-selective abortion, I also conducted interviews with healthcare managers and regulators, policymakers and social workers. My purpose was to better understand the nature and impact of population and health policies, how government regulators perceive and respond to sex-selective abortion, how population health policies and regulations are monitored and whether there is any disjuncture between policy and practice. I also attended workshops on the SRB and sex-selective abortion in Việt Nam to observe the terms of the debate and approached managers, policymakers and social workers in the fields of population and health. Also, since March 2008, when I commenced this PhD research, I have accessed the websites of popular newspapers in Việt Nam and collected published materials on sex selection from bookstores and other outlets, both in print and online.

I have prepared this study convinced of the need to illuminate a practice that is rarely discussed openly and to spark informed debate on a matter of wide social relevance. At the same time, I am mindful that the experiences described are sensitive and emotionally fraught for many of those involved. I took a nonintrusive approach to this research, which was based on established relations of mutual trust, respect and openness with respondents. Honesty, openness and respect in my dealings with respondents were the essential prerequisites of gaining findings of any value into their world views and experiences. Pseudonyms have been used throughout the study in keeping with the undertakings of confidentiality made to my interlocutors. This strategy has been used to bring into the public sphere matters for informed debate without violating the privacy and wellbeing of the respondents who trusted and collaborated with me in this study.

This book represents a holistic account of the phenomenon of sex-selective abortion in Việt Nam. It describes in detail the technologies, procedures and settings that facilitate sex-selective abortion. Women are at the centre of my investigation of reproductive behaviour and the analysis situates their decision-making and experiences within the context of their families, communities and society. The study adopts an ethnographic and interpretative approach, paying close attention to the circumstances of those involved in sex-selection practices and the meaning sex-selective abortion holds for them. These findings are embedded in an analysis of contemporary values, policies and institutions that shows that the private dilemmas and forms of social suffering that constitute the experience of sex-selective abortion are matters of far-reaching political and social significance.

1

Chasing the gender dream[1]

Having a child today as compared to having children 20 years ago is quite different. These days we can make a conscious choice about whether or not to have children, and we can also choose the preferred sex of prospective offspring.

— Dr Bách, public hospital, Hà Nội[2]

When I was conducting fieldwork in Hà Nội in 2009, many people asked me whether there was any way to increase a woman's chances of conceiving a boy. Although a number of research and media reports describe the practice of sex selection, what is less well-known is how and why it occurs. The aim of this chapter is to contribute to a conceptualisation of how people experience and make sense of technology and other sex-selection methods to have a child of the desired sex, and how reproductive technologies affect women's lives, bodies and identities. Dealing with two phases of sex selection—preconception sex determination and sex diagnosis during pregnancy—this chapter explores the traditional and modern methods used to determine the sex of a foetus. It investigates the expectations women bring to these methods and discusses the socioeconomic context in which the market for such sex-determination services flourishes.

---

1   This phrase is borrowed from Jennifer Thompson's *Chasing the Gender Dream* (2004). The concept of 'gender' was introduced by feminists in the 1970s. The distinction between 'gender' and 'sex' is very important. Sex has a biological meaning, while gender is psychological, cultural and historical. According to Jyotsna Gupta (1996), gender theories result from imposing social, cultural and psychological meanings on biological sexual identities.
2   Bách is a pseudonym. The names of all the informants in this book have been changed to ensure their anonymity. In addition, because of the sensitivity of the topic, the location and date of the interviews are not always included.

Preconceptions of sex selection

Attempting to choose the sex of one's offspring is not a new concept. For centuries, a variety of 'home remedies' have been recommended for sex selection, such as the timing of intercourse in relation to ovulation, the position used during intercourse, the alteration of vaginal acidity and the mother's and father's diets. Not until the 1970s, however, did more sophisticated sex-selection techniques become commercially available. In this section, I explore the methods people use for preconception sex selection in Hà Nội today. As Tâm, a 41-year-old mother of two daughters, explained: 'I have combined both traditional and scientific methods to ensure I had a boy, but in the end, I found out I am carrying another girl.'

In contrast with the bustle usually associated with working hours, the corridor of the Department of Family Planning was quiet during this particular summer lunchtime. After a long time waiting in the heat and humidity, most patients had gone to find somewhere to have lunch and refresh. Tâm's husband was going out to buy her lunch, so, in the quiet of noon, Tâm and I sat outside the counselling room and she spoke to me sadly while holding a bottle of water.

Tâm was an accountant for a supermarket and her husband a teacher in a Hà Nội university. They had two daughters, one aged 13 and the other seven. When their youngest daughter was four years old, Tâm's husband decided he wanted to have a son, even though having a third child would violate the one-or-two–child policy and would affect her husband's career. 'My husband has a patriarchal nature. I have always followed his directives,' Tâm told me. She became pregnant soon after removing her IUD. 'At that time, I let it be natural, did not make any interventions. When I was 14 weeks pregnant, I had an ultrasound scan and the doctor said I was carrying a boy.' Needless to say, Tâm and her family were delighted to be having a boy. To guarantee her husband's promotion at work, Tâm had to move away and give birth to her son in secret. She left her son with her parents-in-law when he was only six months old. She and her husband sometimes visited the boy at weekends. Unfortunately, her son drowned in a pool when he was only 18 months old. It was very hard for Tâm to cope with this serious loss; she cried day and night and lost 5 kilograms in a month.

She tried to continue her story, but could not hold back tears, which she wiped away with her hands. I consoled her and gave her a paper napkin to dry her eyes. She clutched the water bottle tightly, and then sipped from it to calm her emotions. There was a short silence before she continued. 'I was not young, so I did not want to have more children. But my family-in-law, all they want is a boy. Being a good wife, I have tried to conform to the desires of my husband and my parents-in-law,' she said, her voice choking with emotion.

Tâm spoke louder when she told me of her plan to ensure she conceived another son. At the beginning of the lunar year, she went to the Hương pagoda and prayed for a son. The fortune teller there told her if she had a boy in the Year of the Tiger, he would bring good luck to her family. Tâm and her husband decided to have a child that year, but it had to be a boy, not a girl. Tâm went to healers for herbal decoctions, detected her ovulation over three months and followed the strict regimen and lunar calendar from Đỗ Kính Tùng's *Sinh con theo ý muốn* [*Having Babies of Desired Gender*] (2002). She tried everything she could to ensure she would have a boy. 'I have combined both traditional and scientific methods to ensure I had a boy, but, in the end, I found out I am carrying another girl,' she said hopelessly. Our conversation was interrupted when her husband returned with a cup of rice soup for her. I knew she needed a quiet space to have lunch, so I left her there.

Like Tâm, many Vietnamese women are using sex-selection services combining both traditional and scientific methods to try to meet the demand to have at least one son. The following are some methods of preconception sex selection women in Hà Nội are practising.

Ultrasonography

It was a Sunday afternoon in a very cold winter. My colleague, who was in the 22nd week of pregnancy, called me and asked whether I could accompany her to a private clinic to have an ultrasound scan. She told me she had found an obstetrics and gynaecology clinic whose owner was a 'famous' doctor.

The clinic was in the doctor's house in a small tortuous alley. The prenatal check room was also the ultrasound room. The room was about 15 metres square, tidy and contained a new three-dimensional ultrasound machine, which was connected to a large screen on the wall, on which patients could see their foetus during scanning. The ultrasound machine was next to a small examination bed and, to the left of the door, was a bench for those who were waiting. A small medicine cabinet and a patient care bed were separated from the rest of the room by a white curtain. On the wall there were some documents advertising the obstetrics and gynaecology services provided by the clinic and their price. One of the services available was 'detecting ovulation' (*canh trứng*), which cost VND100,000 (about US$6).

When we entered, the doctor was absorbed in scanning, while a nurse was writing the results in a medical book. Both ignored the other people in the room. A young woman was lying on the bed, having a vaginal ultrasonography. The doctor read the results out in a loud voice: 'The diameter of the left follicle is 3 mm; the diameter of the right follicle is 4 mm.' He then asked the woman to move to the patient care bed for a vaginal check. The doctor put on a glove and used his forefinger to check her cervix. He said to the nurse: 'Cervix opening size is 4.1.' After the examination, the young woman sat next to me while the doctor wrote in the medical book. I was curious and asked the young woman, 'Why did you have the vaginal check? How long have you been pregnant?' The young woman whispered:

> I came here to detect my ovulation. I just got married last week. My husband and my husband's family want to have a boy, so my husband told me to come here to detect my ovulation.

Our conservation was interrupted by the summons from the doctor. He gave the young woman some tablets and reminded her to follow the guidelines he had noted in her medical record. Before leaving, the woman asked the doctor diffidently: 'What are the implications of detecting ovulation? I do not as yet know what the reasons for detecting ovulation are.' The doctor laughed and replied:

> By detecting ovulation, we can determine when you are most fertile and when you should have intercourse in order to ensure a high probability of having a son. If you want to have a son, you should have more ultrasound scans. Today is Sunday, so you should come back on Wednesday. You may have to have ultrasound scans for several menstrual cycles before you conceive.

The term *canh trứng* ('detecting ovulation') appears on clinics' advertising signage and in the daily conversations of women in Hà Nội. Detecting ovulation has become a new 'reproductive fashion', and is used not only by women who already have daughter(s) and want to conceive a son, but also by women who want their first child to be a boy. Twenty-one of the 35 women in my case studies told me they had spent some months detecting their ovulation to find the ideal time to conceive a son. Thảo, the mother of two daughters, told me about her efforts:

> I met a woman in a private clinic when I was waiting to have a gynaecological check-up. She said she had ultrasound scans to detect her ovulation and had then conceived a boy. I asked her where had the ultrasound scans. She could not remember at that time, but she sent me the address by [text message] later. I had several ultrasonography investigations per month. Having determined my ovulation time, the doctor told me the appropriate method for intercourse to ensure I conceived a boy. I paid VND100,000 [US$5] for each ultrasound scan to detect the ovulation. I began to have … ultrasound scans every day from the 12th day to the 18th day of my menstrual cycle. When the doctor detected my ovulation day, she suggested the appropriate method of intercourse. The doctor told me what kind of food I should have. She said I should have vegetables and milk. She guided me on how to have intercourse, and she advised me to lie down with my legs crossed after intercourse. I had to follow the doctor's guidance. For example, the doctor [told me when it] was my ovulation time, and [that] I should have intercourse at 8 pm, [and] must do so punctually.

The amount of money the women spent on ovulation detection was considerable. On average, Thảo had to pay VND500,000 (US$25) for each visit and about VND1.5 million (US$75) during the three months she wanted to detect her ovulation. For women who had ultrasonography for more than 12 months, the cost was about VND5–6 million (US$250–300).

Using ultrasonography to detect ovulation has become popular in Hà Nội's obstetrics and gynaecology clinics, especially private ones. As one doctor told me: 'At the beginning, this method was used solely for infertility treatment, and then it has been misused for predicting ovulation to determine the sex of the child.' Some doctors in private clinics predict ovulation using a combination of ultrasonography, examination of the vagina and cervix and prescription medicine. The 'reputable' private clinics attract women with the doctor's success in diagnosing foetal malformation, detecting ovulation and determining the sex of the foetus. The situation described below was observed at a private clinic.

My sister-in-law and I attended a private clinic at 6.30 am on a Sunday. She was excited to inform me:

> I booked an appointment to have an ultrasound a week ago. This clinic is crowded because it is run by a famous doctor who is working for one of the biggest obstetrics and gynaecology hospitals in Hà Nội.

When we arrived, many people were already waiting outside the clinic. The husbands were drinking tea or coffee or eating breakfast in a nearby roadside shop while their wives waited. At 7.30 am, when the door opened, the women rushed to the reception desk where the nurse opened a notebook containing a long booking list. Some women were sent away because they had not made a booking. Only one woman, from Bắc Giang province, about 60 km from Hà Nội, was accepted for a scan without a booking. However, the nurse reminded her: 'Next time, you must book before coming here.' The nurse read out the names of the women on the booking list and gave them tickets. Most of these women sat in the waiting room, which was about 10 metres square. Some of those at the top of the list sat at the front of the ultrasound room, which was about 8 metres square and was equipped with a three-dimensional ultrasound machine. At 8 am, the tedium of waiting was relieved by the appearance of a doctor. He was clearly in a hurry and did not greet the waiting women. He turned on the ultrasound machine and urged the woman with the first appointment ticket to lie on the small bed so he could begin the scan.

I sat by the door, where four women chatted while waiting. Three were pregnant—14 weeks, 23 weeks and 35 weeks—and a fourth had no children and was trying to conceive a boy. She said:

> My husband is the only child in his family. My husband's family wants [me] to have a son, but I want to have a limited number of children. I have used this service to ensure that I have at least a son. If I have had a son, I need have only one child or I will not need to care about the sex of the next baby.

The woman who was 14 weeks pregnant already had a daughter. She had already had an ultrasound at another clinic two weeks earlier, where the doctor told her the sex of her baby was unclear because of its position. Now she was worried this new scan might also fail in determining the sex of her baby. The woman who was 23 weeks pregnant consoled the 35-week pregnant woman, saying:

If the doctors in this clinic do not tell you the sex of your baby, you should go to another clinic. But the doctors in this clinic usually tell me the sex of my baby when I ask. They sometimes tell me the sex of my baby when I do not ask.

While waiting for their scans, these women enthusiastically discussed the ways to conceive a boy and to determine the sex of a foetus. Talking about and knowing the sex of the foetus is a popular conversational topic at ultrasound clinics as well as in day-to-day life in Hà Nội.

Talking about detecting ovulation by ultrasonography, Dr Bách, a 58-year-old male doctor, told me:

Normally, the proportion of fertilisation of Y and X sperms is 50:50. With intervention, this proportion is higher, around 60–70 per cent, or even higher. Therefore, the rate of having a son is higher. At the beginning, this method was used in infertility treatment. But now, it is known that the rate of having a son is higher if conception occurs soon after ovulation. This principle helps people to determine the sex of the child before conception.

There is no large repository of evidence to which any doctor can point to to say that timing sexual intercourse around ovulation increases the chances of conceiving a son, although it does, of course, increase the chances of conception. Like Dr Bách, many practitioners use the magisterial language of doctors to convince clients the idea is true. One has to wonder how much practitioners' adherence to this idea is related to the fact it is a good earner. The best-known technique for influencing gender without the use of medical procedures is the Shettles method, described by David Rorvik and Landrum Shettles in *Your Baby's Sex: Now You Can Choose* (1980). The book was first published in 1971 and has been in print ever since. The method is based on the premise that Y sperms are smaller and more delicate but faster than X sperms, which are bigger, tougher and slower. Y sperms have more motility in the ovulatory mucus of the mid-cycle near ovulation; therefore, boys are more likely to be conceived. However, Ronald Gray (1991) performed the first meta-analysis of this method and showed that it did not work. In fact, he found there were more girls than boys conceived if intercourse was practised at this time. C. R. Weinberg et al. (1995) suggest the length of the follicular phase (the time between menstruation and ovulation) is related to the sex of the baby, and that cycles with shorter follicular phases are slightly more likely to result in male babies, while cycles with longer phases are more likely to result in females. This theory, however, has also been disputed. Gray and his colleagues (1998) then undertook a large prospective multicentre study that completely disproved the idea that the sex of the foetus can be selected through the timing of sexual intercourse. Even if doctors can detect ovulation, which they probably can, this will not increase the likelihood of conceiving a boy. But some research has been taken up selectively and forms the basis of a scientised consensus among the medical profession in Việt Nam. This may be in part because in Vietnamese culture the medical profession is organised hierarchically.

Interestingly, using the ovulatory mucus to determine ovulation is not encouraged in Việt Nam, although it is probably as effective as episodic ultrasonography and much more effective than 'counting days'. In contrast, in Australia, teaching women to detect changes in the ovulatory mucus is one of the first things doctors do when their patients want to conceive. Recognising changes in the consistency of the mucus is a method that can be entirely managed by women themselves, without technology. This raises questions about whether doctors and sonographers in Việt Nam are mainly interested in increasing their profits by encouraging the use of new reproductive technologies.

Ovulation prediction kit

As well as ultrasonography to detect ovulation, women have been advised to use ovulation prediction kits, the most popular variety of which is a urine-based kit.

The kits detect the luteinising hormone (LH) surge that occurs in the body before ovulation begins to help women work out the best time for intercourse. Ovulation generally occurs 24 to 48 hours after the LH surge. Most kits are relatively inexpensive and can be purchased at pharmacies or doctors' offices. There are many brands available—Acon, Wonfo, Clear-Blue and so on—and they vary in price from VND7,000 (US$0.35) to VND20,000 (US$1) per kit.

Lụa told me her story.

> I used the ovulation prediction kit. I started to use the kit after menstruation. I tested every day. I bought 10 kits, which cost VND70,000. On the 12th day of my menstrual cycle, I saw two lines on the kit, and then we had intercourse. I heard about this method from a colleague. If I use ultrasound to detect ovulation, it costs VND70,000 each time and I would need several ultrasound scans a month.

The ovulation prediction kit is considered a 'scientific' method of detecting ovulation. Women want to use this method because it is cheaper than ultrasonography and the kits can be used in the privacy of their own home.

Following the Chinese birth chart and the advice of fortune tellers

Some people believe that the position of the Moon at the moment of conception determines the sex of the foetus: a positive sign indicates the child will be a boy and a negative sign indicates a girl. Calculating this sign is difficult as it is based on the angular relationship between the Sun and the Moon. The Chinese birth chart is based on this theory and is related closely to lunar cycles. The chart predicts the sex of a child based on the mother's age and the month of its conception. Figure 1 shows a 'speculative calendar' book. The columns show the mother's age at conception and the rows show the month of conception—the two factors used to predict the sex of a child.

CÓ THỂ SINH TRAI HAY GÁI THEO Ý MUỐN

Tháng thụ thai \ Tuổi vợ	18	19	20	21	22	23	24	25	26	27	28	29	30	31	32	33	34	35	36	37	38	39	40	41
1	0	+	0	+	0	+	+	0	+	0	+	0	+	+	+	0	+	+	0	+	0	0	+	+
2	+	0	+	0	+	+	0	+	0	+	0	+	0	0	0	+	0	+	+	0	+	+	+	0
3	0	+	0	0	+	0	+	+	+	0	+	0	+	+	+	0	+	0	+	+	0	0	0	+
4	+	0	+	0	0	+	+	0	0	+	0	+	0	0	0	+	0	+	0	+	+	+	+	0
5	+	0	+	0	+	+	0	+	0	+	0	+	0	0	0	+	0	0	+	0	+	0	0	+
6	+	+	+	0	+	0	+	0	+	0	0	+	0	0	0	0	0	0	0	+	+	+	+	0
7	+	0	+	0	+	+	+	+	0	+	+	+	0	0	0	0	0	0	0	0	+	+	+	+
8	+	0	+	0	0	0	0	+	+	+	+	+	0	0	0	+	0	+	+	+	0	0	0	+
9	+	0	+	0	0	+	0	+	0	+	+	+	0	0	0	0	0	+	0	0	+	+	+	0
10	+	0	+	0	0	+	0	+	0	0	+	0	+	0	0	0	0	+	+	+	0	0	0	+
11	+	0	+	0	0	+	0	+	0	+	0	0	+	+	+	+	+	+	+	+	+	+	+	0
12	+	0	+	0	0	+	0	+	0	+	0	0	+	+	+	+	+	0	+	+	0	0	+	+

Chú ý: Bảng này là tài liệu của một triều đình phong kiến để các bạn tham khảo. Khi dùng bảng này, tuổi người vợ và tháng thụ thai đều tính theo âm lịch. Dấu + là trai, 0 là gái

Figure 1. A speculative calendar for predicting the sex of a child based on the mother's age and the month of conception. Such calendars are published annually in Việt Nam

Note: The explanatory text reads: 'This table is the document from feudal court records. When using this table, please remember the mother's age at conception and the months are calculated by the lunar calendar: (+) = boy; (0) = girl.'

Source: *The Speculative Calendar 2008*, p. 108.

According to ancient cosmology, a full lunar cycle lasts 12 years, with each year named after one of the 12 animals of the zodiac or *Chi* (Mouse [*Tý*], Buffalo [*Sửu*], Tiger [*Dần*], Cat/Rabbit [*Mão*], Dragon [*Thìn*], Snake [*Tỵ*], Horse [*Ngọ*], Goat [*Mùi*], Monkey [*Thân*], Chicken [*Dậu*], Dog [*Tuất*] and Pig [*Hợi*]). Many people still believe that year in which they are born will affect their personal characteristics and future. Most of the women I met in this study were due to give birth in 2010—that is, *Canh Dần* (Year of the Tiger). The Year of the Tiger is a good birth year for boys because they will be as strong as a tiger, while girls born in this year will face problems, such as finding it difficult to marry or becoming part of a broken family. Therefore, parents do not want to have a daughter in the Year of the Tiger. Each lunar year is also identified by the element-based *Can* system: 1. *Giáp*; 2. *Ất*; 3. *Bính*; 4. *Đinh*; 5. *Mậu*; 6. *Kỷ*; 7. *Canh*; 8. *Tân*; 9. *Nhâm*; 10. *Quý*. Women born in the *Can* year *Canh* will feel lonely. *Mậu* year babies will become widows. The year 2010, *Canh Dần*, was not a good one for having a female baby according to either the *Can* or the *Chi* systems. This system also requires both parents and their children to have compatible birth years. Incompatible ages include Mouse–Horse, Buffalo–Goat, Tiger–Monkey, Cat/Rabbit–Chicken, Dragon–Dog and Snake–Pig. The compatible years are Mouse–Buffalo, Cat/Rabbit–Dog, Snake–Monkey, Tiger–Pig, Dragon–Chicken and Horse–Goat.

Relying on a fortune teller to decide whether to have more children or to terminate a pregnancy was common among the women I met. Some followed the advice of fortune tellers who claimed to have the ability to predict the year in which a couple could conceive a son. Vân, a mother of three daughters, believed a fortune teller's advice that she and her husband could have a boy if she became pregnant in 2009, the year I met her. Her brother told me: 'My sister had her fortune told at the beginning of the year. She was told that she would have a boy in this year, so she tried to get pregnant.' Vân, who lived in a rural area and was educated to secondary school level, was not the only person to believe in the prognostications of fortune tellers. Lê, Cúc and Thương—all of whom lived in urban areas and held bachelor's degrees—had similar beliefs. Lê told me her story:

> The fortune teller said to my husband that we would have a boy this year, and then my husband persuaded me to get pregnant. I did not want to have more children, but I had to indulge him. (Lê, 31 years old, abortion at 12 weeks)

Other women wanted a son because they believed this would relieve their misfortune. Lụa told me:

> The fortune teller said my husband and my daughter were of incompatible birth years. If we had a boy in a Tiger year, the father and boy would be of compatible age, and it could reduce the incompatibility between the father and the daughter. (Lụa, 28 years old, 13 weeks pregnant)

Following a strict dietary regimen

Knowledge about the dietary requisites for conceiving a son has become increasingly widespread throughout Hà Nội. Following a strict diet is one of the most popular sex-determination methods—one women have learnt from anecdotes, published books, healers or even doctors. Lụa told me about her eating strategies aimed at conceiving a son:

> After having ultrasound scanning to check my ovulation, the doctor recommended that we [she and her husband] should eat more protein and have tonics. She advised us to eat potato and sapodilla. I did not eat eggs, but I ate a lot of potato and sapodilla during the course of one month. I also ate more meat and bean sprouts than usual. I did not drink milk at that time.

There are many anecdotes about diets and sexual positions that help people conceive a child of the desired sex. Books on these topics are widely available in bookshops—including in that of the obstetrics and gynaecology hospital where I conducted my research. These books include chapters on sex selection; some provide information about special diets, how to calculate ovulation and even ways to weaken the X sperms. All are bestsellers. The owner of one bookshop told me: 'We sell tens of these books a day. These books sell much better than anything else on our shelves.'

The following information is from a book offering guidance to conceive a child of the desired sex:

Having a son

For male

- Abstain from sex in the days prior to the conception attempt.
- Have intercourse only once during ovulation.
- Eat food high in potassium and sodium. Do not eat fermented food such as yoghurt.
- Sex position: The male partner should penetrate the female partner from above, thus ensuring that sperms have the appropriate conditions to go quickly to the uterus, then to the uterine tubes where the fertilisation occurs.

For female

- Soak the vagina in sodium bicarbonate solution before having intercourse. This solution helps to produce the appropriate alkaline environment in the vagina.
- Continue to lie down after having intercourse to keep the sperm in action. (Đỗ Kính Tùng 2002)

Thương, a woman hoping to have a son, read many of these books. She said:

> I have changed my regimen over several months. I need to eat salted food and supplementary nutrition such as sodium and potassium that are contained in banana, potato … Food that is rich in calcium should not be in the diet because it helps to have a girl baby. (Thương, 36 years old, two daughters, 15 weeks pregnant)

Eating is just the first step. The next step is detecting ovulation (*canh trứng*), which is not easy. Thương explained:

> I have had to go to a private clinic to have an ultrasound scan on the 12th day of the menstrual cycle every month. The doctor inserts a device into my vagina to check the ovisac size and to predict the ovulation around the middle of the menstrual cycle.

Thương had an ultrasound scan eight months after she began the regime, but had not yet managed to conceive—her 'project' was not yet finished. Sometimes her husband was not home during her ovulation; sometimes they 'met' too early. She also went to a private clinic in Hoan Kiem district that is famous for providing services to aid conception of 'a child of the desired gender'. The provider was the former head of a hospital department in Hà Nội. The doctor calculated Thương's ovulation for her and guided her through the regimen to follow. The doctor also pumped natri-bicarbonate solution into Thương's vagina to 'improve' the environment for the sperm.

The acid–alkali method of sex determination was developed between 1932 and 1942. In 1932, Felix Unterberger of Konigsberg, Germany, suggested that alkaline semen produced boys; therefore, a weak douche of bicarb soda (sodium bicarbonate) should aid in the conception of boys (cited in Quisenberry and Chandiramani 1940: 503). In the 1940s, repeated tests and experiments could not replicate the earlier results and the idea was disproven as a way of determining foetal sex (Quisenberry and Chandiramani 1940). Interest in the acid–alkali method faded; however, it has now flared up again in countries such as Việt Nam, along with the development of new sex-selection techniques.

In some cases, women who followed the directions in books on sex selection succeeded in having a boy. There is no scientific evidence that such techniques are guaranteed to produce boys; however, the information from these books has been circulated widely via photocopies or word of mouth. Thu told me:

> My neighbour has two daughters. She followed the directions in the book *Having Babies of Desired Gender* and she now has a boy. She gave me this book and advised me to follow the directions. She said that I would have a boy if I followed the directions in this book. (Thu, 23 years old, two daughters, 13 weeks pregnant)

Traditional medicine

One day, three months after having an abortion, Tâm called me, sounding excited. Her colleague had given her the address of a healer who could help couples conceive a son. Her colleague had used the herbs provided by this healer and consequently gave birth to a boy. Tâm and her husband wanted to try this herbal remedy. She asked me whether I wanted to accompany her on her visit to the healer. It was an opportunity for which I had been waiting a long time, so I was happy to accept her invitation. We went early the next morning to the healer's house, in a small town about 30 kilometres from Hà Nội.

It was not difficult to find the house as locals were used to providing directions. The healer's house was spacious, with a wide corridor with two long benches on which people could wait. A man wearing a large gold necklace welcomed us when we arrived, and we followed him to the guest room. He introduced himself as the healer's husband. The healer was sitting on a bed next to a table and writing something in a book. After an exchange of greetings, she asked Tâm and her husband about their children. When Tâm told her about their desire to have a son, the healer laughed loudly and said: 'No worries. You have found the right place. I can help you achieve your dream. My clients are from many areas, like Quảng Ninh, Thái Bình and Nam Định provinces, even from Korea.' The healer took Tâm's pulse and then her husband's and said:

> If you want to have a son, your left follicles should be stimulated. If your left follicles rupture, you will have a better chance of having a son. You should use my herbs to stimulate your left follicles. These herbs should be used for 20 days. It helps to improve your health, to stimulate your left follicles, and increase alkali in your womb. If you are lucky, you can get pregnant in the first month after using these herbal decoctions. If not, you should continue to use these herbs for another month. In the next month, you only need to use the herbal decoction for 10 days. You can come here and I will detect the ovulation day for you by feeling your pulse. But if you live far from here, you can detect the ovulation day with an ultrasound or ovulation test kit. In addition, you should boil dried perilla leaves and soak your vagina in this solution before having intercourse. You must eat and drink following these guidelines [she handed Tâm a printed sheet; see below]. From now on, you should abstain from sex until your ovulation day. If you have intercourse before the ovulation day, the chances of having a girl will be higher. These herbs cost VND600,000. (Herbal healer, Sơn Tây, Hà Nội, 2009)

Tâm paid the money for two big bags of herbs. When we left, two other couples were outside waiting for their turn. Tâm and her husband returned home, full of hope.

Guidelines for using herbal medicines

For wives

- The medicinal herb package is divided into 20 sachets.
- Boil the contents of each sachet with 1.5 litres of water and 1 teaspoon of sugar until the decoction has been reduced to 1 litre. Divide this decoction into three parts and drink before meals.

For husbands

- Have a full breakfast with rice and an aromatic banana.
- Have lunch with two uncooked chicken eggs.
- Have dinner with orange juice and 200 grams of bean sprouts every two days.
- Increase the quantity of food with high folic acid like animal viscera, protein like beef, chicken, fish, pork … and vegetables like potatoes, pumpkins, green beans, seaweed, tomatoes, carrots, and water spinach …

Abstaining

- Do not use antibiotic medicine while using the herbs.
- Do not have sexual intercourse between the days of menstruation and the ovulation day and have intercourse only once on the ovulation day.
- Husbands: do not drink alcohol.
- The couple: do not eat food high in calcium like shrimp, crab, bone, milk, boiled egg.

How to detect ovulation

- If the menstruation cycle is 28 days, the ovulation date is the 14th day after menstruation.
- If the menstruation cycle is 30 days, the ovulation date is the 15th day or the 16th day after menstruation.
- If the menstruation cycle is 32 days, the ovulation date is the 17th day or the 18th day after menstruation.
- If the menstruation cycle is 35 days, the ovulation date is the 19th day or the 20th day after menstruation.
- If the menstruation cycle is 40 days, the ovulation date is the 22nd day or the 23rd day after menstruation.

Source: Herbal healer, Sơn Tây, Hà Nội, 2009.

Healers in Hà Nội and surrounding areas have been profiting in recent times from the 'thirst for boys'. When women use their herbs and then give birth to a boy, rumours circulate that the healers possess 'having-boy herbs' and they quickly gain a reputation for the efficacy of their treatment. To illustrate the nature of the market for 'having-boy herbs', I relate the following observation.

A healer in Ba Đình district (Hà Nội) has become famous for providing herbs that help couples conceive a child of the desired sex. One day, my colleague and I went to his home. When we expressed our concern about having a child of the desired sex, the healer gave us a long lecture, which was similar to the contents of the various sex-selection books that have been selling like hotcakes in many bookshops. He said if we wanted a son, we should eat salted food, meat, fish, potato, and so on, and should not eat food high in calcium. He gave us a list of guidelines about the dietary regimen and how to calculate ovulation. My colleague bought two herbal remedies for VND500,000. When I asked the healer about how to ensure conception of a daughter, he expressed surprised because his customers only ever want to have sons. After thinking for a while, he said the way to conceive a girl was the opposite of that for a son, so I should eat food containing calcium.

Eleven of my 35 core women used 'having-boy herbs', following advice from neighbours, friends or relatives familiar with the procedure. Phi told me her preconception plan of action with the aim of having a son:

> My friend guided me. She had three daughters and then she had a son. I accompanied her to meet a healer. He gave me some herbs and the steps to follow in order to have a son. Afterwards, my friend took me to a doctor to detect ovulation. The doctor said she saw a mature follicle. I had an ultrasound scan on the following day. The doctor said this follicle had been released and advised me to have intercourse that night. Her advice coincided with the healer's advice. I used both ultrasound and herbs. (Phi, 38 years old, two daughters, 15 weeks pregnant)

Going to the pagoda to pray for a son

Praying to conceive a child is a custom in Việt Nam. In spring, after the Tết holiday, many people go to the Hương pagoda in Hà Tây province, which has a reputation for the occurrence of miracles after the performance of a prayer for a child, called *cầu tự*. In Hương pagoda, there is a cave with stalactites that are known as Son Mountain and Girl Mountain. I visited the pagoda in the spring of 2009, where crowds filled the main cave, praying to the Son Mountain (*Núi Cậu*) altar for a son. Two altars, one for Son Mountain and one for Girl Mountain (*Núi Cô*), sit opposite one another. The Son Mountain altar was crowded, while the Girl Mountain altar was deserted. People from the northern, southern and central provinces had made the pilgrimage to the pagoda to pray for a son. In the pagoda precincts, there was a booming trade in services facilitating prayers and writing petitions for a boy. Shops lining the various paths to the main cave displayed boy dolls; I had seen such dolls in the houses of some of the women I met during my research. Lụa had two of these dolls in a glass cabinet in her home. She and her husband went to Hương pagoda to pray for a boy during Lunar New Year. 'I prayed for luck to be bestowed on my family. If the god feels pity for me, he will give me a boy,' Lụa told me.

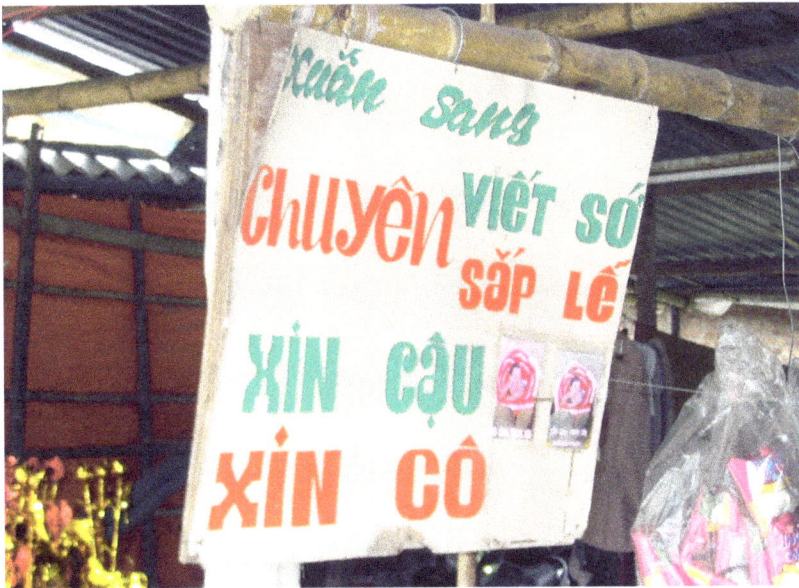

Plate 1. Services offering prayers and petition writing
Source: Photographed by the author, Hương pagoda, 2009.

Plate 2. A crowd of people face Son Mountain, while a solitary woman approaches Girl Mountain

Source: Photographed by the author, Hương pagoda, 2009.

Plate 3. Boy dolls in a shop at Hương pagoda

Source: Photographed by the author, Hương pagoda, 2009.

The majority of the women in this study who did not have a son were earnestly craving for one. Their recourse to the preconception sex-determination methods described above gives expression to the intensity of that desire, which was itself a manifestation of the intense expectations to which they were subject and which they internalised as a strong subjective preference. In such a context, I contend, these women wanted to feel that they had done everything they could, within the range of technical and moral possibilities, to have a son and that they had made use of the full spectrum of modern and traditional resources in the Vietnamese cultural repertoire. Their active, serial consultation of medical specialists, healers and fortune tellers conformed to a traditional reliance in Việt Nam on an array of esoteric techniques, authorities and powers believed to be efficacious and responsive. In this tradition, Vietnamese people have demonstrated an orientation towards not only accepting fate, but also actively attempting to alter it and align it with their desires.

Moreover, even the women who used these methods and did not conceive a son found peace with themselves, their family and other consociates because they knew they had tried. As such, sex determination could also be seen as a woman's conformity to the demands of her social and cultural contexts. By publicly and at great effort endeavouring to determine the sex of her child, she has demonstrated her conformity to the social ideal of a good mother and member of her lineage and society. That she may fail to meet the social expectation to produce a son is demonstrably not for want of desire or effort on her part. Such strenuous efforts to meet expectations are, in turn, themselves determinate, giving rise to sex-determination services, techniques and theories, in the process benefiting a retinue of practitioners and providers of such services.

Sex determination during pregnancy

Is it a boy or a girl? This is a question all expectant parents are curious about. Women who intend to have a sex-selective abortion are particularly keen to know the sex of their foetus in the early stages of pregnancy and they use a variety of methods that they hope will predict this correctly. Examining contemporary methods of sex-selection in Hà Nội helps us understand how women engage with the healthcare system and how the decision to engage to do so is influenced by a variety of socioeconomic variables, including women's social status, their access to and the perceived quality of services and the distribution of knowledge about effective methods within and between healthcare professionals.

Folk techniques

As well as consulting specialist practitioners to determine the sex of their baby, people turn to a large number of folk techniques. Some of the more common of these include the spinning or swaying of wedding rings, the size or shape of a pregnant woman's belly and various theories related to food cravings, foetal movements and so on.

The wedding ring over the belly: Attach a wedding ring to a strand of the pregnant woman's hair or a piece of string. Have the woman lie down and dangle the ring over her belly. If the ring starts moving in circles, the baby is a boy; if it moves from side to side like a pendulum, the baby is a girl.

Pregnancy cravings: If a pregnant woman is craving sweet foods such as fruit juice, chocolate or cakes, she is having a girl, but if she is craving sour or salty foods, she is having a boy.

Pregnant belly: The shape of the pregnant belly is well-known for determining whether the baby is a boy or a girl. If a pregnant woman is carrying low, it is a girl. If she is carrying high, it is a boy.

Foetal movements: If the foetus usually moves on the left side, it is a boy; on the right, a girl is in sight.

Pregnant woman's appearance: If a pregnant woman looks better than ever during pregnancy, she is carrying a boy. If she does not look well, she is carrying a girl.

Left or right: During pregnancy, if a woman favours sleeping on her left side, she is carrying a boy, but if she favours her right side, she is carrying a girl. Similarly, if, when someone calls from behind her, she turns around to the left, the baby is a boy; otherwise it is a girl.

Feeling the pulse

Feeling the pulse is a traditional method of diagnosing the sex of a foetus, which originated in ancient Chinese medicine. The accuracy of this method has not been evaluated, but people are likely to believe its efficacy if the healer correctly predicts the sex of the baby. The question is why women continue to use this method even if they think ultrasonography is more accurate in diagnosing the sex of their baby.

One of my friends was very excited to inform me soon after her wedding that she was six weeks pregnant. She said she was very curious about the sex of her baby and her husband would be happy if it was a boy. At this point in gestation, an ultrasound cannot identify the sex of a foetus, so she decided to have a healer take her pulse to determine the sex of the baby, and she invited me to go with her.

We went to meet the healer in the afternoon, but had to wait a long time to be seen. After a few minutes of feeling my friend's pulse, the healer said: 'You are not healthy. Do you feel a dull pain in your belly and waist? Are you usually tired and hungry in the late afternoon?' (I think most pregnant women have these symptoms!) He added: 'You are carrying a boy, but it is in foetal derangement. I will write a prescription for you.' My friend was worried and bought 10 packs of herbal medicine from him, costing VND300,000. In an effort to impress us, he explained:

> A male has pure Yang Qi, while a female has pure Yin Qi. Once a woman is carrying a male foetus, the Yang Qi will show in her pulse, which is totally different from the pure Yin Qi in her original pulse. If Yang Qi is cached in a pregnant woman's pulse, that indicates the foetus is male. Conversely, the Yin Qi displays in a female foetus and the pregnant woman's pulse will remain Yin Qi. (Traditional healer in Hà Nội)

Nineteen women in my sample of 35 had their pulse taken to diagnose the sex of their foetus. Cúc told me about having her pulse felt:

> My neighbour and I had our pulses felt when I was four weeks pregnant. I went to three different places for the procedure. Two healers said the foetus was a boy, with 80 per cent accuracy, and one healer affirmed it was a girl. I was curious about the sex of the foetus. The healers could tell me the sex of the foetus at an early stage. (Cúc, 30 years old, one daughter, 13 weeks pregnant)

Although most of the women supposed the ultrasound result was the more accurate one, they still used the pulse method to set their minds at ease.

Why do women make recourse to these medically unproven methods to learn the sex of their foetus? Again, a woman's reliance on such methods is a response to the intensity of the hope felt by herself and her family that she is carrying a son. Women's answers to my questions suggest that recourse to these practices gives voice to the anxiety women feel in the early stage of pregnancy. The strength of their desire to know the sex of their foetus reflects both the personal importance to them of having a son and the high emotional stakes of the venture. Consultation with specialists provided some degree of consolation and the opportunity to air their hope and anxiety. It also suggests that the desire for efficacious knowledge in Việt Nam is particularly strong. As we have seen, women use the pulse-feeling method in early gestation when no other available methods can provide answers about the sex of the foetus. Furthermore, this method of foetal sex determination is very simple. Even if the diagnosis eventually proves incorrect, it satisfies a woman's thirst for knowledge about a matter of high importance to her at a critical juncture of her pregnancy. It is this thirst for knowledge that the arrival of prenatal ultrasound-scanning technology has answered.

Ultrasonography

According to sonographers, prenatal determination of foetal sex by ultrasonography during the second and third trimesters of pregnancy is based on the demonstration and size of the penis in the male or the labial folds in the female; however, there is no appreciable difference in the size of the penis and the clitoris until after 14 weeks of gestation (Feldman and Smith 1975; Efrat et al. 1999). One study of the determination of foetal sex by ultrasonography showed that 'the accuracy of sex determination increased with gestation from 70.3% at 11 weeks, to 98.7% at 12 weeks and 100% at 13 weeks' (Efrat et al. 1999: 13).

Assessing the use of ultrasonography in Hà Nội, a doctor told me:

> Nowadays, using ultrasound to determine the sex of foetuses is popular. Most pregnant women want to know the sex of their foetus … it is just natural curiosity. People with a feudal mindset or male chauvinists have used ultrasound to determine the foetal sex followed by sex-selective abortion. That is a deviation in the use of reproductive technologies. The original aim of using ultrasound in reproductive health care was to check the development of the foetus and to diagnose foetal malformation. Providers have used ultrasound to determine the sex of foetuses with a monetary aim. (Dr Toàn, male, 54 years old)

Most of the private obstetrics and gynaecology clinics in Hà Nội are equipped with ultrasound-scanning machines. To attract clients, many private clinics have also invested in 'colour' three-dimensional or 'four-dimensional' ultrasound machines made by brands such as Toshiba, Medision and Volusion. Most ultrasound machines in Việt Nam are imported from Japan or the United States. The price of a new machine ranges from VND1.2 billion to VND1.5 billion (US$60,000–90,000). Originally, most imported machines were second hand; they had been in use for 10 years and were sold on to private clinics in remote provinces at 10–20 per cent of the price of new ones. The sale of cheap ultrasound machines is comparable with the sale of motorbikes from the 1980s–1990s from Hà Nội to other provinces, especially rural areas. At present, many private clinics in Hà Nội have new ultrasound machines, which are more modern than those in the public hospitals. The acquisition of a new and modern ultrasound machine is a marketing tool for private clinics. With the fee for each ultrasound scan being VND200,000–250,000, the capital investment can be recouped in one or two years.

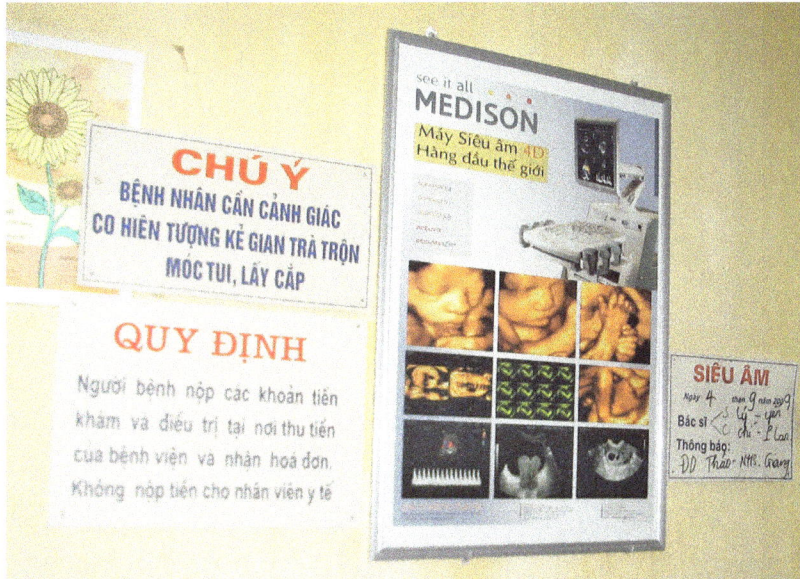

Plate 4. Ultrasound machine advertisement in a hospital
Source: Photographed by the author, 2009.

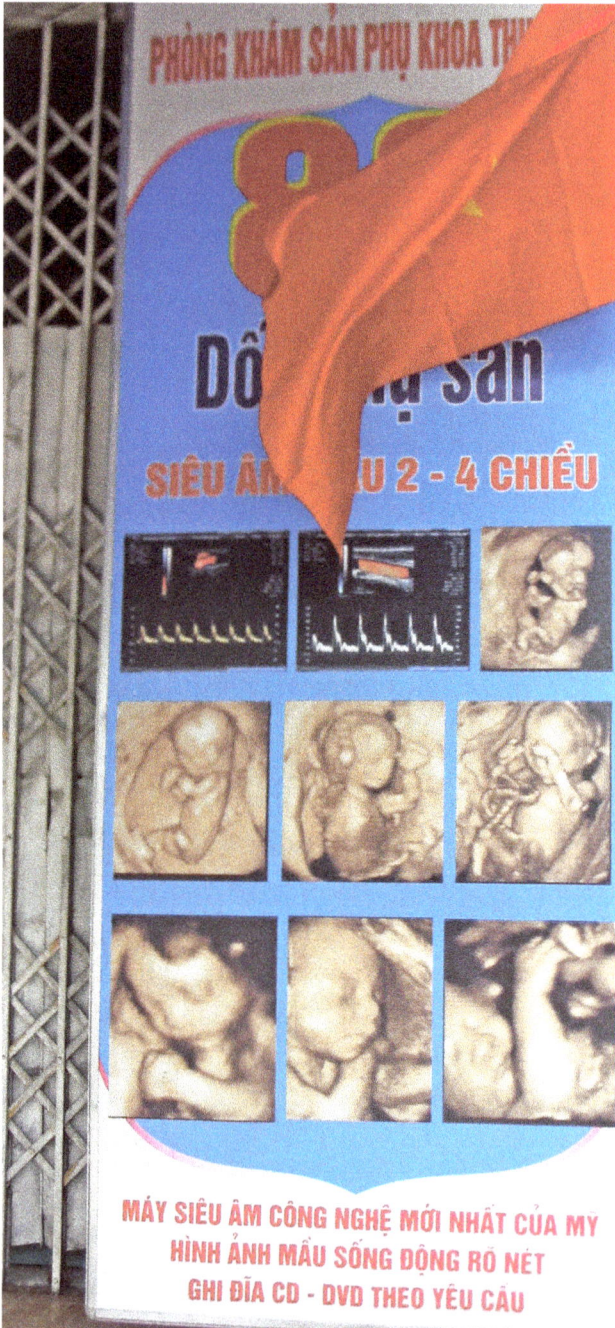

Plate 5. Ultrasound machine advertisement in a private clinic
Source: Photographed by the author, 2009.

Commenting on sex determination, a doctor told me:

> Diagnosing the sex of foetuses in early gestation is one of the
> marketing methods of private clinics and it brings a great reputation
> to the sonographers. Most women are curious to know the sex of
> their babies, but a number of them want to know the sex of the foetus
> for sex selection. Determining the baby's sex by ultrasound is about
> 70 per cent accurate at 12 weeks of pregnancy, and nearly 99 per cent
> accurate in the 14th to 16th week of pregnancy if the technicians are
> experienced. At this gestational age, abortion is still safe according to
> medical standards. (Dr Bách, male, 58 years old)

Indeed, the technical ability and reputation of a doctor/sonographer
are evaluated by the accurate diagnosis of the sex of the foetus in early
gestation. Doctors are in competition to diagnose the sex of a foetus
as soon as possible after conception. Some private clinics print colour
images of the foetus in which the genital area is prominent to prove
their abilities to potential customers and the quality of their ultrasound
machine (see Plate 5).

Since the Ministry of Health outlawed prebirth sex selection by
ultrasonography, public hospitals are no longer allowed to inform
women of the sex of their foetus. However, if pregnant women are well
acquainted with a staff member, they may be able to find out. The sex
of the foetus is not noted in medical records, but the patient may be
informed indirectly through comments such as, 'It looks like its father',
'It looks like its mother', 'It's wearing a dress' or 'It's wearing pants'.

In contrast, while doctors in public hospitals rarely inform the patient
of the sex of their foetus, doctors in private clinics readily pass on this
information to pregnant women. Why do they do this? In the public
hospital system, a doctor's income is not determined by the number of
patients they see, whereas in private clinics the number of patients seen
directly influences a doctor's income. Providing information about
foetal sex together with a colour picture of the foetus can be considered
an effective marketing method for private clinics. Private clinics in
cities and towns compete for patients by acquiring modern ultrasound
machines and informing patients of the sex of their foetus. The fame
of a doctor spreads quickly if they are known to provide accurate
diagnoses. If a doctor did not inform patients of the sex of their foetus
at the 12–13-week stage, those patients would be unlikely to return to
that clinic.

It is generally the case that ultrasound identification of sex is accurate for a male foetus from 12 weeks, and from 13 weeks for a female. However, ultrasound operators may not be called to account if they make a misdiagnosis. With so many terminations, the sex of each aborted baby is not always known. If a male baby has been inadvertently aborted, in many cases, no one would ever know. The scope for abuse is obvious. Women want to conceive boys and seek as much help as they can to achieve this. Once women conceive, ultrasound scans can identify sex, but if a mistake is made and the baby is aborted, very often the mother may not know.

A doctor who owns a private clinic admitted:

> If we do not reveal the sex of the foetus, clients will go to other clinics. Nobody waits until after giving birth to know if the baby is a boy or a girl. If we do not inform the clients about the sex of their foetus, we will lose our clientele. (Doctor, female, 46 years old)

Knowing the sex of the foetus is a demand not only of the prospective parents, but also of society. Instead of the mother's and baby's health being the primary topics of inquiry, pregnant women are often confronted with questions about the sex of their foetus. One woman, 15 weeks pregnant, confided:

> At the beginning, I did not care about the sex of my baby because I am carrying my first child. But I have been asked the sex of the baby every day. When I answered that I did not know, people did not believe me. Some people teased me that I did not dare to tell the sex of my baby because I was carrying a girl. Their behaviour made me annoyed. I am now very anxious to know the sex of my foetus, so I have been to three different clinics to have ultrasound scans. (24 years old, first pregnancy)

Ultrasonography is one scientific option for women contemplating sex selection and, compared with other methods, it is considered one of the most accurate. Lê told me:

> It is scientific. I believe 80–90 per cent accurate in ultrasound, and 60–70 per cent in feeling the pulse. But I wanted to have my pulse felt to satisfy my curiosity until I could have an ultrasound. At that time, ultrasound could not yet tell me the sex of my baby. I was very happy when the healer said it was a boy when I was six weeks pregnant. (31 years old, two daughters, 12 weeks pregnant)

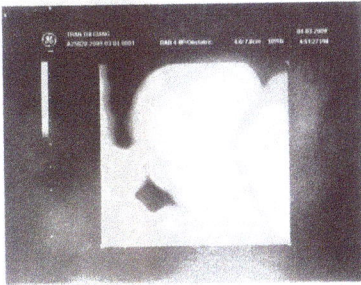
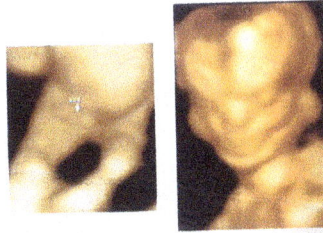
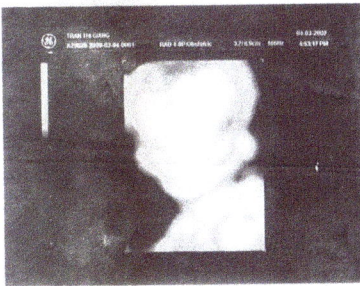
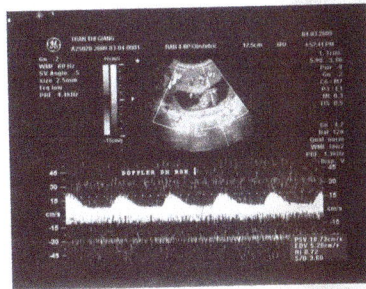
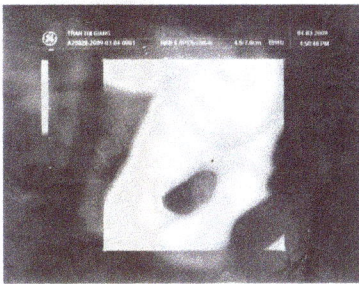

Plate 6. Results from a three-dimensional ultrasound scan in Hà Nội
Source: Photographed by the author, 2009.

Interestingly, the women who had a sex-selective abortion had several ultrasound scans because they wanted to be sure they were not aborting a male foetus. The number of ultrasound scans a woman has is closely linked with sex-selective abortion. Cúc told me her story:

> When I was 12 weeks pregnant, I had ultrasound scans in two clinics in Hà Nội, and I had another ultrasound scan in this town. I had three ultrasound scans in one day. The doctor in this town said the scan

was not clear enough to see the sex of my foetus, but the doctors in Hà Nội said it was a boy, with 80 per cent accuracy. I was very happy. The images of the foetus have been burnt on a DVD. I played the DVD at home to see the images. I tried to look with hope in my heart. I had other ultrasound scans in the following week in this town, and then the doctors said it was a girl. I went to the clinic in Hà Nội again, and that doctor also said it was a girl. I took the DVD to the doctor in a private clinic in this town and asked him to look at the images for me. After watching, he confirmed it was a girl. I was so disappointed, but I still did not believe it was a girl. I waited one more week and had three ultrasound scans, in private clinics and at a district health centre. All the doctors said it was a girl. I had eight ultrasound scans in total, seven times by colour ultrasound machine and one time by black-and-white ultrasound machine. It cost me about VND2 million for the ultrasound scans. (Cúc, 30 years old, two daughters, 13 weeks pregnant)

Among my 35 core cases, most of the women (21) had four or five ultrasound scans per pregnancy. Two women had eight scans. There were only four cases recording just three ultrasound scans.

Amniocentesis and chorionic villus sampling (CVS)

Foetal sex determination is usually done with ultrasonography, but it can also be done with amniocentesis[3] and CVS.[4] The sex of the foetus can be accurately determined if a pregnant woman undergoes CVS at 10–11 weeks or an amniocentesis test at 15–16 weeks. Amniocentesis and CVS are genetic tests and are more accurate than ultrasonography; however, CVS carries the risk of harming the foetus and inducing a miscarriage. Amniocentesis is usually quoted as having a 1–2 per cent loss rate and an additional 1–2 per cent infection and/or problem rate (leaking membranes, preterm labour, and so on). CVS reports about a 2 per cent loss rate. There have also been reports linking CVS with disorders such as amniotic banding syndrome (Alfirevic et al. 2017).

---

3   Amniocentesis is a procedure performed at 16–18 weeks of pregnancy, in which a needle is inserted through the woman's abdomen into her uterus to draw out a small sample of the amniotic fluid around the baby. Either the fluid itself or cells from the fluid can be used for a variety of tests to obtain information about genetic disorders and other medical conditions of the foetus.
4   Chorionic villus sampling (CVS) is the removal of a small piece of placental tissue (chorionic villi) from the uterus during early pregnancy to screen the baby for genetic defects. CVS can be done through the cervix (transcervical) or through the abdomen (transabdominal).

Although amniocentesis and CVS are considered the most accurate methods to diagnose foetal sex, they are not used as commonly as ultrasonography. They carry a risk to the baby and the pregnancy and are managed closely in the laboratories of public obstetrics and gynaecology hospitals. Three women among my 35-woman sample used this method to check the sex of their foetus. They wanted confirmation for fear of aborting a male foetus and, if it was a female, to have the abortion before it was 'too late'. Yến's story helps us understand why and how she had genetic testing to determine the sex of her foetus.

Yến is from a village in a rural area about 40 kilometres from the centre of Hà Nội. Her family's economic circumstances are not as difficult as most villagers whose sole income comes from farming, because she has a sideline making curtains. She usually goes to Hà Nội to obtain orders from clients. She had a son, but, unfortunately, he died by drowning two years before I met her. 'I have cried every day since his death,' she said. Yến and her husband wished to have another boy, but it was not easy, as they were both in their mid-40s. Yến's cousin felt sorry for the couple and advised them to have ovulation detection in a private clinic run by a famous doctor in Hà Nội. Yến 'followed' a doctor to detect the course of her ovulation for a year. The couple was very happy when Yến became pregnant. They consulted three healers and all said her foetus was a boy. The couple waited nervously until Yến was 12 weeks pregnant. At this stage, the doctor said the foetus might be a girl, but he could not be sure. Yến saw the doctor again the next week. The couple's hopes collapsed when the doctor said her foetus was a girl with 90 per cent accuracy. Yến had two more ultrasound scans in two other clinics, but received the same result. The couple decided to have an abortion because they wanted to have a boy. 'I have two daughters already. I do not want to have another daughter. If I keep this foetus, I won't have the opportunity to have a boy,' Yến explained. The couple wanted to confirm the sex of the foetus at this stage of gestation so they could abort it before it was 'too big'. The doctor whom Yến had 'followed' suggested that amniocentesis was the only way they could determine the foetal sex with 100 per cent accuracy; however, Yến would be at risk of miscarriage following the procedure. The hospital could do this test, but it would only do so to test for chromosomal abnormalities or other specific genetic disorders on a doctor's advice. The doctor gave Yến the address of a private clinic whose doctors could provide the same procedure. This clinic did not have the equipment to test the resulting sample; however, its doctors also worked for the laboratory of a hospital, so they could have the sample tested there and provide the result to their clients. Because such activities are illegal, they are conducted in secret. After much soul-searching, the couple decided to have amniocentesis. They accepted the risk of miscarriage to ensure that they would not abort a male foetus. They paid VND500,000 for the test. After one day of waiting, they were given the result of 'female'.

Such screenings have led to frequent instances of clinical uncertainty. Cúc, Yến and other women believed in the new reproductive technologies and spent a lot of money to detect ovulation and determine the sex of their foetus, after which they had a sex-selective abortion. These new technologies may help some women achieve their aim of having a son and making their lives happier. Meanwhile, women who do not have a son can lose respect or face divorce or banishment.

Conclusion

'Chasing the gender dream' makes us consider the reproductive trends enabled by new reproductive technologies, which both facilitate the birth of sons and put more pressure on women to have sons. These days, the pressure to have at least one son is also felt by women who are having their first child. To meet this desire, women have combined different methods to determine the sex of their foetus, such as ultrasonography and fortune-telling, feeling the pulse and herbal remedies. Traditional and modern preconception sex-selection methods and foetal sex diagnosis during pregnancy are responses to the uncertainties women feel and to their hopes and desires. Ultrasonography has assumed a central position in sex determination during pregnancy. With its advantages of a high accuracy rate, comparatively low cost and ease of access, ultrasound scanning has become increasingly popular. The market for new reproductive technologies addresses the desires and anxieties pregnant women face and transforms couples without sons into eager consumers.

The complexity of women's relationship with this technology is such that it cannot be assumed that women are passive vessels, simply acting in culturally determined ways with little reflection on their own condition. Indeed, the findings here suggest women's relationship with new technology is grounded in existing pragmatism. If the benefits are apparent, and if the technology serves their aims, most women will avail themselves of what is being offered. 'Pragmatic women' (Lock and Kaufert 1998) are willing to use whatever technology can provide to protect themselves.

One could contend, however, that the use of ultrasonography for nonmedical purposes and for profit is enhancing patriarchal and technological control over women. Feminists support this view, arguing that new reproductive technologies have put women in the hands of medical engineers (Gupta 1996). The natural process of reproduction can now be technologically engineered and the meaning of fertility has changed. One woman said to me:

> If I want to have a son, I must follow the doctor's guidelines. We only have intercourse when the doctor says 'it is time'. Our intercourse depends on the doctor, not on our love. (Nhung, a patient in an obstetrics and gynaecology clinic)

With the intervention of new technologies such as ultrasonography, many couples no longer have 'normal' sexual relations and 'produce' their sons in 'unnatural' ways. Sarah Franklin (1993) believes such technologies are changing not only our lives, but also the concept of life itself. Women's bodies have come to be seen as 'cyborgs' for the production of the desired kind of child.

When ultrasonography is used for sex determination and is followed by sex-selective abortion, the question is who benefits from the technological intervention? In Việt Nam's contemporary commercialised healthcare system, where new reproductive technologies are easy to access, there is considerable risk of their overuse. This study also shows that the number of ultrasound scans taken has a direct relationship with seeking a sex-selective abortion. The overuse of new reproductive technologies driven by market mechanisms rather than policy guidelines leads to sex selection. Providers diagnose the sex of the foetus because they want to attract clients to their clinics. Individual private practitioners have a direct profit motive in offering technological services. As one doctor said, 'ultrasound has been disguised' and 'it is a deviation' from the intended use for reproductive technologies (Dr Bách, male, 58 years old).

This study shows that women in Hà Nội today are concerned about the sex of their babies and seeking knowledge about their own bodies. They are using the new reproductive technologies as well as 'traditional' methods to achieve their aim of having a son. However, in so doing, they become victims of these new technologies.

Michelle Stanworth (1987) believes reproductive technologies can be a double-edged sword: they offer women greater reproductive choice and agency, but they also make it possible for the medical profession, the state and society to exert control over women's lives. When such new technologies create competencies in sex selection, they also create a huge human dilemma. The ability to select the sex of one's child helps women build the kind of family they desire—giving them acknowledgement, status, pride and happiness. But the new technologies also clearly become key tools in systematic gender discrimination. From a pragmatic, short-term and individual perspective, these technologies can be seen as 'good', whereas in a long-term, collective perspective, their effects may be adverse, such as men being unable to find wives and women facing greater exposure to sexual violence. Margaret Lock and Vinh-Kim Nguyen (2010: 141) write:

> More than any other kind of biomedical technology, those that affect reproduction bring to the fore an inherent tension among individual desire, perceived family interests, and that which is deemed appropriate for the nation, and indeed the world as a whole. These tensions are rife today because, as individuals and families are pressured to reduce their family size to conform to efforts to standardise the 'population problem', a global circulation of ultrasound technology has permitted families to take a certain amount of control with respect to the sex of their off-spring.

The development of reproductive technologies and their routine use increase moral dilemmas—vivid evidence of the interface between prenatal testing and human experience. The implementation of new technologies has placed women in an arena where medicine, social values and culturally determined meanings of motherhood are closely intertwined.

2

Sex-selective abortion decision-making: Beyond 'a woman's right to choose'

Control over fertility is a concern of women everywhere, whatever their differences in terms of socioeconomic condition, religion, caste or class. The concepts of agency and autonomy are central to feminist discussions of women's reproductive decision-making. The common interpretation of autonomy among liberal feminists identifies it with 'individual independence', 'self-determination' and the right of the individual to choose (Gupta 1996). However, Margaret Lock and Vinh-Kim Nguyen (2010) argue that the individual 'choices' and 'rights' assumed by Western liberal thought carry little favour in Asian cultural contexts, which are dominated by hierarchical, relational and consensual social identities. The relevance of Western concepts such as autonomy and choice needs to be tested in a Vietnamese context. How do they fit into the local socioeconomic, cultural and political contexts? How does a woman's decision about whether or not to undergo an abortion affect and reflect her status and autonomy in that society? This chapter reveals how Vietnamese women make decisions about sex-selective abortion by examining their stories and analysing the factors that influence their decision-making. To begin, I recount Huệ's story.

Huệ and her husband were both serving in the army. Their decision to have a third child was not an easy one because it meant violating the one-or-two–child policy, which would affect their careers. Huệ's husband was the oldest of four siblings; he had two sisters and a brother. His brother's son had died the previous year of blood cancer, while his brother's wife had been sterilised after having two children. Huệ's father-in-law was a kin group head in his village. His family had responsibility for worshipping the ancestors as well as other tasks related to his kin group. Having a boy to maintain the continuity of the family line was therefore very important for Huệ's husband's family. Although the couple was living in Hà Nội, they regularly visited the husband's home village, where they were constantly reminded of their responsibility to have a son. Huệ's husband did not attempt to force her to have a son, but he looked very sad whenever the subject was mentioned. The couple hesitated about having another child even though they were under pressure from their family. However, one day, Huệ's husband came home looking particularly sad. He told her what was wrong only after persistent questioning. He told Huệ he had been invited to a wedding party at his friend's house with a group of construction workers. When they were sitting around the dinner table, his mates joked that he could not sit with them at the table because he had no son. A strong man then held him down on the floor, where the women and children were eating. His eyes were moist with tears and he could not eat any more. This event made a deep impression on Huệ, motivating her to have a son by any means.

Several months later, Huệ fell pregnant. The couple was anxious to learn the sex of the foetus as soon as possible. Huệ and her husband were disappointed when ultrasound scans revealed it was a girl. Huệ had six ultrasound scans before having an abortion. She and her husband attended the hospital several times before deciding to proceed with the abortion. During that time, the couple could not sleep. Huệ said:

> Deciding to have this abortion was one of the most difficult decisions in my life. I terminated my pregnancy. Although it was normal, I feel I have done wrong towards my child. But if I had kept this pregnancy, we would lose our careers and have no chance to have a son.

Huệ's reproductive decision reveals the tension between traditional norms (having sons to continue the lineage—a woman's duty towards her husband's family) and modern society (population policy, new reproductive technology, keeping up appearances). It tells us about the moral, political and social values that women are obliged to bring to their reproductive decisions. In this chapter, I argue that low fertility in tandem with the development of new reproductive technologies and strong patriarchal pressure have imposed increased pressure on women to conceive sons. In this context, women's actions as reproductive agents conform to social norms. When women decide to have a sex-selective abortion, their decision is framed by the negotiation between morality and the social conditions in their particular cultural context.

To understand why women choose to terminate a pregnancy because their foetus is the undesired sex, it is necessary to know the social, cultural and political contexts in which reproductive desires are constructed and negotiated. Based on in-depth discussions with and observations of women undertaking sex-selective abortion, this chapter explores the factors that influence this trend and illustrates them with reference to the specific circumstances of women seeking sex-selective abortion. This is followed with a discussion of the decision-making process itself, identifying the key people with whom women consult and other factors that have a bearing on their decision-making.

Sociological and cultural contexts of sex selection

Son preference and patriarchal norms

As in many patriarchal societies in Asia, in Việt Nam, son preference is a prominent aspect of the culture (Johansson et al. 1998). Vietnamese anthropologist Vương Xuân Tình (1994) identifies five key reasons parents want sons:

1. Men have always played an important role in the means of production (heavy physical labour is shouldered by men).
2. Men hold the responsibility to carry out the rituals associated with the cult of the ancestors.
3. According to customary law, only sons can inherit their parents' property.
4. Because of the tradition of patrilocality, a daughter is considered to be 'the child of another family'.
5. Sons represent political and economic interests.

In an agricultural society, male labour is essential. Farming families need men to undertake the heavy work in their fields. Traditionally, having a son was considered necessary to maintain and extend the lineage. Ancestor worship is very important and only males can perform the rituals associated with this. If a man dies without a son, his lineage is considered to be broken. Parents customarily live with their oldest son in old age and he consequently inherits the family's property. A daughter, however, will be married early and live in her husband's house after marriage. She provides little or no support to her original family; hence, any 'investment' in a daughter is lost to the family. Daughters are considered 'flying ducks' because they are lost to their parental family after marriage (Vũ 1992; Johansson et al. 1998; Tran 1999). One of several Vietnamese proverbs brutally illustrates this patriarchal order: '*Nhất nam viết hữu, thập nữ viết vô* [To have one son means you have a child, but to have 10 daughters means you have no children].' Another proverb derides men who live with their in-laws as 'dogs in the pantry': '*Con trai ở nhà vợ như chó nằm gầm chạn* [The man who lives in his wife's house is like a dog lying in the pantry].'

Son preference is one reflection of a patriarchal society in which women's status is low, and is just one aspect of the broader phenomenon of male preferencing (Haughton and Haughton 1995). According to Ha Tran (1999), Confucian values lie at the core of traditional family structures in Việt Nam, in which the father is the household head and makes the major decisions relating to finances, the organisation of work and childbearing. The traditional view of Vietnamese women is '*Tam tòng, tứ đức* [Three obediences and four virtues]'. The three obediences are: obedience to the father when unmarried; obedience to the husband when married; obedience to the eldest son when widowed. The four virtues are: proper employment (being proficient and diligent in traditional skills related to housekeeping, farming and the running of a small business); proper demeanour (being neatly dressed and behaving in a decorous manner); proper speech (soft and pleasing tone of voice); and proper conduct (respect for her parents, husband and eldest son, showing consideration towards relatives, self-effacement and modesty) (Tran 1999).

Son requirement and female and male identities

In a patriarchal society, bearing a son is very important for determining a woman's position in her in-laws' family and in society. Many contemporary Vietnamese women are still greatly concerned with the necessity of having at least one son. If couples do not produce a son, women will be placed under great pressure. Women are blamed for infertility or 'sonlessness'. In these situations, women are labelled as being 'unable to give birth', whereas men are teased and offered sympathy. Thus, women have a vulnerable and uncertain position among their in-laws until they have produced at least one son. Women who do not have sons are considered inferior to those with a son. Many women confided in me about their families' dissatisfaction with them not having a son.

Within a family, sons are the major source of women's value. Sonless women become weak and vulnerable in a marriage. Many women in this study believed their main duty after marriage was to give birth to a son for their husband. Even though their husbands may not discuss the matter, the women always understand that their husbands want a son. 'He did not mention that we had to have a son. He did not say, but he was sad to have no son. I felt pity for him so I tried to get pregnant' (Phi, 38 years old, two daughters). The once common custom of seeking a concubine for a man whose wife cannot give him a son has not been entirely superseded in contemporary society. In 'feudal' or precolonial times, a man was allowed to take multiple wives, while a woman could only ever have one husband. The failure of the first wife to give birth to a son was a common reason for a man to have extramarital affairs or take a second wife (Phạm Văn Bích 1999). Knowledge of this tradition still affects women without sons. Many women with whom I spoke shared Phi's worry:

> Perhaps my husband is not now concerned about having a son, but when he thinks of his old age he might become concerned about his lineage and want to have a son. So, I have to beware of this. (Phi, 38 years old, two daughters)

Sons are vital to maintaining the continuity of their family line. Van Hy Luong (1984) suggests the male-oriented model of Vietnamese kinship emphasises the male-centred continuity of the kinship unit. In terms of the model's internal logic, polygyny is intended to ensure this continuity (Luong 1984). Traditional society has its own solutions to the problem of not having a son: take a concubine or adopt a boy. However, for Kinh people (the major ethnic group in Vietnam), because an adopted son has different blood, the popular option is to appoint a nephew to be the male heir (*thừa tự*). The nephew will inherit his adoptive parents' property after they die and have responsibility for worshipping the parents and carrying on the cult of the ancestors.

In my fieldwork, I heard many stories from my core cases about married men they knew of having extramarital affairs or taking extra wives if their first wife had not produced a son. This phenomenon was a significant factor influencing their own decision to have a son at any cost. One couple described to me the case of the husband's sister. The sister was very successful in trade and was the family's breadwinner, but she had only two daughters. She was now past reproductive age. Her husband had an extramarital affair with a single woman and they had a son. Rather than divorcing, the official wife provided financial support to raise her husband's son.

I also know of a family with an 'official' and an 'unofficial' wife living together in a village in Hà Nội, where I conducted community-based research and focus group discussions. The unofficial wife moved in with the husband and his family when they had a son together, and they all lived together openly. Women attending the focus groups confirmed that there were several cases like this in their village. This phenomenon is a significant worry for women without sons. As Thu said:

> In my village, some women who have only daughters experience domestic violence. The husbands threaten that they will get extra wives. Their situation made me think about myself. I should be aware about this phenomenon. (Thu, 23 years old, two daughters)

The phenomenon is not opposed strongly by local authorities or other villagers. Some people showed sympathy for these women, but advised the official wives to accept the solution. Of course, women suffer great misery in this situation and the behaviour of their husband violates the official law on monogamy.

As sociologist Phạm Văn Bích (1999: 18) notes:

> Ideally members of a family were expected to subordinate their personal interests to those of the family as a whole. Personal interests could not run counter to the family interests but should comply with the latter. Each person had to discipline him- or herself, and subdue his or her personal desires and aspirations if those ran counter to the communal standards.

According to Mai Huy Bích (1993: 11):

> Traditional Vietnamese society is established from [a] village community and this community is composed of families. The communal characteristic of Vietnamese people is supplemented by the influence of Confucianism. The communal characteristic is manifested by the family's domination of the family members. The individual freedom is very limited. Individual interests must have a strong attachment to the interests of the family.

Therefore, in this context, women have to place the interests of their husband, their family and their husband's lineage (to which they belong after marriage) first. Otherwise, they will face public criticism. Women grow up with the knowledge that their duty after marriage is to selflessly serve their families, to be passive and obedient and to continue the family line by bearing sons.

The successful bearing of sons is considered central to the identity of men as well as women. Men cannot have an important position in their kin group if they do not have a son, and they will become the subject of gossip. The case of Huệ is a vivid example of a woman without a son. Huệ and her husband were facing the conflicting pressures of the need to ensure continuity of the family line for the sake of their relatives in the home village and the ruin of their careers if they had a third child.

Having a son is important for male identity when other aspects of masculine identity may be in question. For men who reside with or near their wives' parents (matrilocality), having a son is especially important. A Vietnamese proverb says: '*Thà ở xó chuồng heo còn hơn ăn theo quê vợ* [Better to stay in a piggery than live in your wife's homeland].' Men who live in such circumstances may feel they have lost their freedom and are sneered at by others. This was the case for Liên's husband, who felt pressure to have a son by way of compensation.

Liên's husband, Minh, is the second son of a poor family. He left secondary school to work in construction. In 2005, he met Liên while he was building a house for her brother. Liên was a hairdresser and once owned a barber's shop. After marrying, the couple decided to live in Liên's home village because they thought they could earn more money there. Minh's older brother was living with his parents, so they did not oppose the couple's decision. Liên and Minh's household economy is stable thanks to income from a small rented barber shop. Their two daughters were born in 2006 and 2007. Minh is happy with his capable wife and two beautiful girls; however, he is concerned that he has no son. He confided:

> My wife's family is precious to me, but I still feel that I am in a disadvantageous position when living in my wife's homeland. I really want to have a son to have some moral support. (Minh, 34 years old)

Living for family and kin

Sons are of particular importance because they carry on family lines and are responsible for their parents not only in their old age, but also after their deaths. Another Vietnamese proverb says: '*Trưởng nam bại, ông vải vong* [If there is no son, there is no cult of the ancestors].' The cult of the ancestors is central to the spiritual life of the family and is based on the belief that one's spirit is immortal and relationships continue between the living and the dead. Vương Xuân Tình (1994) notes that, customarily, sons—especially first-born sons—have been given the responsibility to carry on the cult rituals and celebrate the funerals and death anniversaries of their parents, while daughters are merely required to contribute to the commemoration of the death anniversaries of their own parents. If a family does not have a son, these rituals have to be celebrated by the son of a consanguineal family. It is said that a married woman is no longer part of her natal lineage and cannot go to the lineage shrine (*nữ nhân ngoại tộc, bất nhập từ đường*). This is still the case in some areas of Việt Nam, as illustrated by one of my female interlocutors, Loan, whose origins were in the Red River Delta.

Loan's motivation to have a son was driven by concern about who would take responsibility for the family's cult rituals. She was under pressure because of the experience of her mother-in-law, Mrs Thoa, who had no brothers. After Mrs Thoa's parents died, responsibility for the family's cult rituals was passed on to her father's nephew. She could not celebrate her parents' death anniversaries in a proper manner. Mrs Thoa explained this custom:

> According to elders [*các cụ*], daughters cannot carry out cult rituals. Even though a daughter celebrates her parents' death anniversary, her parents will not receive the things that she offers because the altar in her family household belongs to her husband's ancestors. Her parents' spirits cannot go there.

Because of this, Mrs Thoa has to celebrate her parents' death anniversaries in her cousin's household. Her cousin's family, however, is very poor and he cannot afford to have a nice altar, so the cult rituals are practised on a wardrobe. Moreover, the nephew's wife is HIV positive. Because of the stigma around HIV/AIDS, no one else will attend Mrs Thoa's parents' death anniversaries. This has left Mrs Thoa bitterly disappointed and she urged her daughter-in-law to try to have a son by any means. Mrs Thoa worried that if her son's family did not have a male heir to take care of the cult rituals, her experience would be repeated.

According to Confucianism, families are patrilineal—if a family does not have a son, the family line is considered extinct. The extinction of the family line is considered one of three major filial impieties, along with not taking care of one's parents in their old age and bringing one's parents into disrepute. Confucius is quoted as saying: '*Bất hiếu hữu tam, vô hậu vi đại* [Having no son to continue the family line is the biggest filial impiety].' One man told me of his motivation for having a son:

> Having girls means that we serve for others, not for us. First of all, a girl is to encourage my wife, the second is for society [a girl will become a wife and will have a productive funtion for the society she belongs to]. Girls are considered a pancake in water [*Bánh đa nhúng nước*, a popular term in Vietnam meaning nobody wants it]. There is nothing for me. Having a son is similar to when an old tree dies—there will be a young tree. That is a circulation; old bamboo will have sprouts. (Vỹ, 42 years old)

Mead Cain (1993) asserts that gender inequality in the access and control of resources is a critical factor driving strong son preference among women. The need for a son is closely linked to the customary law on property inheritance. Since 1945, the laws have assumed the equality of men and women.[1] However, under customary law, men and women are not equal, especially with regards to the inheritance of

---

1   The Land Laws in 1993, 2003, 2013 regulates that women and men—as 'all people'—are equal under the laws. For example, the 2013 Constitution notes that 'Male and female citizens have equal rights in all fields. The State shall adopt policies to guarantee the right to and opportunities for gender equality. The State, society and family shall create the conditions for women to develop comprehensively and to improve their role in society. The Constitution prohibits gender-based discrimination' (National Assembly of Vietnam 2013: Article 26).

land and houses. Land has high value, so the division of land according to customary law provides motivation for having a son. Phi confided in me:

> My father-in-law has a feudal mentality. He constantly reminds us to have a son, but my husband refuses to talk about it. My father-in-law is going to divide the ancestors' land for his descendants. Only sons and grandsons can receive a portion. If I have a son, my family can have more land.

Customary practices of gift distribution within patrilineages can be symbolically wounding as well, reminding women of the value placed on sons. Some women in my study told me how displeased they were when their sons received gifts/dividends after ancestor-worshipping days while their daughters were given nothing.

Community pressure

According to Mai Huy Bích (1993: 11), traditional Vietnamese society is established at the level of the village community, which is made up of families. The communal characteristic of Vietnamese society is supplemented by the influence of Confucianism manifested in the domination of the senior male over other family members. Individual freedom is very limited, and individual interests must be subsidiary to the interests of the family. The community plays an important role in shaping people's reproductive desires and behaviour. As with Huệ's husband, many sonless men are laughed at and many sonless women are taunted with comments such as 'không biết đẻ [not knowing how to give birth]' or 'kiếp trước ăn ở thế nào [your previous incarnation was not good]'. Gossiping about sonless men and women exerts pressure on families. Many women justified their decision to try to become pregnant with a son by referring to this social pressure. In addition, having a son is evidence of a family's virtue. For men, having a son is a demonstration of masculinity, success and filial piety.

Most women I interviewed said they were blamed and felt anxious if they did not do all they could to have a male heir. Sex-selective abortion is therefore one solution to a failed attempt to conceive a son. If a woman had a son after her efforts, the couple's status increased considerably and her effort was praised. If, however, a woman had yet another daughter, the couple would be ridiculed.

> If I have a boy, people will congratulate me. But if I give birth to another girl, they will laugh at me. They will say that I have a flock of flying ducks. (Na, 49 years old, two daughters)

Women who have several daughters will be mocked for two reasons—not having a son and having too many children according to current social standards.

In rural Việt Nam, the strength and political power of a lineage depend on the number of male heirs. It is said that the greater the lineage, the stronger is its power. Therefore, having a son improves a man's and his lineage's position in the community. Pressure from family, gossip within the community and the concept of responsibility to have a son force sonless couples to try to have male heirs by any means. Women are under the most pressure; they are valued for having a son and are said to have fulfilled their duty to their husband's family only after giving birth to at least one son. They are held in low regard by their husband's family if they have only daughters. Some sonless women are neglected, spoken to scornfully, beaten ruthlessly or threatened with replacement by other wives. Accordingly, they take the initiative to find ways to have a son.

For Vietnamese people, the opinions of those around them are very important.

> Communal assessment is regarded as the highest standard and modifying its members' behaviour and attitudes accordingly. Each person has to discipline him/herself, and subdue his/her personal desires and aspirations if those are contradictory to the communal standards. Otherwise, a person would be labelled a 'social disgrace' and as 'losing face'. Members of a family were expected to subordinate their personal interests to those of the family as a whole. Everybody has an obligation to take care of and obey the older generation. (Phạm Văn Bích 1999: 18–19)

State policies and their perverse effects

Public policies have a significant influence on people's decision-making with respect to fertility. Some researchers have argued that parental discrimination against a female foetus is exacerbated by strict population policies—for example, China's one-child policy (Goodkind 1999a). In Việt Nam, the one-or-two–child policy is the central component of the Family Planning Program initiated in 1963 (Vũ 1992). After *Đổi Mới* in 1986, the government began promoting the norm of a small family with only one or two children for each couple. Small families have a lower probability than larger families of including a son. Annika Johansson et al. (1998) indicate that the need for sons is still strongly felt in North Vietnamese culture. In addition, the one-or-two–child policy introduced new and potential contradictions regarding women's fertility. On the one hand, women who do not have a son worry about not producing a male heir. On the other, they feel pressure from local authorities to keep to the two-child limit. Yong J. Yoon (2006) used a demographic model to predict that a low birth rate would lead to an increase in the SRB because of sex-selective abortion.

Public policies on social security, the market and healthcare services also influence son preference in the contemporary context. Social security systems are very weak in Việt Nam; people must be self-reliant. Elderly people usually depend on their children, primarily their son(s). For farmers, there is no financial security once they are beyond working age. Hence, sons play a valuable economic role for their ageing parents, and this is the dominant factor driving son preference. Noticeably, in this study, a large number of the women having a sex-selective abortion were farmers (10 of 35 cases).

Sons usually become important providers when their parents are weak or ill. With poor health insurance and most healthcare services paid for out of their own pockets, elderly Vietnamese can incur high expenditure as a result of age-related health problems. The payment burden is placed on the son. A manager of a public hospital told me:

> At present, we have poor social security. Obviously, sons have an important role in their families. Perhaps some families have lost their fortune because of their sons, and some families are prosperous thanks to their daughters. However, they are only a minority. Basically, when old parents are weak or ill and when their families have important affairs, sons have the main responsibility. Old people who can no longer work depend mainly on their children, not on social security. When the social security systems are improved, son preference will not be as pressing. To me, son preference is not irrational. I do not dare to say it is a legitimate aspiration because if I say that I will violate the law and policy on gender equality. (Manager, male, 52 years old)

While cadres can receive more social insurance from the government, nongovernment workers, especially farmers, have little social security. As Bélanger explains (2002: 330):

> Since the liberalisation of health care and the introduction of user fees, peasants who face health problems need to borrow considerable sums of money to gain access to health-care services. This change in social policy likely has increased the value of sons to their parents.

The farmers in this study also mentioned their worries about this issue. Trang's husband said:

> My brother is a cadre. He works for a state bank and has social insurance. He can feel secure when he retires. My wife and I do not have permanent jobs; we are self-employed, so we have to take care of ourselves. We want to have a son to rely on when we are in old age. (Male, 46 years old)

Women cadres who depend on the state and the Communist Party have greater incentives to respect the population policy so as to maintain their job security and ensure promotion. Meanwhile, women engaged in other occupations have greater freedom to choose the number of children they have. Previous research indicates that cadres are more likely than others to incur sanctions for not respecting the one-or-two–child policy. Therefore, they are likely to be under more pressure than others to have only two children while also trying to have at least one son (Goodkind 1994; Bélanger 2002). Interestingly, mothers who are cadres tend to have a higher male SRB for children of third and higher birth orders (Bélanger et al. 2003).

A significant number of women in this sample who underwent sex-selective abortion were cadres (10 of 35 cases). Employees of the state or the party who had more than two children—violating the population policy—usually hid the birth of any subsequent child to avoid being penalised. Thương was one such woman.

At noon one day, Thương and I sat outside the surgical room, waiting for her turn to have an abortion. Thương opened her phone and showed me a photo. 'Look at my daughters. They are twins,' she said. 'They are beautiful,' I said. She told me with a proud voice: 'They are beautiful and obedient. I love them so much.' Then she lowered her voice:

> My husband and I thought that two daughters were enough and we did not intend to have more children. But my husband is the only son in his family. We are both government cadres; I am a teacher and he is a director of a company, so we cannot have a third child. In order to have another child, I have to offer one of my daughters for adoption. My husband's sister adopted my daughter; however, they are only adoptive parents on paper. My daughter is still living with me.

The social value placed on having a son coupled with policy-led restrictions on family size can lead to outcomes other than sex-selective abortion that are also damaging to girls. Rachel Burr (2014) looked at what it means to be a good child in Việt Nam and suggested that ancestral worship—still widely practised throughout the country—was key to this. Families emphasise the need for a son to continue worship practices into the next generation. While the high value placed on the boy-child has been tempered by the influence of the state's social policies and modernity, the eldest boy in a family still often holds preferential status. Burr observed of an orphanage in Hà Nội that it comprised two-thirds girls and one-third boys. The girls were usually the eldest child or second-born girl in a family. According to Burr (2014), these girls are 'victims' both of the one-or-two–child policy and of the traditionally informed pressure on women to produce a son.

Social change and the sex of children

The desire for children of a particular sex is affected not only by population policies, but also by rising living standards and other social changes. Writing about the People's Republic of China, Robin Burgess and Juzhong Zhuang (2002) show that socioeconomic factors can affect the preference for sons. In Việt Nam, economic rationality and new social norms about 'having fewer but better children' have influenced women's decisions about the desired number of children. The costs of raising children have been rising rapidly, and parents want to 'invest' more and more in their children despite limited finances. For instance, parents in Hà Nội compete to send their children to specialised schools despite the high fees. As one village farmer said:

My parents could have nine or 10 children because they just needed to provide enough food and clothes for us. It is said that '*Trời sinh voi; Trời sinh cỏ* [God gives elephants; God gives grass]'. We cannot do the same because we need to raise our children with nutritious food and a good education.

The high cost of having children is an important concern for parents. In economic terms, children are seen primarily as a burden, not as an asset—daughters more so than sons in this view. According to one woman who decided to have a sex-selective abortion:

The cost of raising and educating children is very expensive nowadays. I only have the capacity to raise and pay for the education of two children. I think I will have only two children instead of three in order to have a better life for them. We have a strenuous life, working hard in agricultural jobs. We do not want our children to work hard like us. (Thu, 23 years old, two daughters)

However, some women considered having more children and wanted to have a son once their economic situation improved.

I did not think about having a third child before. Recently, my family's economic condition improved, and we can now afford to raise more children, and we would like to have a son. (Hậu, 35 years old, two daughters)

A large number of women in this study who sought a sex-selective abortion had a high school or tertiary education (24 out of 35 cases). They are not easily categorised as educationally disadvantaged or lacking basic awareness of social norms and state policies. A study of the association between educational levels and the child sex ratio in rural and urban India reports that women's higher status may not lead to greater equality between male and female children. Women with greater 'empowerment' are simply more likely to resort to modern strategies to have at least one son. These women have more knowledge about the methods believed to influence the sex of a child, such as selective diet, the best time for conception and the use of ultrasonography. Elizabeth Croll (2000) argues that gender equality among adults does not necessarily lead to gender equality among children. A study of sex-selective abortion in India suggests the higher a woman's socioeconomic status, the more likely she is to be involved in sex selection (Ganatra et al. 2001). Similarly, my findings suggest a high propensity to use sex-selective abortion among those of higher status, which likely reflects both greater awareness of and greater access to sex-determination and abortion services, as well as greater ability to afford these services.

Some new factors are complicating sex preferences for children in contemporary Việt Nam. According to one Vietnamese proverb, '*Có nếp, có tẻ* [It is better to have both glutinous and ordinary rice]'. The meaning, as explained to me, is that people prefer to have children of both sexes. In a traditional peasant family, a daughter was welcomed if she was the first child because she could help her parents (Phạm Văn Bích 1999). It was also said that '*ruộng sâu, trâu nái, không bằng con gái đầu lòng* [having a piece of fertile land and a fertile buffalo is not as valuable as having a daughter as your first child]'. However, the shift to smaller families and changes in social and economic responsibilities have imposed new pressures on women to have at least one male heir. Many couples now want their first child to be a son and are likely to feel anxious if it is a daughter instead. If their first child is a son, the outcome is described as *ăn chắc* (gaining the certainty of having at least one son)—meaning parents need not worry about the sex of their second child. Interestingly, statistical data from the UNFPA show that, unlike most countries, in Việt Nam the SRB is skewed for the first-born child. In 2009, the SRB was 110.2 for the first birth, 109 for the second birth and 115.5 for the third birth (but 132 if the first two children were daughters) (UNFPA 2015).

Although most couples want at least one son, they do not want too many sons. In rural areas, the average land per capita is limited and declining. Having many sons to provide labour was not the main motivation of the people with whom I spoke. In fact, it is said that '*tam nam bất phú, tứ nữ bất bần* [with three sons, one will not be rich; with four girls, one will not be poor]'. In addition, the customary expectation that a son and his family will live with his parents after marriage (i.e. virilocality) means some couples worry about having too many sons, especially in urban areas with limited land. One man told me:

> I want to have a boy because I think about my family line. Actually, raising a boy is harder than raising a girl. Parents worry more about the economic situation for a boy than for a girl upon marriage. (Na's husband, 52 years old)

Some social trends indicate that the preference for sons is not likely to disappear in the near future. Anthropologists have noted that liberalisation and globalisation in Việt Nam have been accompanied by a resurgence of traditional social, cultural and religious practices that contradict the expectation that modernisation will render obsolete traditional ways of life. These trends include restoration of the household economy, patrilineage and ancestor worship (Werner 2002; Luong 2003; Taylor 2007). To some extent, the revival of such traditions has been endorsed by the Vietnamese state as it seeks to maintain a national identity for the sake of economic and political security, and for its own authority.

Farmers are being influenced by the ideal of smaller families, while simultaneously experiencing pressure from family and kin networks and the prestige accorded to traditional notions of the importance of having a son. The case of Ngọc helps us understand the pressures leading such parents towards sex selection.

When I met them, Ngọc and her husband were sitting in the hospital corridor eating a frugal lunch of rice and vegetables. Ngọc's husband told me that the abortion Ngọc was about to have was, for them, a great expense. Ngọc was 33 years old and the couple already had two daughters. Now, she was 13 weeks pregnant.

> All our savings have been spent on this affair [the abortion]. We are farmers and earn just enough to survive on. Raising two children is already difficult for us. We intended to have two children only, but my parents complained too much. In death anniversaries and festivities, elders often asked when we would have a son [khi nào thì có thằng cu]. That makes us anxious. My wife tried to get [a son with] this pregnancy, but we are not lucky. (Ngọc, 33 years old, two daughters, 13 weeks pregnant)

In short, while traditional factors still influence son preference, modern factors are also playing a role in people's perceptions about having a son. Women in contemporary Việt Nam suffer a great deal from the clash between the intense demand for a son and the pressure to have fewer children.

Women's decision-making on sex-selective abortion

In the remainder of this chapter, I explore how the decision is made to have a sex-selective abortion. Rosalind Petchesky (1984) points out that feminists support women's right to choose, but they pay less attention to the social and material conditions under which those choices are made. The sections that follow examine the conditions under which women make decisions, paying attention to the significant social others with whom they consult. I then discuss other factors influencing their decision-making.

Women's position in reproductive decision-making

Looking at the relationship between gender and development, Elisabeth Croll (2000) asserts that there is no neat correlation between the status of women and that of girls, and there are some improvements in women's status that have led to a decline in fertility but have not reduced the preference for sons. The question is why the increase in the status of women does not lead to a similar increase in the status of girls. It could be due to generational differences and the position of women within their husband's family (Croll 2000). Aida Seif El Dawla et al. (1998: 99) suggest that 'women's relationship to their bodies is shaped by such negotiations among needs, desires and obligations; ownership of the body is both personal and socially determined'.

In a patriarchy, women have limited authority within the family and therefore also limited authority in decision-making. According to traditional Vietnamese customs, a married woman belongs to her husband's family. Her childbearing is considered a family issue and decisions related to it must be approved by her husband's family, especially the elders. Although the situation for women in Việt Nam has improved because of the legal recognition of gender equality, some traditional values persist in everyday life. Women's position in relation to their husbands, family members and others involved in reproductive decision-making can help us understand their attitude to son preference.

Husbands

Traditionally, Vietnamese family lines are continued through men, and women join their husband's household on marriage. In this patriarchal family structure, Vietnamese women have limited authority. Childbearing is considered their main duty and decisions about it must be approved by their husband's family. While women in such situations may feel they lack power, most also accept these arrangements and even actively employ them (Gammeltoft 1999).

Husbands play an important role in women's decision-making in general, including in abortion decisions. All the women in this study had to consult their husband when making decisions and gain his approval. While couples may discuss such issues, the final decisions are not always made by the wives. As Huyền said:

> I did not want to have this abortion. I felt it is immoral. If my husband did not insist on having an abortion, I would not have done so. (Huyền, 36 years old, two daughters)

The contradictions inherent in the decision to have an abortion can lead to violence, spousal neglect or extramarital affairs. Some women, such as Huyền and Lụa, were forced against their will to have an abortion by their husbands.

Lụa called me at midnight in tears. Initially, her husband had been very happy when she became pregnant for the second time. During the first few months, he looked after Lụa's health by bringing her food and a cup of milk before going to bed. Everything changed, however, when he found out she was carrying another girl. He advised her to have an abortion, but she did not agree. She thought it would be immoral to have an abortion just because the foetus was female. After that, her husband stopped taking care of her as before and he began to come home very late. He also received strange phone calls and messages. Lụa recognised there were problems with their relationship and eventually discovered that her husband was having an extramarital relationship with his hairdresser. In an effort to avoid their happiness being destroyed, Lụa decided to have an abortion.

These is a close connection between abortion and violence. Reviewing the data of the effects of intimate-partner violence on women's reproductive health and pregnancy outcomes from various countries,

N. N. Sakkar (2008) asserts that such violence affects women's physical and mental health, reduces their sexual autonomy and increases the risk of unintended pregnancy and multiple abortions. A study conducted by Angela Taft and Lyndsey Watson (2007) found that, for women under 27 years of age, domestic violence was associated with the decision to terminate a pregnancy (and also with unwanted pregnancy and poor pregnancy outcomes). Although the women in my study are a littler older than Taft and Watson's subjects, there is now international evidence of the relationship between domestic violence and the decision to terminate a pregnancy.

Conversely, in some cases, women elected to have a sex-selective abortion even though their husband had not placed any pressure on them. Women who are 'empowered'—highly educated and economically independent—are less likely to be influenced by their husbands. For these women, the most influential factor in their decision-making is the social benefit of having a son. Thương and Na both gave their reason as the fear of 'losing face' because of having many daughters. Na said:

> If I had another daughter, people would laugh at me instead of having compassion. (Na, 49 years old, two daughters).

This analysis clearly points out the role of cultural values and social norms in reproductive decision-making.

Parents-in-law and other family members

In Việt Nam, women often mention the contrast between women's formal rights in society and their lack of rights within their families (Gammeltoft 1999). A number of studies indicate that women in Việt Nam have a weak position in reproductive decision-making (Johansson et al. 1998; Trần 2005), as the entire extended family becomes involved. The pressure on women from their extended family to choose an abortion is enormous, with the opinion of the elders particularly important.

Rural women typically have close contact with their relatives, so they make decisions about abortion only after discussing the matter with them. If women live with their husband's family, they need to consult carefully, especially with their mothers-in-law. In my study, those couples who discussed their decisions with their family were typically living with the husband's parents in the same house. If the matter was discussed within the family, the final decision had to be based on the elders' opinion. Not following elders' advice is considered 'filial impiety' (*bất hiếu*). To avoid dealing with contradictory opinions, some young couples chose to keep silent during early pregnancy and before an abortion. However, such an approach can create conflict within the family. I met two cases in which the couples decided to have an abortion but only told their family afterwards. Both these women were scolded by their husband's family and sent back to their own parents' home by their mothers-in-law. Thuận's case is an example.

Thuận and her husband decided to have abortion without telling their families. When Thuận returned home after her abortion, she could not escape the attention of her mother-in-law and had to admit to the procedure. Her mother-in-law was angry Thuận had hidden such an important matter. Instead of being taken care of, Thuận was sent back to her own family.

In contrast, couples living as a nuclear family usually made their own decisions. They did not want to involve other family members for fear of the elders disagreeing and preventing them from having an abortion. As Phi explained:

> We have our own house and live far from our parents. We did not dare talk to our parents about abortion. If they knew, they would not allow me to do so [have an abortion] and would scold me. (Phi, 38 years old, two daughters, 15 weeks pregnant)

The belief that women belong to their families-in-law after marriage plays an important role in sex-selective abortion decision-making. Where couples receive contradictory opinions on having an abortion, women's natal families usually advise them to follow their in-laws' wishes to avoid any clash between generations, the consequences of which are likely to fall on the woman.

Thu married when she was 18 years old and had two daughters. She and her husband did not care much about the sex of their children. 'My husband loves our daughters so much. He has never scolded them. He said he did not care about having a son,' Thu told me. When Thu became pregnant for the third time, an ultrasound scan revealed she was carrying another daughter. The young couple decided she would continue with her pregnancy, but Thu's mother-in-law encouraged them to terminate. Thu confided:

> My husband said if I got pregnant, I should give birth regardless of the foetus's sex. But my mother-in-law disagreed. She advised me to have an abortion and then try to do something to have a son.

Thu was confused so she approached her own mother. At first, Thu's mother did not want her to have an abortion. She thought it was immoral. In the end, however, she advised Thu to do as her mother-in-law wished to avoid any conflict. Thu said: 'I want to keep this pregnancy, but I worry that if there is any problem, my mother-in-law will blame me'. (Thu, 23 years old, two daughters)

The case of Thu shows that women are usually in a weak position in regard to reproductive decision-making, creating vulnerability and diminishing women's control over their own lives. With different value systems coexisting, women must choose between being a 'good' mother who protects her child and the expectations placed on them by society. The notion of 'goodness' is often associated with behaving in an acceptable manner as defined by the wider society.

In the research on abortion because of foetal malformity, decisions are often made by the entire family (Gammeltoft 2014), whereas in my research, most women who had a sex-selective abortion kept it a secret and rarely discussed the matter with their families. This could lead to psychological problems after the abortion.

Counsellors

Not all women who went to hospital seeking abortion services decided to go ahead with an abortion (see Chapter 4 for further discussion). Counselling can discourage women from terminating their pregnancies and information about the abortion procedure can have an intimidating effect on women seeking to terminate a pregnancy. 'Doctors say the foetus's bones have already formed. The foetus's body will be torn during abortion. It makes me nervous,' Hà (29 years old, two daughters) told me. Counselling involves providing information about the procedure and this tends to spark guilt and anxiety and other strong emotional reactions to the recognisably human form of the foetus. The case of Quý shows that the concepts of morality and emotion between mother and child have a strong impact on women's decision-making. Ultrasound images can also have a strong influence on women's emotions. As Quý (40 years old) said: 'I felt pity when the doctor pointed out the foetus's body and said the foetus was touching her face.' For the abortion provider, these are effective methods to prevent sex-selective abortion. A counsellor told me:

> With women wanting late-term abortions, I usually show them the images of their foetus such as the head, arms and legs. These images bring home to them the nature of the relationship between mother and child. This makes them rethink their decision. (Counsellor, 52 years old)

Counselling plays an important role in abortion decision-making (Trần 2005; Gammeltoft et al. 2008). The key issues are the best way to provide information to women who are considering having a sex-selective abortion and what abortion providers should do if they recognise an abortion is being sought for reasons of sex selection, while respecting women's autonomy and maintaining the standards associated with informed counselling. As Scott Woodcock (2011: 495) points out:

> Counselling involves providing information about the procedure that tends to create feelings of guilt, anxiety and strong emotional reactions to the recognisable form of a human foetus. Instances of such counselling that involve false or misleading information are clearly unethical and do not prompt much philosophical reflection, but the prospect of truthful abortion counselling draws attention to a delicate issue for healthcare professionals seeking to respect patient autonomy. This is the fact that even accurate information about abortion procedures can have intimidating effects on women seeking to terminate a pregnancy.

Other people

As well as family members, employers and even fortune tellers also play an important role in a couple's decision-making about abortion. The cases of Huyền and Cúc provide examples.

Huyền's case

Huyền was a primary school teacher and her husband was a construction worker. They had two lovely daughters. When Huyền was 12 weeks pregnant with her third child, she had an ultrasound scan in a private clinic. The doctor said he was unable to determine the sex of her foetus at that time. Huyền returned to the clinic the following week, when the foetus was 13 weeks old. When the doctor told her the foetus was female, Huyền's husband wanted her to have an abortion immediately. Instead, she sought the opinion of her mother and two sisters. They opposed an abortion because they considered it immoral. Huyền also thought it was immoral to terminate the pregnancy just because the foetus was female; however, she would get into trouble if she had a third child. In the school where she worked, a teacher who had a third child was made to work in the library and take care of day-boarders instead of teaching. Huyền met with the principal to express her concerns. The principal told Huyền if the foetus was female, she should have an abortion. She would experience disciplinary measures similar to those placed on her colleague if she had a third child. Her career would be destroyed and she would not reach her goal of having a son. The principal's analysis quickly brought Huyền to the decision to have an abortion. (Huyền, 36 years old, two daughters, 14 weeks pregnant)

Cúc's case

The nurse gave Cúc two tablets. She trembled as she returned to the corridor where her husband was waiting. She sobbed violently and her husband consoled her for a while. He then took out his mobile phone and called his boss to tell him about the couple's situation. The boss said that if they had a third child, it would violate population policy; however, his boss could help him cover up this violation. Then Cúc's husband called a fortune teller, who said if the couple had a child that year, their family would be unlucky because its birth year would be incompatible with the parents'. Consequently, the couple decided to have the abortion and Cúc swallowed the tablets. (Cúc, 30 years old, two daughters, 13 weeks pregnant)

These cases show there is a tension between morality and practical benefits in regard to abortion. In Huyền's case, her mother and sisters opposed her having an abortion on moral grounds, while everyone else around her was more concerned about the fate of her husband's lineage, the practical benefits or the legality. These two cases suggest that the pressure on women and families to go ahead with a sex-selective abortion can also come from work supervisors or the advice of fortune tellers.

How ultrasound results figure in sex-selective abortion decisions

Ultrasound results are a core factor in abortion decision-making. The development of ultrasound technology has supported sex-selective abortion. The earlier women know the sex of their foetus, the more likely they are to have a sex-selective abortion. Women in urban areas are often the first to experience new technology and then pass information about it on to their female relatives in rural areas. Thu said:

> At the beginning, I did not know the sex of the foetus can be determined at the third month. I only knew the sex of my two daughters when I was in the fifth or the six month of pregnancy. I have only since found out that the sex of the foetus can be determined at three months. My sister lives in Hà Nội and she told me this. I had been intending to keep this pregnancy, but had I known otherwise, I would have had an abortion much earlier. (Thu, two daughters, 13 weeks pregnant)

Ultrasound results can also influence a woman's final decision if she is ambivalent about having an abortion. Women in this study who had a sex-selective abortion had at least three ultrasound scans before making their decision; the majority had between four and six ultrasound scans. Some of the women had a final ultrasound scan just before taking the pre-abortion medication. Hiền's case provides an example of women's emotions and the process of a sex-selective abortion.

The nurse gave Hiền two tablets to take before the abortion. She took them out of the surgical room and sat in the corridor in a very anxious state. Her sister-in-law gave her a cup of water with which to swallow the medicine. Hiền took the cup and put the tablets in her mouth, but then took them out and started crying. After a while, she said she wanted to check the sex of her foetus again. Although she had already had six ultrasound scans, she wanted to check one more time before taking the medicine. She went to a private clinic near the hospital for a three-dimensional ultrasound scan. This proved to be very easy. When we approached the clinic, a young woman in white and blue rushed up to us and asked what we would like to do. When Hiền said she wanted a three-dimensional ultrasound scan, the clinic's nurse gave Hiền a ticket and told us the price, VND200,000 (US$10). I went with Hiền into the ultrasound room while her sister-in-law waited outside. In the damp and gloomy room, a sonographer was scanning another woman, so we sat near the door to wait. On the wall, there was a large frame with many pictures of foetuses in various stages of gestation. There were some half-length pictures focused on the genital organs of the foetus. These pictures seemed designed to show the 'qualifications' of the sonographers in the clinic. Hiền looked at a picture of a 14-week foetus with a steady gaze. She said to me through tears: 'My foetus is the same gestation as that foetus over there. So, it has human form. I feel I am doing wrong towards my child.' It was then her turn for a scan. She was trembling as she lay on the bed. The sonographer quickly checked some foetal development indicators and then carefully checked between the hind limbs of the foetus. He asked Hiền: 'How many daughters do you have?' 'I have only one daughter,' Hiền stammered (in fact, she had two). The sonographer checked again, changed the dimensions of the image of the foetus and affirmed it was a girl. Hiền's eyes filled with tears. The sonographer seemed to understand the purpose of Hiền's visit. He did not check any other indicators and printed the result without recording the sex of the foetus. Hiền hurried back to the hospital and called her husband to tell him about the result. Her husband said if she was sure about the accuracy of the sex determination, she should go ahead with the abortion. (Hiền, 32 years old, two daughters, 15 weeks pregnant)

Duration of gestation and foetal situation

Women in my research were most likely to have a sex-selective abortion in the second trimester. Sixty-eight per cent of my sample had their abortion between the 14th and 16th week of their pregnancy. Other research has produced similar results. A study of induced abortion among 1,409 women in Maharashtra, India, claims that sex-selective abortion took place significantly later in the pregnancy than abortions for other reasons (mean gestation 17.2 weeks versus 9.2 weeks, respectively). In another study, of married Indian women, sex-selective abortions accounted for more than two-thirds of all second-trimester abortions (Ganatra et al. 2001).

The decision to have an abortion is not an easy one. The women in my study had several ultrasound scans before having an abortion to ensure the results were accurate. They were advised of the sex of the foetus during a diagnostic scan taken in the 12th week of pregnancy and then waited one or two weeks to double-check the results. It then took them about another week to decide whether or not to have an abortion. The length of the decision-making process results in most women having a sex-selective abortion in the 14th to 16th week of pregnancy. A late-term abortion is technically more difficult and more dangerous for the woman. In addition, a pregnant woman's nurturing instinct and a growing sense of a relationship with the foetus make many women hesitant to have a late-term abortion.

There is a moral differentiation between early menstrual regulation, when the foetus is considered to be a 'blood clot' or a 'bean seed', and late-term abortion, when the foetus has 'human form'. Many women who had sex-selective abortions supposed that abortion early in the second trimester was acceptable, but they would not have an abortion late in the second trimester because the foetus would be too big by then and would have the form of a baby.

Late-term sex-selective abortion is, however, often conducted. A woman confided:

> Most women have to terminate a pregnancy several times. It is normal if my pregnancy is unplanned, but I should have an abortion in early pregnancy. However, this is a planned pregnancy. I have had an abortion just because this is a girl. It is a pity. (Hồng, abortion at 14 weeks)

Sex-selective abortion has also been occurring among women who are HIV-positive or have a malformed foetus, but several studies conducted in Việt Nam have noted the decision to continue with the pregnancy in these cases if the foetus is male (Trần 2005; Oosterhoff et al. 2008). Pauline Oosterhoff et al. (2008) remark that HIV-positive women often decide to continue with a pregnancy if they know the foetus is male, whereas they might not have continued for a girl-child. Similar decisions have been observed in the case of a malformed foetus (Trần 2005). In previous research, I discovered that a disabled boy is usually more easily accepted than a disabled girl,[2] so the sex of the foetus also strongly affects abortion decision-making in cases of foetal malformation. In this study, the case of Toàn supports this conclusion.

Toàn was from a village about 30 kilometres from Hà Nội. She had a daughter with leukemia. Her daughter's treatment was expensive and Toàn and her husband paid for it with money they earned trading bananas from their village. They were afraid to have a second child in

---

2   The project was 'Population, Development and New Reproductive Health Technology: Pre-natal screening in Vietnam', funded by the Danish International Development Agency.

case it also had the disease. Because of this fear, when Toàn fell pregnant unintentionally and the couple found out at 14 weeks that the foetus was female, they decided to have an abortion. According to Toàn, a girl would suffer more than a boy from leukemia.

Religious sanctions against abortion

Abortion—particularly late-term abortion—is considered immoral in Việt Nam. In this section, I discuss the religious implications of sex-selective abortion. The arguments are based on the morality of the practice, the status of the foetus and the position of women in decision-making.

To understand why women hesitate to have an abortion, it is useful to understand local religious beliefs and perceptions of abortion. The major religion in Việt Nam is the so-called triple religion (*tam giáo*)—a combination of Buddhism, Taoism and Confucianism. There are also other religions with a significant number of adherents, including Catholicism, Protestantism, Islam, Cao Đài and Hòa Hảo. The major religious affiliation, with around 10 million adherants, is Buddhism (Đặng 2003). When asked, Vietnamese people are most likely to identify as Buddhist or Catholic, but they are also likely to follow Confucianism and turn to Taoism for their understanding of the cosmos.

The Vietnamese folk religion blends Buddhism, Taoism and Confucianism with spirit beliefs and local cults. Although one might argue that Confucian values—which strongly influence son preference—provide a context conducive to sex-selective abortion, Confucianism does not endorse killing or violence of any form. Rather, the desired ends are to be achieved through superior ethics and by cultivating social relations. In Taoism, it is believed that one's destiny can be influenced by gaining and deploying esoteric knowledge. In neither case do these traditions offer an ethical basis for abortion, nor do they explicitly forbid the practice. Buddhists believe in reincarnation and that life begins at the moment of conception. This naturally inclines Buddhism away from permitting abortion. Taking the life of any living thing is generally condemned in Buddhism and, according to this stance, abortion is frowned on in Việt Nam (Gammeltoft 2003). Finally, as we shall see, popular belief in the efficacy of spirits sets up a different kind of sanction against abortion—a sanction wielded by the aborted foetus itself.

Although these aspects of religious tradition condemn or prohibit the practice, abortion has always existed. The morality of abortion is related to the core issue of when a foetus becomes a human being. Many people believe that, in the early stages of gestation, the foetus (or embryo) is merely a blood clot (Gammeltoft 1999); therefore, early termination is not regarded as abortion. Early-term abortion in Việt Nam is called 'menstrual regulation' and has not posed any particular moral problems. Conversely, in later pregnancy—usually after three months—abortion is considered morally wrong. One woman compared early and late-term abortions in the following way:

> In early pregnancy, abortion is much easier because the foetus does not yet have a human form. It is just a blood clot. When it has human form, it also has a spirit. If I keep it, it will become a human being. If I abort it, it will have resentment towards me. (Chung, 40 years old, two daughters, 14 weeks pregnant)

Studies of moral perceptions of abortion in Việt Nam point out that attitudes about the ethics of the practice vary widely (Johansson et al. 1996; Gammeltoft 1999, 2002), particularly among different generations. For example, in a study of the side-effects of IUDs among married rural women in Hà Tây province, carried out in 1993–94, Tine Gammeltoft (2002, 2003) found that elders considered abortion at any stage of gestation a sin, while younger people found early terminations morally acceptable. Similar findings emerged in my study. One elderly woman told me:

> In the past, we did not dare to have an abortion. Get pregnant, have a child. Throwing it away [abortion] is a sin [bỏ nó đi thì phải tội]. If we do an immoral thing, it [the foetus] might condemn our family. Young people now have abortions more easily. Abortions are popular, but that is a big sin if abortions are conducted when foetuses have a human form. (Trang's mother-in-law, 68 years old)

Although younger people thought early abortions were morally acceptable, they were very uneasy about late-term abortion. 'Abortion is a sin' was mentioned in most of my interviews. As Nguyệt said:

> I did a wrong thing when I had an abortion just because the foetus
> is female. I feel like a bad person. This is my sin and I can't forget it.
> (Nguyệt, 28 years old, one daughter, 17 weeks pregnant)

Not only women, but also men thought abortion once the foetus had
a human form was highly morally problematic.

> If it is in an early pregnancy stage and the foetus has no human form,
> the abortion is simple. I thought a lot about it when we had to decide to
> have an abortion when its body had been formed. Perhaps it would be
> injected with a toxic drug or cut into several parts before taking it out
> of the womb. I felt guilty when thinking that we killed our baby. (Huệ's
> husband, 48 years old)

Change of heart

Women who had decided to have a sex-selective abortion and looked
for an abortion service might change their mind and decide to carry
to term after their abortion requests had been approved. I met three
women who went to hospital for a sex-selective abortion but then
decided to continue with their pregnancy. Why did they change their
minds? The case of Quý will help us understand more.

Quý came to the counselling room in a state of profound anxiety. This
was the last step of the administrative procedure before her abortion. The
nurse/counsellor told her it was too late to have an abortion that afternoon
because she would need several hours for cervical preparation, so she
was given an appointment for the next morning. Quý went home and
cried. She could not sleep that night or even discuss the matter with her
husband. The next day, the couple decided they would not go through
with the abortion. Two days after this, Quý met with me to talk about her
decision. She said:

> I thought it is immoral to have an abortion when it [the foetus] has human
> form. It has a face, arms and legs. It has a full human form. When I had
> ultrasound scans, the doctor said its hand was touching its face. The
> doctor in the Department of Family Planning said it has a skeleton already.
> I felt pity for it. It also has a spirit. If I destroy it, it will resent me and I will
> be haunted by anxiety.

I visited Quý six months later, when her lovely daughter was nearly two
months old. When I arrived at their home, her husband was standing
at the door waiting for the rain to stop. He had a busy job as a tissue
delivery man. Quý was holding her new baby; she looked ruddy-faced

and seemed happy. The couple's five-year-old daughter was playing around her little sister. The couple seemed very happy to see me again and I presented them with a pink dress for the baby. I held the baby and spoke with Quý's husband while Quý served me tea. Quý's husband told me:

> We decided to have an abortion, but we finally abandoned the idea. If we left it off [bỏ nó đi—aborted the female foetus], we would degrade our dignity. What would happen if our children knew about this conscienceless behaviour? We may have a son, but we would lose our dignity and morality. I told my wife that we could not do that because dignity is most important. It is more important than money. (Quý's husband, 45 years old)

Clearly, the immorality of abortion weighed heavily on Quý and her husband. Although the couple decided to continue with the pregnancy and were pleased with their decision, they have been in agony about not having a son. 'We want to have a son to attain our inner wishes and to satisfy my parents. Otherwise, we feel guilty towards our parents and ancestors. That is Vietnamese culture,' said Quý's husband. Having a third child would be an obstacle for them because Quý's husband made a precarious living from his job. The couple's decision-making was characterised by the struggle to balance the wish to have a son, morality and economic circumstances.

All three of the women who decided not to go ahead with their abortion were satisfied with their decision; however, they still expressed a deep need to have a son. Petchesky and Judd (1990: 367) points out:

> A series of 'negotiations' back and forth between ideology, social reality and desire are involved in abortion decision-making. This negotiation incorporates social and individual need into the shifting ground of moral values.

Conclusion

As this chapter has demonstrated, traditional norms about the value of sons in tandem with new elements such as developing reproductive technologies and changes in fertility rates create strong desires for a son. While one may conclude from the evidence that son preference has shifted to a 'son requirement' in the new social context, the value of sons remains central in the reproductive desires and strategies of a substantial proportion of families in contemporary Việt Nam.

The value placed on sons continues to inform and shape reproductive choices, even while those choices are changing and adapting to the new social factors and technologies. In other words, women's abortion decision-making can be understood as an accommodation of resilient patriarchal norms. Sex-selective abortion is a response to the constraints of such norms, reinforced by the contemporary socioeconomic and political environment. The economic, political and social pressures driving the shift towards smaller families, together with use of new ultrasound technology, push women to pursue having at least one son. In these circumstances, women suffer greatly from the clash between the high demand to produce a son and the demand to have fewer children.

In the context of interpersonal relations, women have to accede to the wishes of significant others such as their husbands, parents-in-law and the state when making reproductive decisions. While rural women typically experience pressure from their kin to produce a male heir, urban women—especially professional women—are more likely to be influenced by the social norms and symbols that structure women's position in families and society. Whatever the circumstances, the evidence suggests that most women's abortion decisions are ultimately made on the basis of not only received moral or religious doctrine, but also the social and political conditions that define their lives. Deciding to proceed with a sex-selective abortion is a complex process. In such negotiations, the perceived necessity for an abortion is often the result of external economic, social, medical and/or interpersonal conditions. Many, if not most, women seeking sex-selective abortion are reluctant to have, or ambivalent about, the procedure. Women are likely to experience confusion as the cultural expectations that shape their decision-making clash with the potential sanctions against them, their maternal desires and duties, and the legal, moral and medical frameworks within which their decisions are made.

We have seen that 'others' are involved in the decision-making around sex-selective abortion—if not in the actual decision-making, then in establishing and maintaining the social norms that make such decisions necessary. The presence of the 'other' in such personal decision-making compels us to question what we mean by individual 'choice', 'autonomy' and 'agency'. We should reconsider the feminist view of reproductive freedom grounded in general principles of 'bodily integrity' and 'bodily self-determination'. I agree that the decision-making self must remain at the core of reproductive rights, but the concept of 'self' reaches far beyond the notion of women's right to choose. Women's 'right to choose' should be considered against the social and material conditions under which choices are made. Where dominant patriarchal ideologies construct a wifely and maternal duty to produce a son, a woman's decision to have an abortion is based on their embedded sense of these ideals. Similarly, we should ask how, when and in what circumstances is a woman capable of exercising control over her body. This research suggests that women in Việt Nam experience a tension in feeling both a sense of belonging to and an alienation from their body.

Based on empirical material from Egypt, Saba Mahmood (2001) reconsiders what we mean when we talk about agency. She writes:

> I want to suggest we think of agency not as a synonym for resistance to relations of domination, but as a capacity for action that historically specific relations of subordination enable and create. (Mahmood 2001: 203)

Considering the evidence of women's sex-selective abortion decision-making in Việt Nam, it makes sense to reconsider 'agency' along these lines. Reproductive agency has specific meanings in different cultures, social circumstances and political contexts; it must consider the significant familial, cultural, social and economic relationships that enable and constrain women as reproductive agents. These findings indicate that responsibility for sex-selective abortion rests not with individual women alone, but also implicates the wider society of which they are a part.

3

Sex-selective abortion:
Dilemmas in the silence

Hiền's face turned pale when the nurse in the surgical room called her name. She trembled as she climbed on to the abortion bed, with a mixture of fear and torment in her eyes. She put her legs in the stirrups and her hands on her belly with her fingers crossed. The doctor sat on a swivel stool, protected from head to toe by white surgical clothing, including a face mask and protective glasses. The nurse was also wearing a mask. In contrast to the noise in the corridors and waiting rooms outside, the surgical room was quiet and filled with tension. I heard the clinking of surgical tools as the nurse prepared them. Hiền looked around nervously, then screwed up her eyes. Without speaking, the nurse gave Hiền an injection of pain medication. Hiền winced and breathed slowly to calm herself. With skilful movements, the doctor inserted a speculum into Hiền's vagina, cleaned it and the cervix with antiseptic solution and grasped the cervix with an instrument to hold the uterus in place. The doctor inserted forceps into the uterus and grabbed a piece of the foetus's body, which he removed. It was streaming blood. Hiền curved her body in pain, her eyes brimming with tears, but she tried to constrain her groan. I experienced shock when I saw a leg being pulled out through the vaginal canal. The doctor continued and, one after another, pieces of the foetus were pulled out. The doctor then used a curette to scrape the lining of the uterus and sucked the uterine cavity with a cannula to ensure its contents were completely removed. Finally, the doctor gathered the extracted pieces of the foetus and laid them on a tray to make sure he had the complete body. The nurse took this tray and put it in a fridge before helping Hiền on to a stretcher. Hiền was transferred to the postabortion room, which was crowded with women.

This is a description of a sex-selective abortion that was undertaken using the D&E method in a public hospital in Hà Nội. The abortion process is marked by pain, stress and, most notably, silence. Although the abortion client and providers uttered scarcely a word throughout this transaction, the evident fear and suffering experienced by all actors prompt many questions. Why was Hiền fearful and nervous? What was the meaning of her tears? Did she cry only in pain or did she also feel anguish for her foetus? What did the abortion providers feel? What for them would have been the hardest aspect of the process—the foetal dismemberment, their patient's trauma or the knowledge they were undertaking a sex-selective abortion?

This chapter will help us understand the meanings of this silence, and to pull aside the curtain shrouding sex-selective abortion in Việt Nam. One objective is to provide insights into women's and abortion providers' experiences and the role of the different people involved in the process. I also analyse the medical, emotional, ethical and policy problems surrounding such abortions through a critical discussion of Tine Gammeltoft's (2002: 328) observation: 'In public life in Việt Nam, abortion as a moral problem is shrouded in silence.' I argue that the public and private silences surrounding sex-selective abortion have personal, sociocultural and political meanings. Analysis of the dilemmas faced by women having a sex-selective abortion and the others involved points us towards deeply grounded sociocultural tensions within contemporary Việt Nam.

In describing sex-selective abortion, this chapter reveals the experiences, emotions and moral conflicts of those seeking the procedure. Researching abortion anthropologically entails uncovering the experiences of all those involved in the process, including women and their families, abortion service providers, health system managers and policymakers. From an anthropological perspective, 'the more widely and attentively these voices are heeded, the more likely the prospects are for reforming related social practices and public policies' (Jing-Bao 2005: 10). This chapter explores sex-selective abortion practices in Hà Nội today by utilising an ethnographic approach.

Sex-selective abortion in a public hospital: 'Removing a table that is larger than the door from a room'

In the public hospital where I conducted my observations, the abortion process had three main stages: the administrative procedure, the counselling sessions and the surgical procedure. In each section of this chapter, I describe the experiences of women and abortion providers during the process and explore the problems in the delivery of abortion services.

Administrative procedures: Bureaucratic formality

On a hot summer's day, the temperature and humidity inside Hà Nội's leading public hospital for abortion provision seemed even higher because of the crowds. The Department of Family Planning, where abortions are conducted, is one of the busiest departments in the hospital. Everywhere—along the corridor, at the counters, outside the professional rooms—clients and their families had to push their way through a mass of bodies. Nurses were sometimes grouchy because patients had not followed instructions or they did not have their receipt. In this hospital, women who want a second-trimester abortion must follow a standard administrative procedure. First, they are given an account number and medical book at the reception desk, before being sent to another gate to pay their fee. They then have an ultrasound scan and a vaginal check in the examination room and are given a medical record. They must bring this record to the counselling room, where the counsellor helps them fill in the record and their consent for the abortion. They return to the examination room to have blood and urine tests, before attending the accounting table to pay for the tests before the samples are sent to the laboratory. They need to wait several hours for the results, which they then bring back to the examination room. The nurse in the examination room hands their consent form and medical records over to the board manager. The hospital board manager approves their abortion by signing these documents. After the counsellor makes a final check of the documents, the woman is sent to the surgical room. Women have to pass at least 12 administrative procedures before their abortion.

Several points can be made about the nature of these procedures. First, such convoluted administrative routines are standard in most public hospitals in Việt Nam and similar steps are in place for all surgical procedures, not just abortion. The administrative formalities in this hospital attest to the status of abortion as a routinised medical procedure.

Second, abortion services attract a fee, even in public hospitals. Much of the administrative process entails determining, collecting and recording payment of that fee. Although the government subsidises health care, a large share of the cost of expensive surgical procedures has to be borne by patients themselves. Reproductive health in Việt Nam is significantly market-based, with patients shouldering the financial burden yet also setting the demand for medical procedures of all kinds. The administrative process at this hospital provides a window on to the sex-selective abortion process as a market-based transaction.

Third, the array of medical tests and failsafe procedures in place indicates the level of risk associated with abortion, and especially late-term abortion. Sex-selective abortion is conducted no earlier than the second trimester of pregnancy, because the sex of the foetus cannot be determined any earlier. These, like all late-term abortions, are considered to have a higher risk of complications. As a result, the government has mandated that second-trimester abortions must take place in provincial or national public hospitals. Local clinics are allowed to conduct abortions but not in the second trimester. The shortage of experienced staff and facilities at provincial hospitals means many women come to Hà Nội for a second-trimester abortion, increasing the burden on the capital's public hospitals.

The constrained supply of and high demand for abortion mean the facilities at the public hospital where I conducted my research are always overburdened. The overload of clients increases the waiting time for all administrative steps, so that the administrative process takes an entire day at least. Those women who can, seek out acquaintances who are employed in the hospital to help them. Most women from the provinces, however, have to spend several days completing the administrative procedures. Two women among my 35 core cases chose to have an illegal abortion at a private clinic near their home to avoid these complicated and time-consuming administrative procedures.

In spite of the complexity, confusing nature and often poor standard of administrative services in the public hospital in which I studied, many people still preferred it to a private clinic, because they knew it was safe. One woman's husband said:

> The administrative procedure is so complex. This is the first time we have been to a hospital in Hà Nội. How can we know the procedure? I asked some nurses, but they are irritable. Registration is here and payment is there. It took us a day to do the administrative requirements. We had to continue the day after. I did not know when this procedure would be finished. I do not have any acquaintances in this hospital. We came to this hospital because we thought my wife would be safer here. (Hoa's husband, 39 years old)

We then come to a dilemma faced by hospital staff, some of whom would like to simplify the process to shorten waiting times. The regulations require women to present their identity card and family record book, but this procedure is often waived. Some counsellors want to eliminate these steps to make access to safe abortion services easier for women. One counsellor said:

> Regularly, clients had to show identity cards or family records before having an abortion. But, in fact, clients can have an abortion without showing these documents. Showing identity cards or family records is not necessary and is time-consuming for clients. Administrative procedures should be simple. (Counsellor, 54 years old)

Conversely, other counsellors suggested family records should be collected, because they could help track the number and sex of the children of women seeking an abortion, which would help providers determine whether they were dealing with sex-selective abortion.

Herein lies an important dilemma of the administrative process for abortion in Việt Nam. Hospital staff believe that most patients seeking a late-term abortion are doing so because the foetus is of the unwanted sex. However, at no point in the round of medical tests, form-filling and mandated counselling sessions are clients asked outright whether they are seeking a sex-selective abortion. Women are required to record their reasons for seeking an abortion, but most say it is because they have enough children or because of economic constraints. To my knowledge, 'sex selection' is never recorded as the reason.

When women give their consent for the surgical abortion procedure, they must also accept full responsibility in case of any complications. Women and their families who asked counsellors why they had to give this written undertaking were told it was one of the regulations and if they did not consent, the abortion would not go ahead. Some women and their husbands told me they thought that if there were complications during an abortion, the medical professionals—and not the patients—should bear the responsibility. The explanation I received from abortion providers was more detailed:

> Late-term abortion is dangerous for pregnant women. We have explained the danger for them. If they want to abort, they have to accept the danger. Complications are rare, but they have happened. We require women to do that [provide written consent of their acceptance of responsibility in case of complications] to avoid suffering a lawsuit. (Abortion provider, 52 years old)

The belief among counsellors that they can prevent patients suing by 'making them take responsibility for complications' is a misreading of their own professional ethics, founded on an incorrect assumption. It is true that patients need to be informed, but this is not the same as absolving the hospital of responsibility for complications if the hospital or healthcare provider is at fault.

We can therefore detect a number of silences during the administrative procedure in this hospital. Clients seeking sex-selective abortion must silently endure the ordeal of the hospital's administrative process to receive service in the place considered to provide the safest abortions. Money changes hands, a complex array of checks is undertaken and an agreement is signed, but never is the nature of the transaction made transparent. Instead, women have to take full responsibility for any problems that may happen during a surgical procedure whose very nature is itself not transparent.

Counsellors: The gatekeepers of sex-selective abortion

As noted, counselling is a mandated part of the administrative procedure for abortion service providers. Counselling is provided by nursing staff, who take turns working in the counselling room. These staff—all of them women—have the additional role of helping women complete the administrative steps and form-filling. They are on hand at all stages of the process. As a consequence of their close interactions with clients, most likely learn the real reason an abortion is being sought. This knowledge can create a dilemma between their duty as a public health official and their sympathy for the woman. In their interactions, they elicit admissions that clients probably otherwise would not share. They also exhibit a degree of arrogance and sometimes make accusations against their clients that verge on unprofessionalism. The ethics and effectiveness of these interventions are open to question. However, these intermediaries—unpolished as their services may be—are typically the only staff to make explicit the nature of the transaction taking place in this hospital.

According to international professional standards, abortion counselling should have three basic aims. The first is to aid the woman in making a decision about an unwanted pregnancy. The second is to help her implement the decision. The third is to assist her in controlling her future fertility. These principles should result in a humane and understanding relationship between counsellor and client (Asher 1972). The WHO's (2003b: 26) guidelines on abortion counselling advise:

> counselling can be very important in helping the woman consider her options and ensure that she can make a decision free from pressure. Counselling should be voluntary, confidential and provided by a trained person.

The Standing Committee of the Vietnamese National Assembly passed the Population Ordinance in January 2003 prohibiting sex selection by any means. It encourages any abortion clinic discovering a potential sex-selective abortion to prevent it. Counselling is the unique stage in the abortion process when abortion providers are able—by virtue of the verbal communications counsellors have with women—to uncover cases of sex-selective abortion. The questions raised are: Do counsellors follow the WHO guidelines? Can they act as required? When a sex-selective abortion case is discovered, how do they deal with it? The following observation is of counselling in practice in a public hospital.

'Come in', the counsellor said coldly in response to a tap on the door. The woman hesitated before entering and did not speak. She put her medical book with the ultrasound result on the table and sat opposite the counsellor. The counsellor glanced at the ultrasound result and said rapidly: 'Your foetus is 15 weeks already. It is nearly four months. Why do you want to have a late abortion? Did you see the legs, the arms and the body of your baby?' The woman spluttered: 'I have three children. I did not know I was pregnant—' The counsellor interrupted: 'You have kept this pregnancy intentionally. You have three children, so you have experience with pregnancy.' 'Yes, I knew I was pregnant, but my husband said if it is a boy, we will keep it. We do not want to have another girl,' the woman admitted. The counsellor responded:

> Late-term abortion is not simple. Boy and girl, tuhh, tuhh … Which era are we living in? Before having an abortion, you need to pay for medicines and the blood and urine tests. The fee for these tests and medicines is more than VND1 million. With the abortion procedure there is always a danger of haemorrhage or injury to the uterus. In case of excessive bleeding, you will need a blood transfusion and you will have to pay for it. If your uterus is punctured, which can cause severe blood loss, the uterus will be removed. You have to take responsibility in these cases. If you want to have an abortion, you need to fill in a consent form. Take the form over there and fill it in.

The woman kept silent. She was embarrassed as she filled in the form and gave her reason for the abortion as 'have enough children'. (Author's observation in counselling room)

In practice, this counselling session has not met the ideal espoused in the professional literature and the WHO guidelines. The counsellor was haughty and dismissive and outlined the potential complications in an abrupt manner. Her client was shamed and/or frightened into silence. The counsellor's blunt accusations apparently succeeded in extracting from the woman the real reason for the abortion—it was indeed for sex selection. However, the counsellor's intervention ended at that point and the woman provided a legally acceptable reason on the paperwork and went ahead with the abortion.

Why is such counselling not done according to international protocols? One reason is the weakness of available human resources. Although this public hospital is considered one of the leading obstetrics and gynaecology hospitals in Việt Nam, providing counselling in accordance with the WHO guidelines is impractical because of the lack of trained staff and the heavy workload. As noted, there is no specialised abortion counsellor in this hospital and the nurses take turns working in the counselling room. Some experienced nurses have been trained in counselling by reproductive health projects funded by the Pathfinder organisation and the UNFPA. These nurses are aware of the requirements for abortion counselling, but they are unable to achieve the appropriate standards because of general work pressures. This hospital's Department of Family Planning is usually crowded, with 50 to 70 abortion cases a day. An experienced nurse/counsellor (52 years old) told me: 'I know the abortion counselling standards, but if I follow the appropriate standards for abortion counselling, I can counsel only 10 patients a day.' However, the remainder of the staff had not been trained in counselling. A young nurse/counsellor (36 years old) said: 'I have never been trained in abortion counselling. I have heard other nurses talking to patients and I imitate them.' The WHO guidelines on counselling are idealistic, but are they feasible? How can they be applied when resources and health system support are lacking? These questions are highly pertinent in Việt Nam.

There seems to be more at stake here than just the counsellors' presumed lack of education and their failure to internalise international abortion counselling protocols. Institutionally, the public health system does not have in place any mechanism for implementing the state's ban on sex-selective abortion. When faced with the market demand for abortion of this kind, the administrative obstacle course in place in public hospitals presents only a feeble barrier. Nurses and counsellors—the only staff who communicate with clients and understand what is at stake—are thus directly exposed to the conflict between the law and the nature of the services provided. I surmise that, placed in this position, these intermediaries tend to abandon a neutral professional position and step more into the role of surveillance and deterrence.

Observing counsellors and talking with them, I sensed that many were proud of their ability to know, even without being told, a woman's 'real' reason for seeking an abortion. Most nurses/counsellors affirmed that they could guess a sex-selective abortion case by a woman's characteristics, such as the timing of her pregnancy and the gender and number of her existing children. A nurse/counsellor said:

> I can guess if it is a case of sex-selective abortion. If a woman has two or more daughters, or a woman has one daughter and her child is not small, and she has a late-term abortion without any medical reasons, she may well be having a sex-selective abortion. (Nurse/counsellor, 50 years old)

Counsellors and nurses also seemed to believe their role was to deter women from having a sex-selective abortion. The information they exchanged with clients was provided not with the intention of offering them neutral advice for contemplation, but rather to actively dissuade them from going ahead with the abortion. In one counsellor's opinion, when a case of sex-selective abortion is identified, it is important to mention three issues: the inaccuracy of sex determination, the potential complications of abortion and the moral issues.

> First, I tell them that the accuracy of ultrasound in sex determination is not 100 per cent; sometimes, albeit in a small number of cases, it is inaccurate. Second, they should be counselled on abortion complications. Third, I mention moral issues. The babies are human beings; abortion like that is immoral. (Nurse/counsellor, 50 years old)

For this counsellor, airing such issues in a counselling session might help dissuade a woman from having a sex-selective abortion. She reasoned that a woman might decide to keep the foetus when she heard about the possibility of complications or was prompted to consider the moral or religious issues related to abortion. The following exchange between a nurse and a client is an example of this approach.

As the clinic was less crowded than usual one day, some of the Department of Family Planning staff gathered in the counselling room to chat. A woman, about 30 years old, arrived to ask about the administrative procedure for an abortion. She said she was 14 weeks pregnant and wanted an abortion. The senior nurse asked, 'How many children do you have?' 'I have a four-year-old daughter,' the woman replied diffidently. The nurse said: 'Your child is not too small. It is time to have your second child. You want to have an abortion because the foetus is female, don't you?' The woman remained silent. The counsellor continued: 'Where did you have your ultrasound scans?' 'I have had several ultrasound scans in different places. They all said it is a girl,' the woman said confidently. 'Are you sure about the accuracy of the ultrasound scans?' the nurse asked doubtfully. She continued:

> Do you know you can have complications such as haemorrhage or perforation of the uterus if you have an abortion? You have only one child and you may become infertile. Furthermore, the baby in your womb has a face, body, arms and legs. Are you not afraid of her resentment? The baby in your womb is normal, but you want to abort her and put her in the fridge. Do you want to see the foetuses in the fridge? If you do, let us go and see them in the next room.

At this point, the woman panicked and hastily left, without saying goodbye. (Author's observation in a counselling room)

We can see from this example that the nurse's attempt to dissuade the client by overwhelming her with a variety of confronting arguments was so effective that the young woman abandoned the scene in panic. Although such an approach may deter some women from having a sex-selective abortion, there is a need to discuss the ethical issues involved. This counselling method may not prevent all women from having a sex-selective abortion, because there are other places they can go. Moreover, as John Asher (1972) mentions, the aims of counselling are to help women explore their feelings about their situation and make a decision without being judged by providers. Some women reported that, while the thought of abortion was not traumatic at first, it became so during the counselling process. The counselling did not relieve their anxiety. Conversely, counsellors tended to pass judgement and try to impose their own moral, ethical or religious beliefs.

Women said they were under a lot of stress and wanted to be able to discuss their feelings with someone in private. My observations show that little or no communication occurs between health staff and clients before and during the surgical abortion procedure or afterwards in the recovery room. This is a result not only of providers being too busy, but also of the providers' attitudes.

> Providers should ask our situation and give us counselling. I have been urged to hurry up when I was still indecisive. The clinics are crowded with patients and staff have a heavy workload, but sometimes the staff are very authoritarian. (Hà, 39 years old, 15 weeks pregnant)

While empathetic counselling is generally recommended, women in this study have been judged by staff or not given the opportunity to share their feelings and discuss their difficulties. As a consequence of poor counselling, women face a multitude of anxieties and psychological issues or end up seeking multiple sex-selective abortions. Similar limitations in terms of counselling in abortion care in Việt Nam were found in recent qualitative studies (Trần 2005; Gammeltoft and Nguyễn 2007).

The evidence suggests women would be receptive to counselling that helped them vent their feelings of ambivalence. Not all women who came to the hospital looking for an abortion service decided to proceed. At the same time, the great number of abortions taking place in an institution that lacks adequate counselling might, by default, sway those who are ambivalent. As Cúc said:

> At first, I thought it [abortion] was a sin. When I came to the hospital, I saw so many women who had had an abortion. Some women were in later pregnancy than me, so I was not as worried as before. [There were] numerous [women having] abortions, not only me. (Cúc, 30 years old, 13 weeks pregnant)

Cúc's comments suggest that counselling could make a difference at this stage.

It needs to be noted that in the overwhelming number of cases I observed, counselling staff did not prevent sex-selective abortion from going ahead, despite the sometimes blunt efforts at dissuasion employed. In several cases, once their stern lecture was delivered, they ushered women through the remaining formalities with little fuss. What accounts for the failure of these state agents to prevent acts in contravention of the law? I suggest that, ultimately, these women's membership of the same sociocultural milieu as their clients, and their own experiences of the kinds of dilemmas they face, led them to understand intuitively and sympathise with women's circumstances and accede to their decision to have the abortion. Nursing staff were split between their role as public health professionals and their membership of the same sociocultural milieu as their clients. This perhaps accounts equally well for the 'noisy' irritability and haughtiness staff displayed towards clients and their 'silent' acquiescence to the abortions.

How should nursing staff approach sex-selective abortion seekers? Should they—can they—change their clients' preference for a son? Many are conscious of the role of counselling in sex-selective abortion, but are confused as they have not been adequately trained. Some nurses/counsellors were mindful of the social consequences of sex-selective abortion, but they did not know how to share this with their clients. A nurse/counsellor shared her thoughts:

> Maybe we can tell women that if they want to abort female foetuses and try to have sons, their sons will not be able to get married. In neighbouring countries like China, men cannot get married. In the future, men will find it difficult to get married because of the shortage of girls. At the same time, girls will choose rich men to be their husbands. Men who are not rich and live in rural areas will find it difficult to get

married. Perhaps people have not thought about these matters. I think so, but I do not know how to talk with women effectively. (Nurse, 52 years old)

A number of studies report that partners play a positive role in decision-making and support throughout the abortion process (Beenhakker et al. 2004; Becker et al. 2008). This is especially relevant in patriarchal societies and for sex-selective abortion. In evaluating the role of counselling for women's family members, a nurse/counsellor said:

There are cases of women who have had several sex-selective abortions. A number of women feel pressure to have a son from their husbands or their husband's family. So, the people who provide this pressure should be present at the counselling.

She added:

Counselling for a woman's husband is very important. If they are not counselled directly, they will not know the danger of abortion. If we counsel only women then they can pass on the information to their husbands and their families, but I am sure they cannot convey everything that they have been advised. (Nurse/counsellor, 52 years old)

Although counsellors understand the importance of counselling a woman's family members, it rarely happens. The reasons are not only their overloaded work schedules, as mentioned above, or the lack of training in abortion counselling, but also the fact that counselling as an intervention lies halfway between providing deterrence and providing sympathy. This has led to men and other relatives who accompany women to abortion clinics being neglected. The shortcomings associated with counselling mean men experience their own personal crises while their partners undergo abortion. Furthermore, lack of knowledge about abortion-related complications and contraception, as well as son preference, can contribute to women repeatedly seeking sex-selective abortion. Tuấn and Hùng are examples.

Tuấn's case

Tuấn looked tired as he sat outside the operating room. Behind the closed door, his wife was in pain undergoing an abortion. He told me he had been unable to sleep and had a headache from the stress of struggling with his conscience. He did not want his wife to have this abortion because he felt sorry for his baby and he was worried for his wife's health. However, if they had this baby, they would not have an opportunity to have a son. He wondered about the accuracy of the ultrasound result. He said he would be inconsolable if the foetus was male.

While we were talking, a nurse who was an acquaintance of his rushed over to inform Tuấn that his wife's abortion had been successful. He sighed in relief and told me: 'My worries have been lessened, but I feel sorrowful. Anyway, the baby is our child, it is my blood. I feel heartbroken and anxious.'

Hùng's case

I saw Hùng sitting in the postabortion room while his wife was resting after her procedure. He looked tired and his hair was ruffled. I sat next to him and asked about his circumstances. He confided to me that he did not want to see his wife in this situation and he felt pity for her. She also had an abortion the previous year. He said:

> My wife has had two abortions. She had an abortion last year in May, when she was 17 weeks pregnant. Last time she had ovulation detection in order to conceive a male foetus, but unfortunately it was not successful.

I asked if he wanted to pursue his dream of having a son. He was not sure at that moment, but he wished there was a way to ensure he could have a son. He said he would pay tens of millions of dong if he could have a son without becoming implicated in sex-selective abortion.

In summary, it is not easy to follow the WHO guidelines on abortion counselling in clinical settings such as those in Việt Nam today. Because counsellors have not been trained for sex-selective abortion cases, they improvise their own rough-and-ready approach. At times the nurses can be intimidating and offensive. It should also be noted that their improvisations do little to reduce the number of sex-selective abortions. Significantly, their exchanges with clients were the only time in the whole transaction when the pact of silence around sex-selective abortion was threatened. The adequacy of such counselling is impacted not only by poor clinical conditions (lack of and overworked staff and untrained counsellors), but also by counsellors' personal perceptions and by weak regulatory frameworks for healthcare practitioners.

The sex-selective abortion process

In Việt Nam, first-trimester abortion is provided at the central, provincial, district and commune level in both public and private sectors. Second-trimester abortion has been restricted to central- and provincial-level public health facilities because lower-level facilities and the private sector lack trained healthcare providers, adequate medical equipment or the necessary emergency support (MOH 2003).

For second-trimester abortion, D&E[1] has been recommended by the WHO and approved by the Vietnamese health ministry since 2003. In Việt Nam, D&E has been introduced at some central and provincial hospitals and is carried out at 13–18 weeks of pregnancy. D&E requires preparing the cervix with mifepristone and must be done by skilled and experienced providers, with proper equipment.

As well as D&E, saline abortion is still often practised in many provincial hospitals (Gallo and Nghia 2007).[2] This method is used only for pregnancies of 18–24 weeks gestation. It usually requires one week of hospitalisation, which increases the cost and contributes to the hospital's work overload. It is associated with serious complications such as haemorrhage, uterine rupture and sepsis. This method delays women receiving services until after 18 weeks of pregnancy, even if they first present early in the second trimester. Waiting for the pregnancy to advance sufficiently can create a lot of emotional pressure.

The combination of mifepristone and misoprostol is now an established medical method and is highly effective for termination of pregnancy, including in the second trimester (Dalvie 2008), and has been included in Việt Nam's National Standards and Guidelines, which are currently being updated. This method is also starting to be applied in some central and provincial hospitals following regimens of misoprostol alone

---

1   Dilatation and evacuation (D&E) are used from about 12 weeks of pregnancy onwards. D&E requires preparing the cervix with mifepristone, a prostaglandin such as misoprostol or laminaria or a similar hydrophilic dilator; dilating the cervix; and evacuating the uterus using electric vacuum aspiration with 14–16 mm diameter cannula and forceps. Depending on the stage of pregnancy, achieving adequate dilatation can take anything from two hours to a full day. Many providers find the use of ultrasonography helpful during D&E procedures, but it is not essential (WHO 2003a).
2   Saline abortion during the second trimester is effected by replacing 200 mL of amniotic fluid with 200 mL of 20 per cent saline solution, which stimulates uterine contractions, followed by foetal delivery in 12–24 hours (Segen 2002).

to terminate second-trimester pregnancies: 400 mcg of misoprostol inserted vaginally every three hours for pregnancies of 16–19 weeks and every six hours for pregnancies of 20–22 weeks. This method is safe and effective, but the woman must be monitored closely throughout the process (Hoàng et al. 2008).

In the past, if women wanted an abortion in the second trimester, they had to wait until after 18 weeks gestation and undergo a saline abortion, which is associated with serious complications. Recently, for pregnancies of 17–22 weeks, medical abortion has been applied. The new method has been approved for its safety and efficacy. Medical abortion has brought more options for women seeking to terminate a pregnancy, and is safer and more effective than D&E. According to the National Standards and Guidelines, D&E can be carried out at 12–18 weeks of pregnancy. In the hospital where this study was conducted, D&E was used from 12 to 16 completed weeks of pregnancy. A doctor experienced in second-trimester abortion in this hospital explained that 'the little one's bones become hard after 16 weeks, and its size is too big to conduct a surgical abortion. Abortion after 16 weeks pregnancy conducted by surgical methods has a high complication rate'.

He compared surgical abortion after 16 weeks to 'removing a table that is larger than the door from a room'. However, D&E has been preferred for early second-trimester abortion because it reduces the cost and avoids adding to the work overload of public hospitals. The D&E method has been used since 2000 in the hospital where I conducted this study. This method is safer and shortens the hospitalisation time as well as meeting the demands of women who want an abortion early in the second trimester.

Generally, progress in making abortion safe has advantages for women's health care. However, these advantages have been exploited for other reasons. Abortion providers are conscious of these matters.

> Previously, later term abortion was not safe. It is safer now, and complications have significantly reduced. People found that later term abortion is safe, so they have more induced abortions during later stages of pregnancy. (Doctor, 43 years old)

The improvement in the quality of abortion techniques gives women more options. Although this improves women's reproductive health, it can also facilitate sex-selective abortion. Improvements in reproductive health do not cause sex-selective abortion, but such advances facilitate sex-selective abortion when new technologies are used for nonmedical purposes with insufficient management and supervision.

In the hospital where I conducted this research, a hysterectomy[3] is also used as a method of abortion for women with a high risk of complications, such as those who have had several caesareans, those in second-trimester gestation and those who have had 'enough children'.

Vân's case

I met Vân when she was in a state of confusion. It took her three days to complete the complicated administrative procedures at the public hospital. We had several conversations during that time, in which she told me about her pitiful condition.

Vân had all three of her daughters by caesarean section. Her husband's mental health was not good; sometimes he could work, sometimes not, so she had the difficult responsibility of supporting him and their three children. Despite this, she had always wanted a son. A fortune teller told her she would have a boy if she became pregnant in the Year of the Mouse (according to the lunar calendar). Believing the fortune teller, Vân decided to become pregnant after the Tết holiday. She had several ultrasound scans and learned that her foetus was female when she was 14 weeks pregnant. However, she wanted to be sure about the sex of the foetus, so she waited until she was 16 weeks pregnant and had another scan. She was 17 weeks pregnant when she decided to have an abortion. Having had three caesareans, she was considered a high-risk case. Instead of a D&E, her uterus would be cut out with the foetus inside (hysterectomy). Vân was still confused when we spoke before she went into the operating room. When I asked Vân if she knew about hysterectomy, she was in tears and said:

---

3   A hysterectomy is the surgical removal of the uterus. There are four types of hysterectomy. Total hysterectomy is the removal of the entire uterus, including the fundus and the cervix. Hysterectomy with bilateral salpingo-oophorectomy refers to the removal of both ovaries and the fallopian tubes. In supracervical hysterectomy, the body of the uterus is removed, but the cervix is left intact. Radical hysterectomy is the removal of the uterus, the cervix, the top portion of the vagina and most of the tissue surrounding the cervix in the pelvic cavity. Pelvic lymph nodes also may be removed during this surgery.

> The doctor said it is a total hysterectomy [*cắt tử cung cả khối*]. The doctor asked me to sign my consent and I did, but I do not know what it means. I am confused and know nothing. I wonder is it possible to have a caesarean to take out my baby without cutting out my uterus; then I will use contraceptive pills? I will become a man if I do not menstruate.

After this conversation, I took her concerns to the responsible doctors, who explained that conducting a medical abortion in cases like this was highly risky. The rate of uterine rupture in a subsequent delivery is said to be 50 per cent. If the uterus is ruptured, it must be cut out, the woman will need a blood transfusion and there is a high risk of infection. If the woman is in a difficult economic condition and has enough children—two or more—removing the uterus is the best way to save her life and reduce the risk of needing a blood transfusion. A blood transfusion is also very expensive and the patient must pay for it out of her own pocket. A woman can have a caesarean to remove her baby without removing her uterus, but it will be dangerous for her if she falls pregnant again. In cases like this, hysterectomy is now rarely carried out in Western countries. According to studies from the 1970s in the United Kingdom, the rate of uterine rupture in subsequent deliveries was 6 per cent (Clow and Cromptom 1973). These rates are higher in countries where women do not have access to good delivery services.

Discussing the solutions to a case like Vân's, some of the hospital's leading gynaecologists supposed it would be possible to conduct a medical abortion under close supervision in a hospital with adequate emergency facilities. Having a caesarean section to remove the foetus without cutting out the uterus (hysterotomy) is also possible; however, the woman would have to follow this up with sterilisation or contraception because of the risk of rupture in any future pregnancy.

Let me put the discussion of abortion methods aside for the moment. The most important issue here is, once again, counselling. While informed consent counselling that supports women to make a free and fully informed decision is recommended, Vân and other women in this study did not receive adequate information before they decided to have an abortion. They did not know enough about the abortion process. They allowed the doctors to choose for them without knowing all the details and associated risks. Women need to feel comfortable they can make an informed decision about whether hysterectomy is right for them. They have a right to know the risks and potential benefits of the medical options they are being offered and the right to choose among the available options.

Abortion complications

Assessing the real number of abortion complications is difficult as one must rely on complaints reported by patients and diagnoses by physicians and consider the distinction between complications that are a direct or an indirect result of the termination. Some complications are apparent immediately, while others may not become apparent until days, months and even as much as 10–15 years later. In the hospital where I conducted this study, the direct complication rate was not recorded; however, doctors estimated it was about 2 per cent. The most common complication was excessive bleeding (haemorrhage), which was more likely to affect women who had one or more caesarean sections. For these women, doctors usually chose a safer solution, such as in Vân's case.

Data from the Reproductive Health Department in the MOH (2002) showed that haemorrhage was the leading cause of maternal mortality in the country (40 per cent). Unsafe abortion also made a significant contribution to maternal mortality (11.5 per cent) (MOH 2002). Complications are also associated with multiple abortions. One nurse told me of a case she witnessed in 2008, of a woman who had an abortion at 14 weeks. Fifteen minutes after the abortion, the patient started bleeding excessively, and it proved very difficult to stop. After regaining consciousness, the woman confessed she had undergone three sex-selective abortions in two years.

Underreporting and misdiagnosis are widespread because of the shame and grief associated with the loss of a pregnant or recently delivered woman. Neither the family nor the health facilities like to admit to maternal death. It is likely the rate of death due to unsafe abortion in Việt Nam is also underreported because such procedures are not registered at all or are classified as 'haemorrhage' or other causes. Even though data on maternal mortality are unreliable and may understate the reality, it cannot be denied that late-term abortion, including sex-selective abortion, contributes to higher maternal mortality and morbidity.

Seasonal distribution of abortion

One day when the counselling room was quieter than usual, I took the opportunity to have a conversation with the nurse who was working as counsellor. I wanted to know why things were so quiet. She laughed and explained to me: 'It is the 1st day of the lunar month. Women rarely have an abortion on the 1st or in the middle of the lunar month. These times are for worship.' 'The number of clients is different at different times?' I asked. She replied:

> Counting by the working day, there are more patients on Monday and Friday compared with Wednesday and Thursday. It is usually quiet on the 1st and the 15th of the lunar month. According to the season, it is more crowded just before and after the Tết holiday.

A 2005 study by the National Hospital for Obstetrics and Gynaecology produced similar data. Abortion rates across the year ranged from 7.5 per cent to 10.6 per cent, with the lowest rate in June and the highest in January. The abortion rate also varied throughout the week. Friday had the highest rate compared with the rest of the week (22 per cent on Fridays versus 17.6 per cent on Thursdays). The data also showed that 1.7 per cent of clients attended on the 1st day of the lunar month, 2.2 per cent on the 15th day of the month and 4.6 per cent on the 16th day of the month (Nguyễn and Nguyễn 2009).

I have found the hospital deserted on common ritual ceremony days, as in the following observation.

At 3 pm on 15 January, there were almost no clients in the family planning department. The staff were in a hurry to prepare offerings for the first 15th day ceremony of the year (Lễ cúng Rằm tháng Giêng), which is one of the most important ritual ceremonies for Vietnamese people. It is said: 'To make offerings the whole year is not equal to making offerings on the 15th of the first lunar month.'

Nguyệt, 16 weeks pregnant, was sitting in the counselling room. She looked sad and tired. The doctor told Nguyệt her pregnancy could be terminated by D&E, but if she delayed, she would have to undergo a medical abortion. A medical abortion would require more time than a D&E. Nguyệt's husband was away on business and she had someone taking care of her little daughter, so she wanted to have the abortion as soon as possible. However, the nurse in the counselling room advised her to go home and wait until the Monday of the next week because of the 15th-day celebrations. Doctors do not want to perform abortions, especially late-term abortions, on this day.

To explain the differing numbers of clients on different days and the decline during ceremonial days and months, one nurse told me:

> Women want to have their abortion on a Friday because they have two days off on the weekend. People do not want to do something immoral on the days of sacrifice or during Tết because they are afraid that sinfulness is more serious at such times, and unlucky things will happen to them. (Nurse, 50 years old)

Abortion in private clinics: Illegal and unsafe, but profitable and convenient

I met Hoa, who was 15 weeks pregnant, and her husband on a hot summer day in the public hospital. The couple was wet with sweat and confused about finding the abortion clinic. They had come from a province about 70 kilometres from Hà Nội. Although they had left home early in the morning, it was nearly lunchtime when they arrived at the hospital. They had to wait a long time to complete the administrative procedures, which cost VND320,000, by which time it was late afternoon. Hoa had an appointment for an abortion the following day. The counsellor advised her that it would in fact take three or four days for a late-term abortion. The couple did not have relatives in Hà Nội and could not afford accommodation near the hospital. Their small children were at home without a carer, so the couple had to return home by motorbike. In the end, they decided to have an abortion at a private clinic near their home without any tests. Hoa said:

> I was introduced to a private clinic. The price was VND2 million. The fee for an abortion in public hospitals is VND1.2 million. The expenses for food and travel for me and my husband are very high. Abortion in a hospital is safer and cheaper than in a private clinic; however, the administrative process in hospital is complicated and takes a long time, waiting in crowded conditions. Abortion in a private clinic is conducted quickly and secretly, so I decided to have an abortion in a private clinic near my home. (Hoa, 14 weeks pregnant)

Like Hoa, many women chose to have an abortion at a private clinic, where they were at risk of unsafe practices. They were often poor rural women who lacked access to the safer abortion services offered by public hospitals or lacked awareness of the alternatives available to them. Some found out about the private clinics through acquaintances:

> I have never gone to hospital to have an abortion, but I was told that the administrative procedure in the hospital is complicated. I would have to go through many doors to complete the administrative procedures and to have blood and uterine tests as well. It is crowded in hospital and I would have to queue up for a long time … I decided to have an abortion in a private clinic for quickness, although I have to pay more money. My friend told me about a reliable clinic and I went there. I had never had a late-term abortion, so I knew nothing. In the private clinic, I had no test before the abortion. They said they would do an abortion for me immediately for the price of VND2 million. (Tân, 16 weeks pregnant)

Like Tân, many women chose the private and semiprivate sectors because of the convenient operating hours and shorter waiting times, but many also did so because of real or perceived obstacles to gaining admission to a public hospital where the standard of treatment was higher. While wealthy women in the city have more options for accessing an abortion by a trained practitioner, poor women in rural areas have fewer options. Differences in economic resources, geographic location and levels of awareness make for inequality of access to safe abortion.

Recently, a 'sex-selection package' has appeared at some private clinics. Some of the women in my core case group admitted they were offered an abortion after having foetal sex determination by ultrasonography.

> When the doctor said it is a girl, I was very sad. She told me that if I wanted to have an abortion, she could help me. Her clinic also provides abortion services. She consoled me when I worried about the safety. She said she had regularly done abortions at 15–16 weeks pregnancy. (Phương, 15 weeks pregnant)

Assessing the abortion situation in private clinics, a provincial health manager said:

> Illicit abortion in private clinics creates difficulties for evaluating the abortion situation and making policies on this issue. The medical facilities and the skill of abortion practitioners lead to complications.

However, women who want to have abortions have limited knowledge about them. They usually want to have an abortion at any gestation stage in a short time. (Manager, 54 years old)

The WHO (2003b) estimates that almost 20 million unsafe abortions are carried out globally every year. At the 1994 International Conference on Population and Development (ICPD) in Cairo, the international community recognised the pressing need to address unsafe abortion and called on governments to act:

All governments and relevant intergovernmental and non-governmental organizations are urged to strengthen their commitment to women's health, to deal with the health impact of unsafe abortion as a major public health concern and to reduce the recourse to abortion through expanded and improved family-planning services … In all cases, women should have access to quality services for the management of complications arising from abortion. (UNFPA 1994: para. 8.25)

In Việt Nam, since 1989, the private sector has been allowed to provide abortions up to 49 days of pregnancy. Recently, semiprivate services provided by public sector employees working after hours are becoming more common in urban as well as rural areas. The judgement of the WHO (1999: 53) on abortion services in Việt Nam's private sector is as follows:

The number of private sector abortion service providers, with or without official sanction, is unknown but is believed to be growing rapidly in Vietnam's largest cities and towns, particularly in the south of the country.

Regulation of the private sector varies by province, and in some cases includes periodic inspection, short-term training courses and punitive fines. In provinces where the private sector is prohibited from providing abortions, services are provided covertly and are far more difficult to regulate.

The MOH's circular letter guiding Ordinance 07/2007/TT-BYT on private clinics decrees that private obstetrics and gynaecology clinics only conduct 'menstrual regulation' for women who are less than 49 days pregnant (less than seven weeks). Clinics that violate this ordinance are to be fined VND3–8 million and their permits to practice revoked. An official in the Hà Nội health department confirmed that 'private clinics are not allowed to practice abortion, only "menstrual regulation". Billboards advertising the provision of abortion violate the regulation on abortion' (personal communication, 21 October 2009). Despite this, private obstetrics and gynaecology clinics are booming around public hospitals, especially well-known hospitals such as Bạch Mai Hospital, Army Hospital, National Hospital for Obstetrics and Gynaecology and Hà Nội Obstetrics and Gynaecology Hospital. Outside the gate of the Hà Nội Obstetrics and Gynaecology Hospital, I counted more than 20 private obstetrics and gynaecology clinics. Most of these had billboards advertising abortion services. The situation was similar around Bạch Mai Hospital, where there was an 'abortion market' in a nearby street crowded with private clinics offering abortion. Potential clients are invited to have an abortion regardless of the stage of their pregnancy. Describing such a private clinic, a woman told me:

> My friend introduced me to a private clinic to have an abortion. When I went there, I was frightened by the facilities in this clinic. The clinic was simple and untidy; it was in a small alley. It took 30–40 minutes from the road to walk to the clinic. I did not see any equipment or professional tools. If I had excessive bleeding, I would have died before receiving emergency aid. (Cúc, 13 weeks pregnant, Vĩnh Phúc province)

Although private clinics are not supposed to provide second-trimester abortions, these procedures are conducted with inadequate facilities by unskilled providers. Women use private clinics because of their convenient operating hours and shorter waiting times and the wider range of services they offer, including those that are illicit.

Perceptions of sex-selective abortion

Women's perceptions

As I outlined in Chapter 2, termination of pregnancy is seen as a sin in Việt Nam, but there is a moral differentiation between early and late-term abortions. Several of the women in my study who had a sex-selective abortion told me that abortion early in the second trimester was acceptable, but they would not have an abortion late in the second trimester because the foetus was too big and had the completed shape of a baby. Sex-selective abortion is very often the result of a planned pregnancy, which makes it difficult for women to decide to have an abortion. A woman who had an abortion when 14 weeks pregnant told me it was very common for women to have an abortion if a pregnancy was unplanned, but to go ahead with an abortion when the pregnancy was planned just because the foetus was female was a regrettable act.

The two things women were worried about before an abortion were the moral issues and, in particular, the degree of pain. The most common question I heard women ask was, 'Is it painful?' According to some authors, the degree of pain experienced during abortion varies with the age of the woman, the stage of pregnancy, the amount of cervical dilatation and the individual's level of fear (Smith et al. 1979). Helping women relax before and during the abortion procedure can help reduce pain, and adequate counselling can lessen a woman's fear.

A cervical preparation procedure is performed usually three or four hours before an abortion. Prostaglandins may be administered orally or inserted into the woman's vagina.[4] From that point, women have to stay in the waiting room, where the tension is palpable. This is the most stressful time for them. I saw one woman crying before going to the operating room, and she said, 'Mummy doesn't want to do this, but I have no choice. Forgive me.' Some women were still asking themselves, 'Am I doing the right thing?' Clearly, even at this late stage, many were still ambivalent about abortion.

Women in this situation experience 'not only physical pain and trauma, but also moral anguish and emotional turmoil' (Gammeltoft 2002: 313). The emotional wrench is particularly poignant, because abortion is the end of the life of the foetus, the end of a pregnancy that may have lasted for months and a separation of the foetus from the mother. As we have also seen in the sex-selective abortion decision-making process, the perception that abortion is sinful weighs particularly heavily on mothers as they wrestle with their choice. In my study, women had to cope with the anxiety, fear and grief that accompany abortion and the moral pain of shame and guilt without the psychological support of adequate counselling. In these circumstances, ritual activity serves as one means of coping. On the threshold of proceeding with their abortion, women usually seek help and compassion from spiritual beings and powers. The case of one couple, Hải and Huệ, offers an illustration.

---

4   Prostaglandins are locally acting messenger molecules. Prostaglandin-induced abortion is a method for terminating pregnancy in the second trimester in which prostaglandins are administered to induce uterine contractions, followed by cervical dilation.

Hải looked very tired after nearly two weeks of following his wife to a series of clinics to check the sex of her foetus and two days in hospital to complete the administrative requirements for an abortion. It was nearly lunchtime when his wife, Huệ, took a drug to prepare for her abortion. It would be another four hours before she could have the procedure. She felt pity for her husband, so she urged him to go home to rest as their house was not far from the hospital. Before her husband left, Huệ reminded him to burn incense and pray for her safe abortion. After he left, she told me she had not slept well the previous night. She had woken at four in the morning and burnt incense to ask the spirit of her foetus to forgive her. She said to me:

> There is so much fear that I became ill. I do not want to do this, but I am in a difficult situation. It [her foetus] is too big, with a face and body.

I asked her how these ritual activities helped her. She said: 'To worship is to have sanctity; to abstain is to have goodness [*Có thờ có thiêng; có kiêng có lành*].'

As she prepared for the termination, Huệ sought forgiveness from the spirit of her foetus, for whom she felt attachment, pity and obligation. Her personal anguish was compounded by the private, hidden nature of her act and her perception that what she was about to do was immoral. Her feelings of responsibility and foreboding were reinforced by the formal undertaking imposed on her by the hospital to accept responsibility in case of complications.

My research shows that in thinking about abortion, women confront a dilemma when weighing up the moral and the personal issues while also considering social norms. Having an abortion is a very personal decision, but these findings suggest that, in this context, women's decisions also reflect the collective opinions of those around them and/or the social conventions within which women have to defend their decision.

Providers' perceptions

Doctors in the public hospital I studied did not want to perform late-term abortions because, like their patients, they were aware of the morally problematic nature of such procedures. More importantly, they felt a keen sense of professional responsibility because of the increased risk of complications when pregnancies were terminated in the late stages of gestation. Complicating all this is the fact that the hospital provides late-term abortion because it meets the demand from women for such a service, it boosts the hospital's profits and it meets the aims of the country's population policies. One doctor said:

> Late-term abortion is dangerous, but it has been conducted because it helps women deal with their undesired pregnancies, and the hospital can have more profits by setting a high abortion fee. Abortion also contributes to reducing the population growth rate. (Doctor, 55 years old)

A doctor specialising in abortion described the late-term abortion process as follows: 'To conduct a late-term abortion, the foetus is dismembered, crushed, destroyed, and torn apart.' She considered this savage act to be murder. She said sex-selective abortion was different from termination of unplanned pregnancies because sex-selective abortion was intentional. She said doctors did not want to do this job, but they had to. She has sought psychological balance by undertaking ritual customs. She confided:

> I always think about the moral issues when I conduct this job, but I try to stay in balance between 'materialism' [*duy vật*] and 'spiritualism' [*duy tâm*] in order to avoid mental suffering. I do not want to do this job forever. After I have had to perform a late-term abortion, I go to the pagoda for prayers to balance my psyche. Most women have abortions following unplanned pregnancies, and I think that is normal. What happens if women have to give birth if their pregnancy is unplanned? Who will help them deal with this matter? However, it is different when they have the pregnancy intentionally and have an abortion only because the little one is a girl. Killing a girl to have a boy is a savage action. (Doctor, 47 years old)

Like this doctor, others also found it traumatic to conduct a late-term abortion. They wished there was a method of killing the foetus before it was removed through abortion. A doctor expressed her thoughts:

> I feel less anxious when I conduct abortions for stillbirth cases. I wish there were an abortion method that made the foetus die before the abortion. It would help doctors feel less anxious and less stressful when we have to do this job. It would make me think I am conducting an abortion for a stillborn baby, not a live one. I do not want to kill live babies. (Doctor, 43 years old)

Obstetrics and gynaecology experts in Việt Nam suppose that killing the foetus before abortion is possible; however, this method can be dangerous for the mother's health. In this situation, the mother's health must take priority.

Nurses also did not want to assist doctors in late-term abortion procedures, and were afraid of the moral and spiritual issues involved. A nurse told me:

> I do not want to do this job, but I have to do so. I always feel a chill when I have to perform a late-term abortion. I feel great pity for the unfortunate babies. Their figures are formed, but they have been eliminated. Sometimes, I cannot sleep thinking about the babies' images. I burn incense and pray for the little souls on the 1st and the 15th of the lunar month to relieve anxiety or go to the pagoda to restore peace of mind. (Nurse, 35 years old)

Abortion providers had a range of views about sex-selective abortion. Some supported it. According to these people, women who had two daughters should be allowed to have an abortion. A nurse/counsellor said:

> Many women are in a miserable situation because they have only daughters. If we do not provide a safe abortion for them then they will find other clinics to have an unsafe abortion. However, they should be counselled on health problems related to abortion and they should not have repeated abortions. If they want to have a boy, they should apply preconception sex-selection methods such as detecting ovulation. (Nurse, 38 years old)

A doctor expressed his opinion:

> Nobody would admit that they are having a sex-selective abortion. We have no reason to say they are having a sex-selective abortion either. If we do not provide abortion services for them, they will find the service in private clinics. Private clinics providing abortion services are sprouting like mushrooms. The facilities and sterilisation conditions in private clinics do not meet the standards. It is dangerous [for] patients. (Doctor, 54 years old)

Others opposed sex-selective abortion because they thought it was immoral and should be condemned. Some counsellors tried to persuade women against it by explaining the potential complications and/or highlighting the moral or religious sanctions against abortion. A nurse shared her experiences: 'Some women insisted on having an abortion. I have tried to dissuade them by asking if they would suffer torment or would be condemned by their unborn children' (Nurse, 52 years old).

All doctors and nurses mentioned the dilemma related to abortion regulations. On the one hand, abortion is legal and women have the right to acces it. Providers cannot refuse to provide abortion services. On the other hand, sex-selective abortion is illegal. Most women do not give the real reason for wanting an abortion—that is, because of the foetal sex. The usual reasons given include having enough children already, their last child is still too young or they have been using antibiotics during pregnancy. When a reason other than sex selection is given, providers cannot refuse to provide the service. 'If we refuse to provide an abortion for them, they can find other places with unsafe abortions' (Doctor, 56 years old).

Managers' and policymakers' perceptions

The ICPD in Cairo advocated for prochoice policies to promote reproductive rights. Is there any contradiction between the prochoice stance and 'illegal' sex-selective abortion? The question is whether the right to choose is reduced when both strategies—legal abortion and illegal sex-selective abortion—are implemented through legislation. Therefore the core issue is how to distinguish between a 'sex-selective abortion' and a 'non–sex-selective abortion' if the real reason for the abortion—sex selection—is concealed.

Managers and policymakers therefore face a dilemma between enforcing women's rights to access abortion and forbidding sex-selective abortion. As in China and India, the Vietnamese Government faces the difficult issue of how to supervise sex-selective abortion in a context in which abortion is legal. The manager of a public hospital shared his opinions on the disjunction between population and abortion policies and practices:

> Abortion is a woman's right. Women have a great many reasons for abortion. They can provide any reason. Only women know the reason for their abortion. If they do not tell the truth, nobody knows. We have disseminated the regulations and policies to the health staff. If we catch a case of sex-selective abortion, we will deal with it according to the regulations. However, nobody says they want to have a sex-selective abortion, and no doctors write on the medical record that their case is a sex-selective abortion. (Public hospital manager, 52 years old)

The manager of the family planning department also spoke of the dilemma between the right to abortion and the prohibition on sex-selective abortion. He said:

> Having more children or not is a woman's right. If they give reasons such as having enough children, we cannot refuse. If we refuse, they will sue us. We have no evidence to say that they are having a sex-selective abortion. I suppose the prohibition on sex-selective abortion would be unfeasible and impractical if we only based it on the law and regulations. (Family planning department manager, 54 years old)

The ability of managers and policymakers to deter illegal sex-selective abortion is constrained by their legal obligation to provide abortion for other reasons. A manager said:

> Population policy regulates that each couple should have the number of children they want and have the right to abortion. If we refuse to provide abortion services for them, they will sue the doctor for preventing women from implementing family planning. (Public hospital manager, 57 years old)

Policymakers are aware of the disjunction between public policies and practices.

> We have had the Population Ordinance prohibiting foetal sex selection by any methods (Item 2, Article 7). However, it is not enforced strictly. Nobody has been punished so far. To supervise and identify a case of sex-selective abortion is like finding a sewing needle in the ocean. We cannot do it. Instead of prohibition, we should deal with this matter by addressing the root causes, such as providing social security for elderly people. (Policymaker, 58 years old)

The conflict health officials face between their responsibilities as providers of safe abortion and as enforcers of population regulations is a thorny governance challenge that is primarily of concern to policymakers. However, equally profound conflicts trouble all those who are involved with the practice of sex-selective abortion. Women who undergo these abortions are torn between the pressure they are under to have a son and the emotional stress and ethical doubts they experience. Counsellors and other medical staff are divided between their responsibilities as health professionals and the compassion they feel for their patients. Doctors in the public health system know the practice is illicit, but they feel constrained by the need to offer abortion for the sake of the mother's health. Almost every person I met found sex-selective abortion ethically troublesome. One can see that, although all of these actors participated in the practice in one way or another, for all of them, sex-selective abortion is a peculiarly troubling practice.

Conclusion

In short, the issues surrounding abortion highlight the tensions between notions of equality and authority, freedom and necessity, individuality and collectivity, ethical and legal rights, and the duties and obligations of women, abortion providers, policymakers and others. However, one of the most striking aspects of sex-selective abortion in Việt Nam is that it is largely not spoken about. The silence itself is the result of multiple factors; any single explanation will distort its complexity. The public and private silences surrounding sex-selective abortion have personal, sociocultural and political meanings; people remain silent in different ways and for different reasons. According to Nie Jing-Bao (2005), silence about abortion might signify self-protection, fear, helplessness, self-censorship, anger, shame, anxiety, bitterness, acceptance, embarrassment, indifference, resistance, disagreement, a desire for secrecy, privacy or escape or simply having nothing to say. Looking at the silence around sex-selective abortion from an anthropological approach, I offer some conclusions.

Most of the women in my study who had a sex-selective abortion were 12–16 weeks pregnant. Owing to the time it takes to ascertain the sex of a foetus, sex-selective abortion is usually conducted in the second trimester of pregnancy. Therefore, although the reasons for these abortions were almost never given, we can conclude that sex selection was a factor contributing to late-term terminations. Second-trimester abortions cost more, are more time-consuming and are a burden both to women and to an already overloaded health system. Women suffer mental health problems when they terminate a planned pregnancy late in their term, when their foetus is considered 'normal' and when it is so large that it has the appearance of a fully formed child. This sacrifice is extremely painful and further deepens the silence.

Women who undergo a sex-selective abortion remain silent because they are in a state of confusion, fear and anxiety about the medical, legal and moral dangers of late-term abortion. Undertaking sex-selective abortion almost always under other pretexts, they are unable to obtain adequate advice about their situation from health providers, vent their complex emotions or discuss the alternatives. Women in this situation are faced with the bitter moral issue of 'killing' their own child. Despite its prevalence, abortion is condemned in contemporary Việt Nam (Bélanger and Hong 1998, 1999; Gammeltoft 2002) and is negatively defined in public life as an individual moral failure (Gammeltoft 2003).

Second-trimester abortion entails a traumatic experience for abortion providers as well. Counsellors usually are aware of being involved in a sex-selective abortion and often express their frustrations openly, yet they are constrained in what they can do to help the woman or deter her from having the abortion. Doctors also find late-term abortion difficult, considering the human-like form of the foetus they have to remove. From a cultural and psychological perspective, counsellors and doctors share the values that bring women to hospital. They feel pity for women who have only daughters and want to help them. Counsellors and doctors—who can be considered gatekeepers in the sex-selective abortion process—remain silent about their involvement because they sympathise with the women. Sharing the same moral and religious framework as their patients, many handle their complex emotional and ethical reactions to the abortion process through ritual. From an ethical perspective, public hospital providers also feel constrained by their concern that women who are refused late-term abortion may undertake unsafe procedures in private clinics.

The silence surrounding abortion can be interpreted as being not only rooted in the sociocultural context, but also reflecting current public policies. Women and healthcare providers confront disjunctive regulations that are yet to be debated in public. Public sector abortion providers remain silent about sex-selective abortion because of the dilemma they face between their obligation to provide legal and safe abortion and the ban on sex-selective abortion. The regulation forbidding sex-selective abortion, of course, makes sex-selective abortion seekers and providers fearful of revealing their activities. Therefore, the silence in this context is simply to avoid trouble.

One of the difficulties in prohibiting sex-selective abortion is the lack of public debate on policies and regulatory systems governing professional health practices. In practice, the Population Ordinance is clearly perceived as difficult to enforce because there are no other forms of regulation of healthcare professionals' work. We know that the SRB—an indicator of sex-selective abortion—has been rising rapidly in recent years even though the government prohibited sex-selective abortion in 2003. Policymakers know it is very difficult to prohibit prenatal diagnosis of sex because ultrasonography is so widely available. It is also extremely difficult to prove and prosecute any violation of the relevant legislation. Health managers are aware that the abortion services offered through the booming private sector in urban and semi-urban areas create not only a high risk for women's health, but also the conditions for sex-selective abortion. However, social and academic debates about the negative effects of these policies and to propose effective alternatives are yet to occur. Free public discussion is not a complete solution in itself, of course, but it constitutes an essential social mechanism for understanding the nature of the problem and devising effective solutions.

4

After the abortion: Suffering, silence and spiritual relief

I visited Thuận at her home in a suburb in Hà Nội three days after her abortion. She had given me careful instructions for how to find her house and begged me not to ask anybody for directions as she was fearful that other villagers would learn she had undergone an abortion. Although it was not easy to find her house, I did not dare to ask anyone on the way. When I arrived, an elderly woman opened the gate and introduced herself as Thuận's mother-in-law. Thuận lives with her husband and his parents. Her brother-in-law's family lives in the neighbouring house.

Thuận was waiting for me in the guest room. Although she looked tired, she moved with light steps. After exchanging some courtesies, Thuận's mother-in-law left us to pick up her grandchildren from school. Thuận revealed that only her parents-in-law knew about her abortion and she did not dare to discuss it with anybody else, including her sister-in-law who lived next door.

Thuận told me she felt guilty about her abortion; she had burnt all her ultrasound results and medical records. She wondered how the deceased foetus was treated. She had wanted to bring it home to bury it, but could not because burial land in the village cemetery was limited and because she did not want news of her abortion to become public. She said when she was in the hospital she was too embarrassed to talk about the matter with the counsellor. I consoled her, telling her that, according to information I had obtained from the hospital, the deceased foetus would be preserved and then buried in a cemetery. Thuận was relieved to hear this. She felt she had sinned and wanted to assuage her guilt through ritual; when her health had recovered, she intended to have a ritual ceremony in the temple.

When I asked about her health, Thuận reported that she had pain, a foul-smelling vaginal discharge and was experiencing blackouts, dizziness and nausea. I advised her to go back to the hospital if she continued to have these symptoms. Thuận said she was using paper napkins instead of sanitary pads because she was afraid her sister-in-law and neighbours would realise that she had had an abortion. In spite of the fact that she was very tired, she considered herself sufficiently healthy to do housework.

Thuận worked in a footwear factory. She had taken two weeks sick leave for the abortion. When the leave was over, she returned to work because she did not want to raise suspicions and she felt too sad to stay at home alone any longer. Unfortunately, she was still haemorrhaging when she returned to the factory, so she was soon taken to the emergency ward of the hospital.

Thuận's story provides insights into the many ways in which sex-selective abortion is a painful process for women. Added to the physical pain, nausea and other complications Thuận experienced after the procedure was the moral, social and spiritual suffering. Anxiety, shame, guilt and fear compounded her physical symptoms. Stigma and embarrassment crippled her interactions with family, neighbours, work colleagues and medical specialists, preventing her from obtaining adequate care and relief. Also weighing heavily on her mind were uncertainties about the fate of the physical remains of her aborted foetus and worry about its spiritual wellbeing. Representing an acute example of social suffering (Kleinman and Kleinman 1997), Thuận's story highlights the multistranded nature of postabortion suffering and the vulnerable position of women who undertake abortion of this kind.

When I visited women after their pregnancy terminations, one of the most striking features was that they had tried to keep their abortion a secret. This raises questions about women's silence in relation to abortion and what they really think about the procedure. Medical anthropologists have shown that not only is abortion often shrouded in silence, but also women's voices are often absent in representations of abortion (Fletcher 1995; Gammeltoft 2002). In this chapter, I focus on the factors that frame and contribute to women's postabortion silence and how that silence functions in women's lives.

In this chapter, I propose that women's silent suffering and abortion-related fears are key barriers to their effective access to reproductive health care. By focusing on the experiences of a core group of women after sex-selective abortion, I aim for a deeper understanding of women's postabortion experiences. The key materials discussed are narrative accounts of women's experiences of sex-selective abortion and their reflections on the impacts. Their accounts reveal the physical, social, psychological and spiritual suffering women experience after sex-selective abortion and the obstacles they face in receiving adequate care and understanding. The chapter also addresses how these women deal with physical as well as psychological and spiritual recovery.

Physical care after abortion: Coping with complications

Common postabortion symptoms include bleeding, cramping and pelvic pain. Some women have complications such as severe pain and heavy bleeding, foul-smelling vaginal discharge and dizziness. Bleeding after abortion usually lasts from five to seven days; in some cases, up to four or five weeks. For example, Thuận's bleeding lasted nearly five weeks. In trying to hide her abortion, she avoided check-ups and made a valiant attempt to continue working in the factory.

A Vietnamese proverb says that '*một lần con sa bằng ba lần con đẻ* [one abortion equals three births]', which captures a general acknowledgement that abortion has serious impacts on women's health. Rather than admit to an abortion, some women in my study told people they had experienced a miscarriage. According to employment regulations, workers are entitled to 20 paid rest days if they have an abortion certification from the hospital. No women in my study, however, accepted this opportunity. In a similar vein, Jane Zapka et al. (2001) found that women in New England preferred to remain anonymous when using abortion services—a phenomenon referred to as 'the silent customer'. This leads to a decline in medical insurance claims. Because of the social stigma placed on abortion and women's consequent decision to remain silent, these women forgo the benefits guaranteed by state health policy.

In my study, after the abortion procedure in the hospital, women were transferred to an overcrowded postabortion room. Only those patients with medical risk factors were monitored. Medical staff recommended that patients purchase prescription medicine out of their own pocket at a cost of about VND300,000 (US$15). This typically included:

- Zinnat (Cefuroxime, an antibiotic), 10 x 0.5 g tablets, two tablets a day (morning and afternoon).
- Mutose (Streptokinase, a product used in Việt Nam to prevent postoperative clotting), 20 x 10 mg tablets, four tablets a day.
- Edocom-B (Cefpodoxime, an antibiotic), 12 x 100 mg tablets, two tablets a day.

These antibiotics and anticlotting medications are routinely prescribed after abortion in Việt Nam. Some women in this research could not afford the prescription medicine, so they used 'traditional methods'—for instance, drinking *rau ngót* to prevent infection and placental retention (see the details in Trang's case below).[1] For peri-abortion prophylaxis, the UK guidelines for the care of women requesting an abortion—which are the guidelines used by abortion services in Australia—recommend: metronidazole, 1 g rectally at the time of abortion, plus 100 mg doxycycline orally twice daily for seven days, commencing on the day of abortion; or metronidazole, 1 g rectally at the time of abortion, plus 1 g azithromycin orally on the day of abortion (RCOG 2004: 10). According to abortion providers in Australia, the preference is to give one dose each of the two antibiotics at the time of the procedure and none afterwards; some clinics substitute doxycycline for azithromycin because it is cheaper and proven to work.[2] Doxycycline and metronidazole are also available and very cheap in Việt Nam. The current price of doxycycline is VND5,000 for 10 tablets and metronidazole is VND2,000 for 10 tablets. If these antibiotics were provided at this prescription cost (less than US$1), women could afford them.

---

1   *Rau ngót (Sauropus androgynus)* is a vegetable that is popular as a herbal medicine to promote uterine contractions, and therefore to treat incomplete abortion.
2   Dr Christine Phillips, The Australian National University, Personal communication, 25 March 2011.

Women were also advised to have a check-up 10–14 days after the abortion or to return to hospital if they experienced any 'abnormal' symptoms such as haemorrhage or high fever. However, they were not counselled on how to take care of themselves after their abortion. Two-thirds of the women in this study had at least one check-up after their abortion; however, some did not want to return to the hospital where their abortions was performed because they were trying to forget the painful memories associated with the procedure. As Huyền said: 'I did not want to go back to the hospital for a check-up. It brought back bad memories. Instead, I went to a private clinic to have a check-up' (36 years old, abortion at 14 weeks).

Most of the women in this study who lived in Hà Nội returned to the hospital where they underwent the abortion to have follow-up treatment and ultrasound scanning as a precaution against retention of the products of conception. Most of the women who lived a long way from Hà Nội went instead to local private clinics; however, the quality of services and the information provided in these clinics need to be discussed. The following is Trang's story.

I accompanied Trang to a private clinic in a town for her postabortion check-up. She bought a ticket for an ultrasound scan for VND50,000. The nurse showed her to a room just large enough to accommodate a single bed and a black-and-white ultrasound machine connected to a computer that sat on a table. A man in a white coat was sitting in front of the computer screen. He did not speak, but pointed to the bed and indicated that Trang lie down. He then asked curtly: 'What do you want?' She stammered: 'I had an abortion one week ago. I would like you to check if there is any placental retention [incomplete abortion].' With apparent indifference, he glided the transducer over Trang's belly. He grimaced and told her: 'Get up and drink as much water as you can, and stay here until you need to pass water.' Trang hastily exited the room and drank three glasses of water, and then waited outside for more than an hour.

When we returned to the ultrasound room, the man was playing a computer game. He asked impatiently: 'Have you wanted to pass water?' Trang answered in the affirmative: 'I cannot hold it anymore.' He nodded and started to scan. He stopped the scan when a light space showed on the screen. He said to Trang: 'Done. You have placental retention. Drink rau ngót, as much as you can.' He gave Trang the ultrasound result, consisting of a muddy image with the words: 'Monitor placental retention.'

Trang held the result in her hand, clearly confused. She said to me:

> I had this abortion at a leading hospital in Hà Nội in the belief that it would be the right thing. Despite this, I still have placental retention. I thought it was good, so I did not need to have a medical check. My family's economic condition is not good, as you know. I have spent too much money on ultrasound and the abortion during this pregnancy. However, yesterday, I got some blood clots after it had been 'clean' for several days. I was worried, so I decided to have this ultrasound scan. Perhaps the fact that I used a straw broom to sweep the floor caused the bleeding. My mother said women should not touch straw brooms after giving birth or having an abortion.

I asked Trang why she had not returned to the hospital where she had the abortion. 'It is too far and too crowded there. I came to this clinic because it is convenient and private,' she replied.

Like Trang, many women did not see the need for a medical check if there were no 'abnormal' symptoms after the abortion. Some women— mostly those from rural areas—had examinations in poor-quality clinics because they were conveniently located and private. Trang was diagnosed with 'placental retention'/incomplete abortion, but she was not referred to an official clinic with properly qualified staff and, as noted, the advice she was given was to drink the traditional remedy of *rau ngót*.

Appropriate treatment of complications is part of the essential obstetric care encouraged by the UNFPA and first developed by the non-governmental organisation International Projects Assistance Services (IPAS). It includes emergency treatment for complications of miscarriage or induced abortion; family planning counselling and services; management of sexually transmitted infections; counselling tailored to each woman's emotional and physical needs; and community and service provider partnerships (UNFPA 2004). However, the social taboos surrounding abortion, even where postabortion care is legal, limit women's access to postabortion services. Stigma and shame can be intense and can discourage women from seeking treatment.

Abortion stigma and psychological effects

Abortion stigma

Erving Goffman (1963: 3) defines stigma as 'an attribute that is deeply discrediting', maintaining that stigma leads to a negative change in the identity of an individual to a 'tainted, discounted one'. Researchers and activists in the social sciences and public health have further developed this concept, endeavouring to better understand how people with certain conditions, traits, identities or behaviours are 'marked' or perceived as being different. According to Peter Byrne (2000), stigma leads to a diffuse range of adverse experiences, including shame, blame, secrecy, isolation, familial and social exclusion, stereotyping and discrimination. Accordingly, in their framing of abortion stigma, Anuradha Kumar et al. (2009: 627) define it as 'a negative attribute ascribed to women who seek to terminate a pregnancy that marks them, internally or externally, as inferior to [the] ideals of womanhood'. Women who felt stigmatised were more likely to feel the need to keep their abortion a secret from family and friends. Some research shows that concealment of stigma can negatively impact on a person's physical and mental health (Major and Gramzow 1999; Pachankis 2007). Because abortion stigma is poorly understood and generally not measured, there is little research to indicate what negative consequences it may have on women's lives. The case of Hân shows such stigma is constructed and reproduced by various means.

Hân was an expressive woman and her stories seemed never-ending. In hospital, she told me a great deal about her family and her reproductive history. Her husband owned a carpentry shop and she had a clothing shop. Her family was one of the wealthiest households in her village near Hà Nội. She had three beautiful daughters. She underwent a first-trimester abortion 10 years ago when her youngest daughter was one year old.

I contacted Hân by phone two days after her abortion. We had a frank conservation in which she told me she was still tired, but she was healing well. I expressed a wish to visit her at home and she happily agreed. She provided me with careful instructions on how to find her house and I set out to visit her the next day. I phoned her before I left to be sure she was at home. However, when I arrived at her house, her daughter saw me at the gate and said her mother was not at home. When I asked where her mother was, she looked very embarrassed, cast a furtive look towards the house and stammered, 'I don't know'. I phoned Hân again, but now her phone was turned off. I understood that Hân was at home, but did not want to meet me. I asked the little girl to tell her mother that I had visited and left. I was unable to contact Hân afterwards.

I could not ascertain the reason Hân did not want me to meet her at home, even though we had previously conversed openly, although I suspect it was because of the social stigma attached to abortion. Gathering women's experiences of abortion is often problematic because this stigma works against women's disclosure.

At the individual level, those being stigmatised often experience shame, guilt and disgrace, leaving them feeling unable to access resources that could change their situation. Socially, those who are stigmatised are effectively excluded and marginalised, often leaving them without social networks and resources. Fear of community rejection often pushes women to keep their abortion secret. 'We knew about her abortion, but we did not talk about it. It is not a happy story,' Trang's mother-in-law said. Abortion stigma penetrates Vietnamese women's psyche. Internalised abortion stigma—the most common manifestations of which are shame and guilt (Lithur 2004)—therefore leads to negative health outcomes for individual women.

Psychological effects

A number of studies have assessed the psychological effects of abortion on women (Zabin et al. 1989; Teichman et al. 1993; Hunfeld et al. 1994; Cozzarelli et al. 1998; Major and Gramzow 1999). Women's self-reported responses show they experienced both negative and positive reactions to their abortion (Burnell and Norfleet 1987; Mueller and Major 1989). Some had symptoms similar to the grief experienced after the unexpected death of an infant and, for many, this grief began with the decision to terminate the pregnancy. Some women experienced these problems for only a short period, but many others had emotional difficulties long after their abortion. In many cases, the women experienced nightmares, depression and other kinds of trauma for years.

There are many factors that can affect psychological recovery, and some women are at greater risk of psychological disturbance than others. Amy Harris (2004) argues that those at greater risk tend to include:

- Women aborting a planned pregnancy for medical or genetic reasons.
- Women who encounter opposition to their abortion decision from their partner or parents.
- Women who have strong philosophical or religious objections to abortion.
- Women who are highly ambivalent or confused about their abortion decision and/or have had great difficulty making the decision.
- Women who are coerced by others into having an abortion.
- Women undergoing late, second-trimester abortion.

Building on Harris (2004), my research shows that the psyches of women who have had a sex-selective abortion are usually seriously affected. Huyền's case helps us understand more about women's postabortion experiences.

At 9 pm, two days after Huyền's abortion, her anxious husband, Tân, called me to say his wife's emotional state had been unstable since her procedure. She did not want to eat, she cried continuously and she was always angry with him. He implored me to visit to talk with her. I appeared on their doorstep the following morning. When I arrived, Tân opened the door to welcome me, while Huyền stayed in her bedroom. She told Tân to bring me to the room as she wanted to talk with me in private. Tân served me a glass of water and then left us alone. Huyền looked very pale and her eyes were swollen from lack of sleep and so much crying. When she saw me, she began to sob violently: 'I did not think I would be sad like this. I did such an immoral thing that I would kill myself were it not for my other children'. (Huyền, 36 years old, two days after her abortion)

I consoled her and advised her to see an experienced counsellor. Huyền promised she would do her best to overcome this debilitating situation and would call me back if her emotional state deteriorated.

After my visit, I called her husband every day to ask after her. Over the course of the following week, Huyền improved and returned to her teaching job. Work helped her recover, but the memories remained, she said.

Like Huyền, many women did not discuss with others their feelings and experiences of abortion. Why did Huyền choose to share her feelings with me, but would not meet a counsellor or talk with members of her family?

For women who do not want to talk about their abortion, the lack of communication augments accompanying feelings of depression and grief and actions of avoidance and denial.

> I didn't tell anyone else, even my family or my friends, about my abortion because I was scared that they would look down on me for it. It is perceived to be such a bad thing. (Phi, two months after her abortion)

Similarly, JoAnn Trybulski's (2005) study of the long-term postabortion experiences of 17 women found that the women concealed their abortion because of shame or fear of adverse reactions from family and friends.

In most cases, nurses in Vietnamese abortion clinics did not address the psychological and emotional consequences of abortion in their counselling. They were primarily—even solely—concerned about the physical complications post abortion and assumed no responsibility for any psychological or emotional problems. Therefore, women were advised to return to the hospital only if they experienced physical complications. One conclusion of my study is that there is a definite need for psychological postabortion care.

Many women had stories consistent with that of Huyền. Women experienced a variety of postabortion problems, with different emotional strands; however, some common outcomes associated with sex-selective abortion in this research were guilt, shame, anxiety, distress, trouble sleeping and nightmares, but also a sense of relief.

Guilt and shame

Guilt and shame are probably the most common symptoms of postabortion syndrome, and can lead to anxiety, depression and other psychological problems. Putting these reactions in sociological context, Paul Hiebert (1985: 213) differentiates between guilt and shame-oriented cultures as follows: 'Guilt cultures emphasize punishment and forgiveness as ways of restoring the moral order; shame cultures stress self-denial and humility as ways of restoring the social order.' Hiebert

(1985: 212) further proposes that shame cannot be relieved, as guilt can be, by confession and atonement: 'Shame is removed and honour restored only when a person does what the society expects of him or her in the situation, including committing suicide if necessary.' Based on this typology and my interactions with women after their abortions, we might say that Vietnamese society has characteristics of both guilt and shame-oriented cultures.

In Việt Nam, abortion is commonly regarded as a sin, and late-term abortion poses a major ethical problem. The conflict between social morality and women's actions leads them to feel guilt and shame. One woman confided to me: 'I committed a serious sin. I terminated the life of my child-to-be. I felt ashamed when I taught my students about moral issues' (Huyền, 36 years old, teacher, two months after her abortion). Some women thought abortion was wrong and the idea of killing their baby severely impacted their psychological health. Thuận admitted three days after her abortion:

> I feel guilty about my abortion. I regret that I did that. I feel pity for my child … it was my blood. It had a human form and was healthy. It seems I killed my child. (34 years old, abortion at 14 weeks)

Guilt is a burden not only for women, but also for men. Marc Moskowitz (2001: 29–30) has analysed men's psychology around abortion:

> Men are taught that they must be strong, and that showing excess emotion is by its very nature a loss of face … [T]he integral connection between morality and conformity is an essential component discouraging open displays of emotion. This gives an insight into the controlling forces that keep emotions hidden behind a mask of male strength.

Men do not often reveal what they feel about abortion, but this does not mean they don't experience sadness. The reaction felt by men may manifest itself in persecutory or depressive anxiety and psychosomatic symptoms. Although most men in my study did not speak out, they also felt guilty and sad about the abortion. One male subject confided:

> Over the past few days, the atmosphere in my family has been terrible. I am very sad, but I try to encourage my wife. It is said that a man is like a pillar in a house. If I was not rigid, my family could not be stable. However, I thought a lot about my child-to-be. The foetus was too big to have an abortion. It looks like we killed our baby. I feel very guilty when I think about that. (Huệ's husband)

Anxiety and distress

Several studies reveal the relationship between abortion and anxiety (Bradshaw and Slade 2003; Hess 2004; Cougle et al. 2005). There are also theoretical reasons to postulate a relationship between abortion and social anxiety. Women who have an abortion might be at high risk of social anxiety disorder, which Ronald Kessler et al. (1994) rate as the most prevalent anxiety disorder (13.3 per cent of all women who have given birth will experience this). Brenda Major and Richard Gramzow (1999: 736), who examined the psychological implications of the stigma of abortion, suggest the secrecy of abortion 'inhibits disclosure of emotion and generates cognitive processes of suppression and intrusion that are detrimental to mental health'. Most of the women in this study experienced such feelings. One woman told me: 'I have been fearful since the abortion. I am unable to express the exact feelings in my mind. When people mentioned it [abortion], I was stunned and got the creeps' (Hồng, 27 years old, cadre, three months after her abortion).

Anxiety is defined as an unpleasant emotional state of apprehension. After an abortion, women may feel tension and irritation, which can affect close relationships. Women who were highly ambivalent or confused about their abortion decision, and who had great difficulty making the decision, felt tense in their relationship with their husband and/or in-laws. Loan said:

> I had this abortion mainly because of my parents-in-law. My parents said if they [her parents-in-law] pressured me, I should not have the abortion. I felt that they did not feel compassion towards me, that they only needed a male heir. (33 years old, cadre, three days after her abortion)

After abortion, negative thoughts can plague women and cause a lack of interest in sexual intercourse. For example, Liên told me how her abortion had affected her relationship with her husband:

> Since the abortion, I have had no interest in sex. I pulled away from my husband. Whenever I had sex, I thought of my abortion. I feared becoming pregnant and having another abortion. We went three months without having sexual intercourse. (Liên, 30 years old, six months after her abortion)

Living with bad memories is part of many women's abortion experience. After an abortion, women are often confronted with reminders such as ultrasound images and maternity clothes, although most women in my study did not keep their ultrasound results and images after the abortion. Thuận burnt these images to try to erase her memories.

Family conflict and disharmony

A number of studies demonstrate that the greater the difficulty in deciding to terminate a pregnancy, the more likely it is there will be negative psychological impacts. Women who have had an abortion with a lack of support from their partners or parents, or who had conflicting feelings about the procedure, may be at relatively higher risk of negative consequences (Ashton 1980; Barnard 1990). Loan confided:

> Actually, I did not want to have this abortion. But my parents-in-law wanted me to have it, and then my parents advised me to follow my in-laws' will. If not, this child and I would have been in a miserable situation.

The ambivalence in her abortion decision caused negative feelings. 'I felt pity for my child-to-be. I deeply regret what I have done,' Loan said.

For women who live with their husband's family, childbearing is considered a major issue and decisions related to it must involve and be approved by the husband's parents. The elders' opinion is considered the most important. Some women experienced strained interactions if they had an abortion without the knowledge of their parents-in-law.

Lụa called me at night, whimpering. She had undergone an abortion that afternoon. When Lụa arrived home, her mother-in-law realised she was not well, and Lụa confessed to the abortion. Her mother-in-law became angry and threatened to send her packing. Lụa was forced to humbly apologise and ask for her mother-in-law's forgiveness.

Some elders put pressure on their daughters-in-law to undergo a sex-selective abortion so they could try again for a male heir. However, most—especially the woman's parents—were worried about their daughter's health and considered abortion immoral.

Abortion without the approval of one's parents often causes a clash between generations. Parents-in-law feel they are not respected. Thuận's mother-in-law said to me:

> My daughter-in-law had an abortion without saying anything to me. I only knew about it when she got back from the hospital. That [abortion] is an important issue, but they did not discuss it with us. I was angry with her.

Psychology research indicates that social support can help to reduce postabortion symptoms (Cohen and Roth 1984). A woman is likely to feel more positive if her abortion decision is supported by her husband and family. Conversely, if the decision-making process does not involve the family and/or her husband, she may experience higher levels of depression. Huyền, who had an abortion on her husband's insistence, said:

> I was thinking a lot and intended to keep this pregnancy. On that morning, I did not want to go to the hospital, but my husband insisted that I have this abortion. (Huyền, two days after her abortion)

Sleeplessness and nightmares

A nightmare is a subcategory of dream, distinguished by its frightening and/or emotional content. Nightmares may reflect a real-life trauma or distressing situation or express internal conflict or personal difficulty. Nightmares are said to be symptomatic of fear and anxiety. Psychology research shows that people who have regular nightmares often have psychiatric problems or may be involved in an unstable relationship (Major and Gramzow 1999).

Most of the women I studied reported having nightmares in the three months following their abortion. The following are descriptions of the nightmares women shared with me.

Hoa's nightmare

I dreamed my baby's spirit came to visit me. It wandered about me and then disappeared. I cried like I never had before, sobbing and sobbing. I feel pity for my baby. My mind is empty and I feel that I have nothing left to live for.

Huệ's nightmare

In my dream, I saw a nurse strapping my legs into the stirrups. Then a doctor used some big forceps to pull out my baby, which was covered with blood. There was a lot of pain. Then the nurse wrapped the baby and took it away. I cried out and my husband came to untie me. We searched everywhere but could not find my baby. Then I heard crying coming from a bin, and I saw my baby. But when I held it in my arms, it disappeared.

Huyền's nightmare

I often saw a newborn baby in my nightmare. She was black and blue all over. She was naked and ants swarmed over her. I took her to a river to wash her, but I lost my grip and she sank and I could not find her.

Lụa's nightmare

The house was burning and I heard my daughter crying. I ran around looking for her. I could see and hear her, but she was being consumed by the flames and I could not reach her.

I could empathise with these women because, during my field research, I experienced trouble sleeping and had vivid nightmares. I often saw the operating room and abortion procedures in my dreams. I most vividly recall the nightmare I had after observing the first abortion procedure. In this nightmare, I was helping a nurse to put a foetus in a fridge. After a while, I opened the fridge and saw the bloodied foetus stand up and cry.

Some health staff also confided in me about their fears when they first began to work with abortion patients. On night duty at the hospital, they saw foetuses or heard stamping noises in their dreams, but this stopped when they woke up.

Sleep problems, including nightmares related to the abortion, often involved the 'return' of the aborted child. Having trouble sleeping was a common complication among the women who had sex-selective abortion, and it was usually attended by nightmares. Sleeplessness and nightmares were also very common among the providers.

Relief

Despite the difficulties, the majority of women do seem to cope with negative emotions. Phillippa Goodwin and Jane Ogden (2007) suggest that women who have abortions experience not only distress, but also emotions such as relief and a sense of return to normality. Some of the women in my study felt that abortion was the best way to go under the circumstances: it alleviated the foetus's suffering, as well as their own (*đỡ khổ nó, đỡ khổ mình*). Thus, a sex-selective abortion is painful, but, on another level, it resolves the problems associated with going ahead with the pregnancy.

Women were conscious that abortion was 'the best thing' rather than 'the right thing'. As one woman said: 'I feel pity for my child who was not born, but I think abortion was the best thing in my situation' (Lụa, 28 years old, two months after her abortion). This way of thinking helps control negative feelings.

Some studies have emphasised women's experience of relief as a positive outcome over and above the negatives (Adler et al. 1990; Armsworth 1991). Feeling relief is a mode of recovery. Some women felt relieved after having a safe abortion when that decision had been difficult to make. 'It was hard to decide to have an abortion. At the beginning, I felt guilty, but then I thought that it was good for me and the child,' said Na (49 years old, one week after her abortion).

In addition, many women gained coping skills that contributed to their postabortion adjustment and gave them the capacity to deal with similar crises. Most of the women in this study increased their knowledge of reproductive health after their late-term abortion. Thirty-five-year-old Hậu, five days after her abortion, said:

> Late-term abortion [*phá thai to*] is not easy. At the beginning, I thought it was not so dangerous. When I heard the nurse's counselling, I was scared because she said it could cause haemorrhage or perforation of the uterus. I was so nervous. It is so dangerous to have late-term abortion in private clinics where they do not have emergency equipment. It is too late to go to hospital when a haemorrhage has happened. From this abortion experience, I know in future I have to choose a good abortion service. Women who choose unsafe abortions disregard their lives.

The abortion crisis can also help women rethink their situation, with some reporting enhanced feelings of appreciation for their daughter(s) and their lives.

I visited Phi three days after her abortion. Phi's daughter welcomed me politely and guided me upstairs to where her mother was lying down. The girl brought me a glass of water and then left us alone. I praised her for being well-behaved. Phi was proud of her daughter and said she had taken care of all the housework since her abortion, in spite of the fact she was only 14 years old.

The care shown to me by my daughter makes me feel guilty about my treatment of my female foetus. In this situation, I am now more aware of the value of a girl. A boy cannot take care of his mother like a girl can. (Phi, 38 years old, three days after her abortion)

Foetal disposal

The treatment of the deceased foetus was a major concern for women and, as outlined above, it could be critical to a woman's psychological state after an abortion. While the malformed foetuses were usually 'taken care of' and buried by the patient's family, some female foetuses from sex-selective abortion were left in the hospital. These families did not dare become involved in the burial because they wanted to keep their abortion secret; however, all worried about how the foetus was treated and experienced guilt.

One summer afternoon, Trang and I were on the way back to her home from the town where she had received a postabortion ultrasound scan. When we passed her village's cemetery, Trang burst into tears and said:

> I feel sorry for my aborted baby. My parents-in-law advised that we [she and her husband] leave it in the hospital. I do not know how it was treated. I regret that I could not bury it. (Trang, 27 years old, 10 days after her abortion)

Curious about Trang's story, I looked into why her parents-in-law had advised her to leave the aborted foetus at the hospital. I knew the abortion of a foetus with human form was considered a bad death. Foetuses are seldom given funerals as fully formed people; rather, the remains are buried in fallow land or hills around the village. Importantly, it is believed the parents should not be involved in the foetal burial. Parents were told that if they had a funeral or burial for their foetus, it would make it harder for them to overcome the loss, the foetus would follow them and would not be reincarnated or would be reincarnated back into their family of origin. Although parents wanted the foetus to be reincarnated, they did not want its soul to be reincarnated into their own family, as it could harm the mother's fertility.

I returned to the hospital where Trang had her abortion and met the staff at its mortuary. They told me foetal remains from second-trimester abortions (after 12 weeks pregnancy) were placed in a fridge. The staff collected the remains every day and stored them in the mortuary. A local funeral company then took them to a cemetery for cremation. The mortuary staff burnt incense and prayed for these foetuses before sending the remains to the cemetery.

Like Thuận and Trang, most of the women I studied were very anxious because they did not know how their foetus was treated after the abortion. They were too embarrassed to raise the issue with the counsellors, who, for their part, did not mention it either. Despite their regrets, these women did not want to bring their foetus home and bury it themselves because they were afraid its soul would return and/or they did not want their neighbours to find out about the abortion. Some of the women went to a pagoda to pray for the salvation of their foetus.

As we have seen, women who undergo sex-selective abortion suffer psychological problems, which can be healed through ritual practices. Therefore, in the following sections, I analyse such rituals and their role in psychological healing.

Foetal rituals and the healing process

In this section, I look at women's ritual practices after a sex-selective abortion. This study confirms the judgement of Tine Gammeltoft (2010) that, through ritual, women seek to (re)establish an identity as a good and caring mother by displaying maternal affection for the child they have lost. However, we should be aware of the more complex cultural, moral and emotional factors involved. It is crucial to locate gender issues within this framework. By examining these issues in the Vietnamese context, we can learn how women and men cope with abortion and the influence of rituals on the psychological healing process.

Vietnamese spirit beliefs and the status of the foetus after abortion

Although in theory there are three main religions in Việt Nam, it is difficult to distinguish between the separate religious communities. The majority of the population is not interested in sectarian distinctions. For example, a Buddhist family may visit a Taoist temple and perform rites belonging to the Confucian cult of the ancestors.

Buddhism encompasses a variety of traditions, beliefs and practices. The following perception of Buddhism is extracted from my conversation with a medium who owned a temple in Hà Nội. Buddhists believe that life is *samsara* (the cycle of birth, life, death and rebirth). When people die, their soul continues to exist and will be reincarnated in another body. Within all forms of Buddhism, there are six 'worlds', known as the world of gods or heavenly beings, the world of humans, the world of asuras (the realm of the demigods), the world of animals, the world of hungry ghosts and hell. The code of morality is contained in the 'five precepts': avoid killing or harming living beings, avoid stealing, avoid sexual misconduct, avoid lying and avoid alcohol and other intoxicating drugs. Abortion is therefore considered a transgression of the first precept. However, Buddhism tolerates abortion in difficult cases.

Buddhism's doctrine of karma and reincarnation has greatly influenced Vietnamese views of abortion and concepts of life and death. Karmic relations are supposed to inspire human beings to act benevolently towards each other to reincarnate into a better life (*siêu thoát*). A requiem ritual (*lễ cầu siêu*) can help the soul find the right way to reincarnate into a better realm. This concept has been particularly influential in defining the significance of unborn foetuses within Vietnamese culture.

According to Vietnamese cosmology, the spirits of the dead will travel to 'the other world' (*thế giới khác*) and can influence the lives of those still living. Ancestral spirits (*tổ tiên*) are considered to be family members who continue to need care and who protect their descendants (Gustafsson 2009). Ancestor veneration is one of the most unifying aspects of Vietnamese culture; it is a vital duty, indicating filial piety. However, according to Confucian beliefs, parents should not worship their children. A foetus is neither an ancestor nor a descendant; its spirit does not belong to the ancestors, but has to wander in the spirit world, both homeless and hungry.

The concept of the hungry ghost also appears in Vietnamese ancestor worship and popular religion. Hungry ghosts are the ghosts of people who have not found everything they need to survive in the afterlife. If a ghost does not have enough food, water, shelter and so on, it will return to this world to feed on the living. The ghost will scare people and then feed on these fears. Performing a ritual can help get rid of these hungry ghosts. Vietnamese people believe the ghosts of their ancestors return to their homes at certain times of the year. The festivals of *Xá Tội*

Vong Nhân and *Vu Lan* (which fall on 15 January and 15 July, according to the lunar calendar) are held to honour hungry ghosts, with food and drink put out to satisfy their needs.

Therefore, the requiem ritual (*lễ cầu siêu*) for the soul after death is very important. Such a ritual should be performed within 49 days of the death, after which the soul will be ready to go to a specific realm (*cảnh giới*). The purpose of a requiem ritual is to aid the soul's welfare and facilitate a timely reincarnation. If the ritual is not performed within this timeframe, the soul can become a hungry ghost.

When Buddhism arrived in Việt Nam, it combined with Confucian beliefs in ancestor worship and concepts such as that of the hungry ghost. It is commonly believed that spirits can return to the world of the living, and if these spirits have not been given sufficient offerings, they will harm their living relatives.

Vietnamese conceive a 'bad death' as dying young, childless, in a violent manner or in a manner that leaves the body incomplete (Malarney 2003; Kwon 2008). Bad death is also defined as *chết oan*—an unnatural death that results in the deceased becoming an evil spirit. Foetuses whose lives are ended through abortion are considered cases of *chết oan*. Someone who has died a bad death should not be brought home. Instead, their body should be taken directly to a cemetery. However, in some cases, those who have had a bad death are not even permitted a burial in the communal cemetery without the approval of the communal board.

Gammeltoft (2010) posits that, if the Vietnamese ritual terrain is conceptualised as a 'positive space' for ancestors and a 'negative space' for ghosts, women and their relatives have invented a third position for the foetus. In other words, a foetal spirit is defined as neither a family member nor a ghost.

Foetuses and infants are thought to have souls, but their souls are distinct from those of adults. Foetal and infant souls are easily wounded. It is popularly believed that a foetal soul occupies the existing physical form of the foetus. In other words, the body of the foetus is formed and then the spirit comes to the body. If the parents do not perform the proper religious rites for the foetus's spirit, it will come back and haunt the mother. Trouble is usually caused by hungry spirits.

Foetal rituals

As an example of how women respond to the pain of losing their aborted child, and the meanings of ritual in psychological healing, I recount Hồng's tale, which she related to me when I met her three months after her abortion.

> After my abortion, I felt anxious and depressed. I was very nervous, stunned and got the creeps when anybody mentioned the abortion. I dreamt of [the foetus] every night. Sometimes, I saw a little white shadow wandering around my bed. I hardly slept and awoke startled. I thought I should do something to overcome these feelings, so I went to meet a fortune teller whom my family often consulted when we needed to do important things such as building a house or getting married. She seemed to know everything about my abortion. When I arrived at her house, she asked me, 'Have you had an abortion?', although I had not mentioned anything about it. She told me she saw a baby spirit following me and advised me to complete a ritual to seek moral forgiveness. I had to have a ceremony to pray for the salvation of its soul. So, I invited a sorcerer [*thầy cúng*] and had a big celebration to pray for it [the foetus]. I wanted to have another child, a boy, so I did not want this baby spirit haunting me. I am not superstitious, but to worship is to have sanctity; to abstain is to have goodness [*có thờ có thiêng; có kiêng có lành*]. I felt some relief after performing this ritual. I think I have sufficient knowledge to be dubious about superstitions, but there are some things that we cannot explain. After my abortion, I experienced many unfortunate things. My arm was broken in an accident. I could not do anything successfully. These emotional states have taken such a toll on my life.

Hồng's feelings and her ritual practices conform to a Vietnamese theory of personhood in which the soul remains present after death, as do the soul's relations with the living. In making offerings, the woman both acknowledges and maintains relatedness with her foetus. Her motivation for performing the ritual is fear not only of bad karma, but also of the capacity of the foetus to cause harm. Overall, the ritual and offerings are motivated by compassion—both for the foetus and for herself.

Foetal ritual and moral relief

Buddhism prohibits the killing of any living creature. For fundamentalist Buddhists, abortion is killing. As described above, women feel helpless and remorseful after abortion, and foetal rituals can help them relieve a general sense of guilt.

Huyền, whom we met in the previous section, was in a serious condition after her abortion. She had improved substantially by the time I met her again. I asked her whether she had seen a counsellor. She replied:

> In hospital, the doctor and nurse did not have time to talk about psychological issues. They also did not care about my situation. I had heard about the temple where I could appease my foetus's spirit. It relieved my sense of guilt after the appeasement. (Huyền, 36 years old, two daughters, abortion at 14 weeks)

While reproductive clinics are not concerned with psychological healing, the foetal ritual plays an important role in this healing process. It provides comfort to women who have had an abortion and allows them to express their grief for the aborted child.

The women in my study experienced considerable spiritual pain, owing to the intensity of their feelings for their aborted foetus and the conflicting experiences in their role as a mother. They condemned themselves and expressed fear of foetal wrath. One solution was to create suitable conditions for the reincarnation of their foetus. When the women believed the spirit of their foetus had been sent on to its next life, their sense of sinfulness was very much alleviated and their fear of foetal wrath was assuaged. Thu expressed her sentiments as follows:

> I had an abortion before; I was very sad after that. But my feeling after this abortion is worse than after the previous one. I felt uneasy and thought of it always. The foetus was too big and it was totally normal. I felt sorry for it. I had a ritual for it in the hope that it can be reborn and have a better life. (Thu, 23 years old, two daughters, abortion at 14 weeks)

The doctors and nurses who conducted the abortions reported similar feelings of emotional unease. As noted in the previous chapter, health staff involved directly in abortion often reported their work was psychologically and morally burdensome. They often attended pagodas to do penance for their work. In the hospital department where a great number of abortions were performed, on the 1st and 15th day of every month, according to the lunar calendar, the health staff would burn incense and make offerings to the god of the soil and the foetal spirits. It was also particularly important that offerings were not missed on the middle days of the 1st (Nguyên Tiêu) and 7th months (Trung Nguyên/ Vu Lan) of the lunar calendar.[3] One nurse observed:

> I went to the pagoda to celebrate requiems on every Vu Lan festival in order to save the foetal spirits in this department and to relieve my fear. I have been fearful ever since I've worked here. (Nurse, 52 years old)

Foetal ritual and reincarnation

In this section, I explore beliefs about foetal spirits and the significance of the haunting foetus in the context of religious and traditional concerns about self-restraint, family structure and morality. Belief in foetal spirits provides us with a focal point for the examination of both religious and gender theory.

By performing rituals after an abortion, women hoped their foetus would be given another life with a higher status, which brought them psychological relief. To a lesser extent, their husbands shared these concerns, so both parents frequently united to give a special blessing to the spirit of their foetus in the hope it would proceed expeditiously to the next life. When a foetal spirit acknowledges its parents' painful sorrow, it will desist from making trouble for them. An elderly woman told me about the risk of being 'followed' (bám theo) by the foetus's spirit if there was no ritual to aid its reincarnation:

> Last year, my sister conjured up the spirits of the dead. The sorcerer said I had two aborted foetuses, but I had not had rituals for them. So they followed me closely. If I want them to achieve salvation, I need to have an incarnation-freeing ritual [đàn lễ giải nghiệp]. (Thu's mother-in-law)

According to one medium, if parents do not perform a ritual after an abortion, the foetus's soul cannot be reincarnated and will return to haunt the mother or other family members. A woman who had a stillbirth told me that, one month after the death, she had an incarnation-freeing ritual performed for her foetus. One night, 30 days

---

3   The meanings of these ceremonies are explained in Chapter 5.

after this ritual, she had a dream in which she saw a woman holding a baby. She was then confident that her child had been reincarnated by virtue of the ritual.

Foetal haunting

It is believed that a woman who aborts a foetus is more vulnerable to being haunted than other members of her family. The foetus might bring its parents problems and misfortune, so they must practise a ritual to appease it. The ritual also expedites the foetus's reincarnation or helps it gain higher status in the spirit world. A spirit that has not received the proper rites can become a hungry ghost and is likely to seek vengeance through evil acts, such as by causing infertility, disease, injury or death for its mother or family. The existence of these kinds of spirits is not unique to Việt Nam—for example, they are similarly represented in Taiwanese traditions in which there are 'foetus ghosts' (*yingling*) and 'foetus-demons' (*xiaogui*) (Moskowitz 2001).

After an abortion, any illness or other familial misfortune is typically interpreted as having been induced by the foetus's ghost. However, the abortion and not the ghost itself is considered the primary cause of such misfortune, which is a punishment inflicted by the spirit of the aborted child if the appropriate atonement rituals are not performed. Two months after her abortion, Phi confirmed this idea:

> People said that abortion led to bad luck. In my case, this was definitely true. My parents and parents-in-law, as well as all the children in my family, were ill after my abortion. (Phi, 38 years old, abortion at 15 weeks)

Foetal ritual and gender issues

In Vietnamese culture, there are a great many goddesses who are worshipped by women who have been marginalised or excluded from their family because of the patrilineal ideology, *bà cô*. They have married out or been pushed out of the household and forgotten or are considered lost to the family. They are excluded from participating in the ancestor cult[4] and occupy an anomalous position because of this exclusion from ritual life. Villagers set up shrines outside villages or on the margins of

---

4   The ancestor cult is based on the belief that some essence of one's ancestors persists and is capable of influencing the physical world.

pagodas to venerate the women whom the ancestor cult has excluded. The spirits of female foetuses are similarly excluded from the ancestor cult. Pagodas are where foetal spirits may be admitted and reside, but admission is granted only after the proper rites are performed. It is worth noting that the processes and aims of these ceremonies differ for male and female foetal spirits. For example, one medium pointed out:

> Male foetus spirits can have a position in the spirit pantheon [*cấp sắc*]. Female foetus spirits have been admitted through Buddha's door [*quy cửa Phật*] only. The foetal rituals for female foetus spirits involve requiem ceremonies [*lễ cầu siêu*].

Offerings during a ritual ceremony for a male foetus include clothes, shoes, horse(s) and swords; for females, clothes, sandals and jewellery (all of offerings are made from paper). The ritual to gain position as a spirit is more complicated than the requiem ceremony and usually requires the participation of at least three exorcists (Plate 7).

Plate 7. Performing the ritual to gain a position in the spirit pantheon for a dead foetus

Source: Photographed by the author, Hương pagoda, 2009.

Men rarely attend foetal rituals—in contrast to popular religious practices such as ancestor worship and sacrifices to the village deity. When I asked why husbands did not attend, the most common answer was 'it is a woman's job' (*việc đàn bà*). Interestingly, male abortion providers also rarely attend these rituals. A doctor who provided abortion services told me he felt anxious whenever he had to conduct an abortion, so he had his wife undertake conciliatory rituals for him at the pagoda.

The rise of foetal rituals: Commodification of moral relief

The aim of foetal rituals is not only to appease the foetus, but also to express the parents' desire that their aborted child will have a good life in the spirit world. Foetal rituals indicate the concern of responsible parents and their willingness to make a sacrifice for their child's welfare. Many women in my study wanted to appease the spirit of their foetus by making special offerings, but only mediums or fortune tellers could give them the information they needed to satisfy the spirits and become well. As an indication of the importance of ritual in the healing process, these women paid a high price for ritual services. Thanh told me why she paid a substantial sum for her foetus's ritual.

Thanh, who was in her late 40s, had an abortion 18 years ago. Because she doesn't regard herself as 'superstitious', she did not have any foetal rituals after the abortion. She is now the principal of a secondary school. Recently, she suffered a serious headache and experienced some trouble with her job; it was recommended she consult a fortune teller. The fortune teller said the spirit of Thanh's aborted foetus would always follow her, and it should be appointed as a servant for a saint. However, the foetal spirit could not take this position without the appropriate ritual ceremony being performed, so it was causing harm to its mother. The fortune teller advised Thanh to undertake a requiem ceremony for her foetus as soon as possible. The aims of the ceremony were to appease the foetal spirit and to help it achieve a position with the saint. As a government employee, Thanh did not want to be seen as superstitious. She therefore decided to have a secret ceremony in a private temple, for which she paid VND20 million (about US$1,200 at that time).

Thanh represents a unique case in this study as she spent a large amount of money on a foetal ritual. However, in three other cases—those of Huệ, Cúc and Thương—women spent VND3–5 million for postabortion foetal rituals. Most women in this study gave VND300,000–500,000 each time they visited a temple or pagoda for foetal rituals.

The commodification of foetal rituals has proliferated in both Japan and Taiwan (Underwood 1999; Moskowitz 2001). Critics have focused on the financial exploitation associated with this ritual practice. In some cases, religious practitioners extract large amounts of money from gullible people. In Việt Nam, the foetal requiem (*lễ cầu siêu cho thai*) can be regarded as a folk ritual, which has boomed in recent times. Fortune tellers, spirit mediums and exorcists have promoted the appeasement of foetal spirits. Some pagodas have organised large ceremonies for thousands of foetuses. For instance, during the Vu Lan festival on the 15th day of the 7th lunar month in 2010, a great ceremony was organised in Vĩnh Nghiêm pagoda, Hồ Chí Minh City, for about 8,000 foetuses. According to one news report, the purpose of this ceremony was to set parents' minds at rest and to encourage people to behave well or appropriately (Thu Mai 2010). On 1 October in the same year, another ritual was organised, in Từ Quang pagoda, for 5,000 foetal spirits, which saw the participation of some 3,000 people. These postabortion ritual practices are rooted in Vietnamese folk tradition and have been reinvented to meet current demand and offer a resolution to the moral dilemmas women face.

William LaFleur (1992) suggested the revival of the *Mizuko kuyō* (foetal ritual) reflected the increasing anxiety about abortion and infanticide in Japan at that time. Foetal rituals in Việt Nam were once practised privately and women's worries about the spiritual fate of their foetus were not of public concern. However, recently, religious practitioners have raised the profile of these rituals, which has elicited a positive response from many women. Once-private foetal rituals have become 'communal abortion rituals'. This phenomenon helps open public debate about the social, ethical and psychological issues related to abortion. Here I make a few suggestions.

First, abortion is a widely used method of birth control in Việt Nam. This does not mean there is no emotional or ethical concern about abortion, and it is also a mistake to suppose that Vietnamese women have an abortion because it is an easy choice. The pressures on women to choose an abortion include the unintended pregnancy of unmarried women, the pressure to produce a male heir and the policy limiting the number of children per family. As demonstrated in this and preceding chapters, the decisions made in deference to these social pressures have profound ethical, psychological and spiritual consequences.

Second, foetal rituals may help individuals air and address feelings of ethical unease associated with abortion that are frequently kept private. More and more pagodas are willing to perform foetal rituals to meet the increasing demand. A communal abortion ritual enables people to resolve some of the moral conflicts that assail them. Marc Moskowitz (2001: 39) claims that there are a number of consequences of public rituals for foetal ghosts:

> [W]orshippers are surrounded by others who have shared the same experience and thus can derive comfort from a sense of solidarity with the other participants at the ceremony. As people go to the temple they are surrounded by hundreds of others who are also there because of their abortions, which potentially reduces their feeling of being more sinful than others.

The monk Đại Đức Thích Giác Thiện, in a requiem ceremony for foetal spirits held on 1 October 2010, said:

> The preaching and the requiem help parents notice that they have done immoral things. The ritual helps people overcome their depression and find peacefulness. Foetal rituals not only bring moral relief for people who have lost their potential child, but also encourage them to have a good lifestyle and serve as a warning about the extended abortion situation recently. (Như Phú 2009)

Third, ritual is part of a healing process in a context in which—because of the stigma, shame and lack of capacity in the modern healthcare system—women do not necessarily receive psychological support from their family and institutions. Ritual is a way for women who have made secret, painful and stressful choices to worship together and to overcome shame and stigma. They can find affirmation and recognition of their private problems among people in a similar situation. This ultimately helps them overcome their feelings of social, cultural and moral marginalisation. Summarising the ritualisation of late-term abortion in Việt Nam, Gammeltoft (2010: 73) states:

By ritually 'remembering' the foetus, abortion-seeking women sought to maintain an identity as responsible mothers; ritual acts of incense burning and prayer were, in this context, moral gestures through which the women sought to (re)establish an identity as a good and caring mother by displaying maternal affection for the child they had lost.

Reproductive life planning

After experiencing the psychological crisis of abortion, the women in my study began to think about their future reproductive life. Many worried about their fertility after their abortion. As we have seen in Chapter 3, women who undergo late-term abortion in public hospitals are usually warned about the impact on their fertility as one possible complication. They might also believe there will be a negative impact on their fertility as a result of being haunted by the aborted foetus. Some women wanted to become pregnant again as soon as possible; the main aim of their sex-selective abortion was to create an opportunity to conceive a son.

Of the 35 women whom I met in hospital and who identified themselves as having undergone a sex-selective abortion, I followed up 26 cases. The remainder declined to take part in the follow-up study, mainly because they did not want to discuss their sad stories or because they felt the visit of an 'unfamiliar' guest could raise suspicions. The dropout rate due to these reasons shows the difficulties of pursuing research on abortion experiences.

Of the 26 cases I followed up, one year after their abortion, four women had become pregnant with a male foetus, three women had become pregnant with a female foetus and had had another abortion, eight hoped to become pregnant again, five did not want another pregnancy because of their negative abortion experience and six had no idea about their future reproductive lives.

The stories of three women that are presented below reveal some of the patterns of women's reproductive lives after their sex-selective abortion.

Lụa's case[5]

When I made my return visit, Lụa looked good compared with my visit immediately after her abortion. She informed me that she was now four months pregnant with a male foetus. She was also happy to let me know that the troubles in her family had settled since she became pregnant. 'Luckily, it is a male foetus, otherwise I do not know what would have happened with my family,' she said. Her husband arrived home, having collected their daughter from school. He asked whether Lụa had been drinking milk. Lụa was very moved by his caring disposition. She whispered to me that his behaviour had changed so much since learning the unborn child was a boy.

Huệ's case

Huệ had been depressed after her abortion, so she arranged for a ritual in a pagoda. She still longed for a son. One afternoon about a year after her abortion, I visited Huệ while her husband was at work and her children were at school. We had a long conversation in which she told me about her health, her life and her reproductive plans since the abortion. She said she felt weaker and experienced headaches more frequently since the abortion. She was looking for Chinese medicine to strengthen both her and her husband's health. The couple had been trying to conceive a boy by using traditional medicine and praying. One day, a friend notified her that a sorcerer could help people conceive a son by performing a religious ceremony. Huệ went to meet this sorcerer, who told Huệ her husband had a debt from his previous life and they would not have a son if he did not pay this debt by holding a ceremony (trả nợ tào quan). Huệ was very worried about this and decided to have the ceremony, at a cost of VND4 million. The sorcerer then advised her that if she conceived in November of the lunar year, she would have a son. In addition, she prayed in many pagodas and bought several kinds of 'having a son' medicine from famous traditional healers. 'I have done my best to have a son. If I can attain my wish, it will be great. If not, I do not regret it because I have done as much as I can,' she said.

Ngọc's case

Six months after Ngọc's abortion, her husband wanted her to get pregnant again. This time, the couple prepared carefully for the conception. Ngọc used Chinese medicine and had an ultrasound to detect her ovulation.

---

5   Lụa's case was described in Chapter 3; her husband forced her to have an abortion.

The couple waited until the foetus was 12 weeks old before having an ultrasound scan to check its sex. They were very disappointed when they were informed it was female, so they decided to have another abortion. Ngọc went to the hospital at which she had the previous abortion, but the doctor there would not perform another one because it had not been long since her previous, late-term abortion and Ngọc had also previously had a caesarean section. Ngọc was puzzled by this and decided to have an abortion in a private clinic. There was no serious problem with this abortion, but she felt her mucus was not normal and smelt strange.

Whether, as in Lụa's case, women achieved their dream of having a son, resumed chasing their dream of a son, as in Huệ's case, or were disappointed and had another abortion, as in Ngọc's case—all these women faced serious challenges. One result of this study therefore is to highlight the concerning fact that women who have sex-selective abortions represent a group at high-risk of having multiple abortions. Repeated abortions create higher risks of harm to both physical and psychological health. A study of women seeking repeat abortions found a threefold increase in psychiatric consultations compared with maternity patients who carried their children to term (Törnbom and Moller 1999).

Conclusion

This study describes the range of emotions women experience during their journey through abortion, and the social, economic, religious and cultural factors affecting their postabortion care. All of these factors influence women's physical recovery and psychological healing. My research shows that women who had a sex-selective abortion experienced sadness, grief, guilt and shame. However, these women's mental and physical health during and after abortion did not receive sufficient attention. They received little support from their family, their community or the healthcare system. As a result, for many, ritual was the preferred method for attaining some degree of psychological healing.

The frequency with which women resorted to rituals suggests they felt they had few options at their disposal to manage the difficulties they encountered. Through ritual, women can fulfil what they believe to be their motherly obligations to their aborted child. Ritual can help heal women's psychological pain and also help them bare the physical strain of an abortion. Foetal ritual not only has religious meanings, but also tells us about morality, family structures and the relationship between women and men in contemporary Vietnamese society. Similarly, Meredith Underwood (1999: 761) claims:

> women use the ritual and symbolic resources available to them in order to overcome the predicaments of their sex. It allows them to negotiate with the patriarchal powers that be and therefore to survive the transgression of their accepted roles as wife and mother.

Sex-selective abortion is a painful and complex experience for women. It is not possible to give one simple, universal explanation of women's feelings about abortion. The silence that surrounds women's experiences of abortion makes them vulnerable to social, psychological and spiritual suffering. Women who had illegal sex-selective abortion felt stigmatised by having to go outside the law to secure their reproductive goals. Women are also vulnerable to being stigmatised because of the perception that abortion is morally wrong. The women's silence about their abortion experiences demonstrates how they are often put in situations they do not control. Patricia Wasielewski (1992) asserts that the power to ideologically define the abortion context is one of the most important factors influencing women's reaction to their abortion. The silencing of women in sex-selective abortion prevents women from achieving full physical recovery and psychological healing. The institutional channels through which they might air their feelings are lacking, and public forums do not provide a safe environment in which women can express their complex emotions and thoughts without fear of distortion. In addition to their fear of social censure, the generally poor quality of medical care—and postabortion care in particular— exacerbates the risk of complications for women after abortion.

5

Social responses to sex-selective abortion

Demographic data indicate the proportion of male to female births in Việt Nam has increased over the past two decades, especially since 2003. The Intercensal Population and Housing Survey in 2014 conducted by the UNFPA provides an estimate of the national SRB as 112.2 male births per 100 female births. Although the government and social organisations have taken a number of measures to try to deal with this matter,[1] the upward trend in the national SRB has not yet been effectively restrained. The rapid increase in the SRB raises questions about the effectiveness of strategies aimed at combating prenatal sex-selection practices. What are the sociopolitical responses to this phenomenon? Why have they had such a limited effect? This chapter reviews current debates about sex-selective abortion, focusing on the social and political responses to the practice and aiming to open discussions about potential avenues for confronting the challenges posed by sex selection in Việt Nam.

---

1   The Vietnamese Government has attempted to address sex-ratio imbalances, including through laws that prohibit the determination and disclosure of the sex of the foetus and any advertising relating to prenatal sex determination. The laws provide punishment such as fines for anyone contravening them.

Attitudes towards sex-selective abortion: Global debates, local dilemmas

In 1990, Indian economist Amartya Sen published an article titled 'More than 100 million women are missing'. It rang an alarm bell for the world about increasing SRBs. The issue of sex selection was first raised at the ICPD in 1994. Section 4.15 of the ICPD's program of action discusses sex selection as a problem arising from son preference and discrimination against girls from the early stages of their lives— compounded by new technologies that can determine foetal sex and facilitate abortion of female foetuses:

> Since in all societies discrimination on the basis of sex often starts at the earliest stages of life, greater equality for the girl child is a necessary first step in ensuring that women realise their full potential and become equal partners in development. In a number of countries, the practice of pre-natal sex selection, higher rates of mortality among very young girls, and lower rates of school enrolment for girls as compared with boys, suggest that 'son preference' is curtailing the access of girl children to food, education and health care. This is often compounded by the increasing use of technologies to determine foetal sex, resulting in abortion of female foetuses. (UNFPA 1994: s. 4.15)

The next year, the Beijing Platform for Action listed practices considered 'violence against women', including prenatal sex selection and female infanticide. It declared that these were:

> Violations of the rights of women in situations of armed conflict, including systematic rape, sexual slavery and forced pregnancy; forced sterilisation, forced abortion, coerced or forced use of contraceptives; pre-natal sex selection and female infanticide. (UN 1995: paras 115, 116).

These two documents created the foundation for several countries either prohibiting or recommending against the use of various technologies for sex identification and sex-selective abortion. For instance, Article 14 of the Council of Europe's 1997 Convention on Human Rights and Biomedicine states that 'techniques may not be used to choose a future child's sex, except where serious hereditary sex-related disease is to be avoided'.

However, the value of restricting prenatal sex selection has been debated vigorously in reproductive forums. Sex-selective abortion intensifies existing debates and brings out new ethical and sociopolitical challenges. If debates about abortion in general are concerned mainly with women's rights versus foetal rights, the challenges with respect to sex-selective abortion include the morality of abortion, the clash of values, the persistence of gender discrimination against women, the meaning of procreation, the boundaries of individual liberty and choice, individual and collective responsibility in the technological age, the importance of the 'common good' and the power and limits of the state to prevent harm and promote social wellbeing (Jing-Bao 2010). The essential question is whether prenatal sex selection should be restricted. The notion of reproductive liberty is the most common argument made against proscribing sex selection. Two articles in the journal *Human Reproduction* capture the spirit of the debate: Claude Sureau's 'Gender selection: A crime against humanity or the exercise of a fundamental right?' (1999) and Giuseppe Benagiano and Paola Bianchi, 'Sex pre-selection: An aid to couples or a threat to humanity?' (1999). The 'liberal' argument for sex selection supposes that the rights of parents are paramount (Dahl 2003). In the meantime, there is widespread opposition to sex selection.

Opponents argue that enacting legislation banning the practice of sex selection will create tensions between the discourses about abortion rights and those about gender equality. Daniel Goodkind (1999b: 52) writes:

> Restricting the practice would seem to interfere with reproductive freedoms and maternal empowerment, the twin goals adopted at the recent Cairo conference. The restrictions may also increase human suffering if sex discrimination is then shifted into the postnatal period.

Goodkind (1999b) raises five ethical issues related to legislative restrictions on sex selection. First, what is the effectiveness of government legislation in reducing sex-selective abortion where a culture of son preference remains untested? Second, the liberal interpretation of reproductive rights is that parents may choose the sex of their children—preferably, one boy and one girl in low-fertility societies. Third, even if a ban on sex-selective abortion was effective, human suffering may be increased if parents substitute postnatal for prenatal discrimination. Fourth, the restriction of sex-selective abortion might undermine individuals' rights to reproductive freedom and could lead to a decline in the availability of abortion services. Fifth, there is no solid evidence that a shortage of females will have a detrimental effect on women's wellbeing.

Drawing on the ethical and sociopolitical debates surrounding the proscription of sex-selective abortion, Nie Jing-Bao (2010) discusses practical problems inherent in state-centred and coercion-oriented approaches to preventing sex-selective abortion: the neglect of reproductive liberty and reproductive rights; overlooking the hidden dangers of state power; inconsistency with existing abortion policies; ineffectiveness in practice; underestimating the costs and resistance involved; simplifying and misrepresenting the key problems to be solved; a lack of sufficient public discussion; and ignoring indigenous moral and political wisdom.

Opponents of sex-selective abortion argue that the issue of reproductive liberty is of little importance because the problem of a severely imbalanced sex ratio poses a great threat to society. Jing-Bao (2010) argues that although reproductive liberty matters, it must be sacrificed for the common social good, according to the 'two concepts of liberty' (Berlin 1969). Meanwhile, some observers discuss the consequences of sex-selective abortion. Analysing the short-term and long-term implications of sex-selective abortion, Danièle Bélanger (2002) indicates that, by terminating a pregnancy because the foetus is female, many women can gain legitimacy, earn recognition and acquire status in their family and community. Sex-selective abortion can therefore help women avoid having more children than they want and allow them to limit the size of their family. Therefore, sex-selective abortion is empowering for women who face pressure to produce a male heir. However, Bélanger (2002: 194) also supposes:

> viewing sex-selective abortion as strictly empowering is unquestionably short-sighted … Sex-selective abortion, while empowering women in the short term, will most likely continue to further threaten their position in the long term.

The long-term consequences of sex-selective abortion include an imbalance in the sex structure of populations, with a shortage of women leading to their detriment through increased violence (or even war due to a shortage of brides) and a decline in women's political power because of fewer women voters (Bélanger 2002).

The Vietnamese Government has been warned that the imbalance in its SRB could lead to a number of social problems in coming years. Former deputy prime minister Nguyễn Thiện Nhân told state media in 2010 that the government was concerned about the increase in the SRB and its consequences. However, despite such statements, effective policies to address this trend have yet to be developed. More fundamentally lacking in the policy response is a clear understanding of the factors behind this trend and of the links between it and the phenomenon of sex-selective abortion. In particular, a better understanding of the relationship between sex-selective abortion and state policies is critical for the formulation of an effective policy response.

How the state and social organisations have responded to the vexed phenomenon of sex-selective abortion is one of the issues with which this chapter is concerned. However, first I consider another question—the extent to which this reproductive practice is itself a response to state policy settings. To situate sex selection within Việt Nam's political context, I review the country's policies on population and abortion. I contend that recent policy changes in these two areas have impacted on sex selection in several unforeseen ways.

Social responses to population and abortion policy

Population policy

The first of these state policies relates to population control. The Vietnamese Government launched the one-or-two–child policy in the 1960s. After *Đổi Mới* in 1986, the government began urgently promoting a norm of one or two children for each couple. In the 1990s, the one-or-two–child policy strongly focused on limiting family size through the provision of family planning services, including abortion (Johansson et al. 1998). The government's population programs were effective in reducing the total fertility rate, from 3.1 in 1994 to 2.3 in 1999 (UNFPA 2007).

The impact of the change in policy on population outcomes, including on the SRB, has been discussed by stakeholders, policymakers and social scientists. Annika Johansson et al. (1998) indicated the need for sons was still strongly felt in North Vietnamese culture. In addition, the one-or-two–child policy introduced new and potentially contradictory pressures on women. On the one hand, women who did not have a son were worried about not producing a male heir. On the other hand, they felt pressure from the authorities to stay within the two-child limit. Daniel Goodkind (1999b) and other authors have argued that contemporary manifestations of son preference are accentuated under the small family policy because, with fewer children, parents have a lower probability of having a son (Das Gupta 1987; Gu and Roy 1995; Das Gupta and Bhat 1997). As documented in this book, sex-selective abortion gives expression to the contemporary preference for sons, representing an attempt by women to reconcile the conflicting pressures they face. Such outcomes may not have been envisaged by population planning authorities and can be seen as an unintended consequence of the population control they espoused.

A second shift in policy settings, the consequences of which were also unforeseen, concerns reproductive autonomy. Influenced by the 1994 ICPD, Việt Nam's population policies advocated self-determination for families regarding family size and other reproductive health matters (Bélanger and Khuat 2009). The emphasis on women's rights in reproductive decision-making was made even more explicit in the subsequent population conference held in Beijing the following year. Reflecting these concerns, the 2003 Population Ordinance issued by the Vietnamese National Assembly states as its goal for citizens:

> To decide the timing, number and spacing of births in accordance with the age, health, education, employment and working, income and child-rearing conditions of every individual and on the basis of equality between the couple. (National Assembly of Vietnam 2003: Art. 10, cited in Bang et al. 2008: 178)

Policies of this kind, which advocate self-determination over reproductive decision-making, reflect global concern about overly prescriptive family planning policies that create dilemmas for individuals whose needs, obligations and/or circumstances conflict with the reproductive agenda deemed desirable by state population planners. In a way that is responsive to these concerns, Việt Nam's 2003 Population Ordinance shifted the responsibility for reproductive decisions on to individuals and families, giving them a greater degree of discretion than before. This emphasis on reproductive self-determination can also be placed within a broader set of changes in Việt Nam, away from centralised or command-style decision-making in social and economic affairs towards a more liberal governance approach. Since the late 1980s, individual households have had the right to make their own production decisions and have had increased responsibility for the consequences of those decisions. The 2003 Population Ordinance reflected this new model of devolved decision-making, in the sense that it accorded families rather than state planners more autonomy over their reproductive decision-making.

Article 10 of the ordinance has been construed as allowing couples to have as many children as they wish. However, it has also provoked internal criticism that free choice is leading to an increase in fertility. The increase in the fertility rate in 2003 (from 2.12 in 2002 to 2.23) created great concern among policymakers. Although the UNFPA (2005, 2006) determined that the fertility increase in 2003 had been caused by the popular desire to give birth during the Year of the Goat—believed to be a favourable birth year—the unexpected development prompted new calls for the enforcement of the one-to-two–child policy. Resolution 47, 'Further Strengthening the Implementation of Population and Family Planning Policy', issued in March 2005, expressed the Vietnamese Government's concerns:

> The surge in population would ruin what has been achieved, reduce socio-economic development and efforts to improve the quality of the population, slow down the country's industrialisation and modernisation process, and make the country further lag behind … The Population Ordinance and existing policies and regulations, which are not consistent with the two child campaign, should soon be revised. Policies on encouragement and incentives to communities, families and individuals with good records on population and family planning should be reviewed and revised accordingly. (Cited in Bang et al. 2008: 179)

One population policymaker said of these issues:

> Some people misunderstood the 2003 Population Ordinance. Article 10 of this ordinance includes two items: 10a and 10b. Item 10a says couples have a right to have their desired number of children. But Item 10b regulates couples' responsibility to comply with the population planning of the state. People, especially cadres and government workers, took advantage of the relaxation of the ordinance to have another child with the hope that it would be a son. (Population policymaker, interviewed in 2009)

This phenomenon reflects a trend of families taking advantage of the more relaxed population policies to achieve their desired reproductive outcomes. While giving individuals—particularly women—greater say over their reproductive lives, the ordinance also inadvertently provides scope for the expression of son preference. Certainly, the impact of different policy options on population outcomes is an issue requiring discussion among concerned stakeholders.

The final population policy I discuss relates to the emphasis on population quality. After achieving state population reduction targets, Việt Nam's population programs have shifted from birth control to the quality of reproductive outcomes. Several studies discuss this shift in focus (Johansson et al. 1998; Gammeltoft 2008). Population quality control programs have focused on the early detection of foetal anomalies with a view to minimising the number of children born with deformities and disabilities. These measures reflect a certain view of what constitutes a 'normal' population as well as a desire to reduce the potential burden on families and the wider economy posed by children requiring extremely high levels of care. The key measures in this program have been the use of prenatal ultrasonography to identify the health status of the foetus and the use of abortion services to abort any deformed, diseased or otherwise 'abnormal' foetuses.

One implication of this concern with population quality is that it is not restricted to central government authorities, but is also widely shared by parents. Clearly, education campaigns and the advice of medical professionals have transmitted the official population quality agenda to society at large, while also authorising and enabling strong interventions in reproductive processes in the interests of obtaining 'quality' outcomes. However, quality does not necessarily mean the same thing to all concerned. For instance, parents who strongly desire a son might regard a perfectly healthy female foetus to be a 'poor-quality' outcome or an all-girl family as 'abnormal' according to their notion of what a normal family should be. At the same time, one can see how parents might feel emboldened by official public health strategies that consider it acceptable to intervene in reproductive processes to achieve desired 'quality' outcomes. They may be similarly enabled to achieve their reproductive goals by the availability of scanning technology and abortion services. In short, one might posit a link between 'public' population quality policies and 'private' sex-selection practices.

Reproductive technologies and modes of intervention that have been made widely available to serve the normalisation of population quality policies are being used by individuals in ways unforeseen by state planners in pursuit of desired reproductive outcomes that are at odds with those of the state.

Abortion policies

Abortion has been legal in Việt Nam since 1954; however, the procedure was still rare until the beginning of the 1980s, when it started to increase, first slowly and then rapidly during the late 1980s, with the reinforcement of the one-or-two–child policy (Johansson et al. 1998). Việt Nam has one of the highest abortion rates in the world (more than 1 million each year), with many women undergoing multiple abortions (WHO 1999). In 2004 and 2005, there were 37.5 and 35 abortions for every 100 live births, respectively (MOH 2005, 2006).

Table 1. Abortion policies and induced abortion statistics for Việt Nam and selected countries, 2009–10

Countries	Government support for family planning	Year	Abortion rate*
Australia	Indirect[1]	2010	14.2
China	Direct[2]	2009	19.2
Canada	Indirect	2009	13.7
Denmark	Direct	2010	15.2
Singapore	Direct	2010	10.8
Việt Nam	Direct	2010	19.0**

* Number of legally induced abortions per 1,000 women aged 15 to 44 years.

** The figure does not include abortions in the private sector.

[1] Indirect support is where the government does not provide family planning services through official outlets, but instead supports the private sector, including non-governmental organisations, in the provision of these services.

[2] Direct support is when family planning information, guidance and services are provided through government-run facilities.

Sources: Data for Việt Nam from MOH (2010); all other data from UN (2013).

Việt Nam's abortion rate of 19 per 1,000 women aged 15 to 44 years represents abortions provided by the public sector only (Table 1). A more recent study (Hoàng et al. 2008) suggests the number of abortions provided in the private sector equals that in public hospitals. The recent very high abortion rate in Việt Nam is an issue about which there has been relatively little public debate.

Since sex selection occurs largely by means of abortion, the two issues are clearly linked. One might consider the ease of access to abortion in Việt Nam, its prevalence and its routinisation to be among the key preconditions enabling sex selection to take place. Abortion services are inexpensive and widely available through public and private providers (Gammeltoft 2002). A great many clinics and specialists provide these services, making inspection and regulation extremely difficult. The high incidence of abortion also makes it difficult for health providers and regulators to determine why an abortion is being sought. Finally, the recourse to abortion as a way for parents to deal with pregnancies that fail to conform to state population planning guidelines also leads to the normalisation of abortion as a family planning measure. When families routinely use abortion to meet the state's reproductive goals, it is a short step to use abortion to secure the reproductive outcomes families themselves deem desirable.

In fact, this is one aspect of Việt Nam's abortion policies that has been debated. Different views exist about how to deal with this matter— for instance, most healthcare managers and population policymakers believe abortion regulations are too open. The conditions for having an abortion in Việt Nam are very simple; according to regulations, pregnancies of less than 22 weeks can be terminated if there is no medical contraindication. Managers and policymakers with whom I spoke proposed tightening regulations on abortion:

> Perhaps it is necessary to reconsider the abortion policy. If abortion is too easy to access, people will take advantage of this in combination with sex determination by ultrasound technology to have sex-selective abortions. If abortion is managed closely, sex-selective abortions may decrease. (Population policymaker, male, 57 years old)

Meanwhile, others had contrasting views:

> Recently, international organisations have required having a simple administration to create good conditions for women to access abortion services easily. If we tighten abortion policy, the number of illegal and unsafe abortions will increase. In some countries such as Romania and South Africa, the abortion fatality rate increased rapidly after a stricter policy on abortion was implemented. The number of sex-selective abortions is a very small number compared to abortions in general—just a few per cent. (Reproductive health policymaker, male, 54 years old)[2]

Legislation is a central part of the political framework around sex selection. However, the managers and policymakers with whom I spoke were conflicted about the right steps to take. The dilemmas are multiple: balancing women's rights, reproductive rights and customary rights; building adequate legislation for the use of new reproductive technology while preventing the misuse of that technology to detect the sex of a foetus; and making safe abortion accessible versus enforcing stricter regulation of abortion. In fact, strict law enforcement could create difficulties in accessing reproductive services and increase the fee for using them, and illegal abortions conducted by unregistered and untrained providers could increase the serious potential health consequences for women. There is a lower incidence of unsafe abortion and a much lower mortality rate in countries where legislation allows abortion on broad indications than in countries where abortion is heavily restricted (Berer 2008).

---

2   This statement indicates the policymaker's limited knowledge. First, the 'simple administration' that international organisations require corresponds to good clinical governance—for example, ensuring doctors and nurses follow rules of best practice—which does not always occur in Việt Nam. This is evident in accounts of abortion practices. The policymaker here has misunderstood the statement as a request to 'tighten up abortion policy', which is not the intention of international organisations. It is interesting that, because there is so little discourse around clinical governance and regulation for good practice among health practitioners in Việt Nam, this speaker, who works in reproductive health policy, has not understood the importance of the push from international organisations for the health system to function in a way that is more resonant with norms of best practice. Second, the example from South Africa is factually incorrect. South Africa moved from a prohibitive stance to a more liberal stance, with legislation that allowed abortion, in 1996. After South Africa legislated the introduction of safe abortion, the mortality rate due to abortion sepsis dropped a little; however, this reflected the poor state of the health system, which was slow to make safe abortion readily available (Coovadia et al. 2009).

Some researchers (Goodkind 1994; Bang et al. 2008; Bélanger and Khuat 2009) argue that parental discrimination against a female foetus is exacerbated by population policy. In this view, 'sex-selective abortions are interpreted as a "public" act, in that they reflect contemporary government pressure, constrained reproductive choices, and lack of political will to stop such acts' (Goodkind 1994: 351). However, in light of the preceding discussion, one might refine this observation to note that, in a context of decentralisation and increasing reproductive autonomy, measures such as family planning and abortion—which were once used to prosecute a state's population and public health agenda—are now increasingly being used by the population at large to advance reproductive agendas that differ significantly from those endorsed by the state. It is in this sense, too, that sex-selective abortion might be considered a 'public' act, enabled as much as constrained by the public policy context in which it occurs.

The response of local and national authorities to sex-selective abortion

Nie Jing-Bao (2010) concludes that the one-child policy, together with greater economic and civil freedoms, contributed to an increased SRB in China. He argues that the problem of distorted sex ratios might not have become so serious if there had been public debate about the issue from the outset. Although they have known about the distorted sex ratio since the late 1990s and early 2000s, Chinese officials have denied the existence of the problem by underreporting the number of female deaths (Peng 1997). They have tried to show that China's SRB is not unbalanced. Of course, free public discussion is not a complete solution in itself, but it would help to identify the problem and to suggest effective measures to deal with it before it becomes serious. Similarly, Việt Nam has responded slowly to the rise in its SRB, which may have been occurring since 1999, when there were 107 boys born for every 100 girls, with an average annual increase of 1 point. However, responding to voters' questions at the 10th meeting of the 9th National Assembly in 2006, the Vice-Director of the Reproductive Health Department of the MOH gave a written reply: 'There is no indicator to confirm the imbalance of sex ratio at birth' ('The imbalance of sex ratio at birth has been an apprehensive issue,' Response to the dispatch 740/VP1, 06/11/2006, MOH). Although the Standing Committee of the National Assembly passed its Population Ordinance in January 2003 prohibiting sex-selection by any means, and the government promulgated the 'implementation decree' for this ordinance in October 2006, government officials only began paying attention to the rise in the SRB when the UNFPA released the results of the 2006 Population Change Survey in Việt Nam. The report warned:

> When inferential analysis (i.e. conclusions deduced from sample data) is added, along with information on the number of deliveries in 2006 coming from health facilities, it can now be confidently stated that the sex ratio of births at the national level is slightly skewed toward boys. However, provinces/cities with high SRB (above 110) need close monitoring and immediate attention. (UNFPA 2007: 4)

In 2006, the Vietnamese Government adopted a series of regulations and policies prohibiting prenatal sex determination and sex-selective abortion. All organisations and individuals were strictly forbidden from performing nonmedical foetal sex determination and sex-selective abortion. To respond to the increase in sex selection and public concern about this issue, the government issued Decree No. 114/2006/ND-CP in October 2006, which stipulated fines of between VND500,000 and VND15 million for people using traditional practices to determine the sex of a foetus or promoting or practising abortion for the purpose of sex selection. However, prohibition of sex-selective abortion is not simple for number of reasons. As we have seen in previous chapters, abortion of foetuses of the undesired sex can be concealed easily by the parent providing other reasons for the abortion. It is also difficult to prohibit diagnosis of foetal sex because the services for foetal sex determination are widely available. And it is hard to procure evidence and prosecute violations of the regulations on foetal sex determination. The feasibility and the enforcement of this decree show some shortcomings that will be considered in the next section of this chapter.

The increase in the SRB in Việt Nam came at a late stage compared with other countries, such as South Korea, China and India, where imbalances in the SRB started to appear in the early 1980s. The increase in the SRB in Việt Nam did not occur before the late 1990s; however, from then on it increased rapidly, gaining 1 point per year. This rate of increase is higher than that measured in South Korea and China during the 1980s (Guilmoto et al. 2009). This phenomenon is commonly explained by the lack of adequate medical facilities and equipment in Việt Nam in the 1980s, such as private clinics and modern ultrasound machines (UNFPA 2009a). Ultrasound technology first appeared in some major hospitals in the mid-1990s and has since become widely available in the private health clinics that have been springing up in urban and semi-urban areas.

In the decade from 2010, Việt Nam was in almost exactly the same position as China had been in the late 1990s. In this regard, it is necessary to reiterate comments by Ian Howie, UNFPA's representative to Việt Nam, in 2006:

> Việt Nam's population dynamics have changed rapidly over the past decade, accompanying swift developments in the country's social and economic structures. There is some evidence that the national sex ratio at birth is currently tilted toward a higher-than-expected number of boys. It is imperative Việt Nam pays close attention to this phenomenon, to ensure it continues on a positive development path and avoids the numerous problems that arise from a skewed gender balance. (Institute for Social Development Studies 2007: 18)

The Vietnamese Government is conscious of the importance of controlling the SRB. In its national gender equality strategies for 2011–20, approved on 14 November 2011, the SRB was one of the indicators targeted. In trying to control the rapid increase, the government has set a target for the SRB to be lower than 113 by 2015 and 115 by 2020.

The Vietnamese Government has provided strong support to reduce the SRB by introducing various regulations banning sex selection. However, it is far from certain how effective the implementation of regulations prohibiting prenatal sex determination and sex-selective abortion has been. The legislative approach that has been adopted in Việt Nam needs further evaluation and discussion to determine whether it is capable of achieving its aims. It is necessary to have comprehensive strategies that involve healthcare providers, social organisations, community members and mass media as agents of change.

The General Office for Population and Family Planning of Việt Nam (GOPFP) initiated an intervention project to reduce the SRB in 18 provinces with a high SRB rate in 2009 and 2010. The specific objectives of the project were to: 1) provide information on the imbalance in the SRB for couples of childbearing age, sonographers, abortion service providers and people who had prestige in the community, to reduce the activities leading to the imbalance in the SRB; 2) implement and enforce regulations relating to the SRB; and 3) encourage and support women and girls through education, reproductive health care and economic development.

Improved knowledge about the incidence of sex-selective abortion in Việt Nam is an essential precondition for effective government action to manage this problem. Evidence from other countries in the region suggests that the rapid increase in the SRB occurs mainly through sex-selective abortion. This study has also confirmed that sex-selective abortions are being conducted routinely in Việt Nam in a covert and tacit manner. However, in a workshop titled 'Creating a Shared Vision to Address the Imbalanced Sex Ratio at Birth in Việt Nam', organised by the UNFPA in collaboration with the GOPFP in November 2010, many Vietnamese government officials in attendance revealed they believed the rise in the SRB was a result of 'traditional methods' of preconception sex selection, such as the timing of sexual intercourse and the use of traditional medicine, and not the use of ultrasonography and abortion. A colleague of mine, who for many years has studied abortion in Việt Nam, attended this conference and was disappointed by this stance. The question is why government officials did not admit that sex-selective abortion was the main cause of the increase in the SRB in Việt Nam. Were they lacking in information about the incidence of sex-selective abortion or were they trying to find alternative explanations to deflect social criticism of their slow and insufficient response to the problem? As the Indian prime minister has noted of his country, sex-selective abortion and high rates of female infant mortality are a national shame. Việt Nam's policies on sex-selective abortion have been copied from countries with an imbalanced SRB, rather than being modified to account for the motives, methods and experiences of those who undergo sex-selective abortion in Việt Nam. Perhaps official acknowledgement of the existence of sex-selective abortion in Việt Nam will require the same measures that led to the earlier government acknowledgement of the increase in the SRB—an admission made only after the 2006 Population Change Survey. The statistical data the survey produced played a crucial role in changing the government's perspective. In a similar way, research on sex-selective abortion in Việt Nam is likely to improve public knowledge of the phenomenon and prompt the formulation of policy to address it.

Healthcare system responses

Prenatal sex selection and health sector reforms

In Việt Nam, the proliferation of ultrasonography—a popular obstetric technology—coincided with economic and comprehensive health sector reforms initiated in the late 1980s. Ultrasound services—especially prenatal scanning—have increased rapidly and have become an important source of revenue for public and private healthcare providers. However, the introduction of ultrasonography in antenatal care is occurring in an ad hoc manner, driven by market forces rather than health policy, which is leading to its overuse (Gammeltoft and Nguyễn 2007; Gammeltoft 2014). In addition, a lack of control over the practice of foetal diagnosis—particularly foetal sex determination—has social implications such as the increase in sex selection.

The *Đổi Mới* reforms that began in 1986 and ushered in economic liberalisation and privatisation have created dramatic changes in social service delivery systems. Renovation of Việt Nam's health sector began in 1989 with the introduction of user fees, private drug sales and gradual legalisation of private service providers (WHO 2003b). Two major changes in the institutional arrangements for the public health sector, driven by state-imposed fiscal constraints and management of health services, were the 'socialisation' of service provision (the encouragement of user-pays) and decentralisation of state budgeting and organisation of public services. Privatisation and commercialisation of the healthcare system have created conditions conducive to the use and abuse of technology for sex determination in Việt Nam. This phenomenon—combined with the weak supervision of abortion—has allowed sex selection to increase. The improved accessibility of private sector health services provides women with greater choice in reproductive health care, but, in this context, it also creates new pressures and avenues for women to achieve desired pregnancy outcomes.

Health system responses

In response to the increase in sex selection, the MOH issued Official Document No. 3121/BYT-BMTE, dated 21 May 2009, prohibiting the use of medical technology for sex selection, to limit the factors driving the imbalance in the SRB. The MOH required all health facilities that offer prenatal screening and reproductive health services to abstain from using technology for sex-selection purposes.

Since this ban was issued, sex determination is no longer conducted openly. In public hospitals, notifications by medical staff to patients about the sex of their foetus have been limited; however, this does not mean they have been eliminated altogether. Compared with public hospitals, private clinics offer numerous services for sex determination. Together with ultrasonography, sex-determination capabilities are now available in most localities, spreading from the large cities to market towns, where villagers can access such technology at an affordable price. Ultrasonography is a relatively easy technique to administer and does not require highly trained staff or much additional operational expenditure. Costs have been reduced largely by competition as the private health sector has developed.

Dr Dương Quốc Trọng, the head of the GOPFP, provided the following solutions to deal with the situation of the SRB imbalance: first, the legal prohibition on dissemination of knowledge on sex selection and implementation of foetal sex determinations and sex-selective abortion services need to be reviewed, amended and supplemented. Second, the power of authorities to prevent, inspect and take responsibility for sex-selection activites should be enhanced. Third, individuals and organisations violating the regulations need to be strictly fined (Dương Quốc Trọng 2012).

Like healthcare managers, most abortion providers think public hospitals should create good conditions for women seeking abortion services to reduce the incidence of unsafe abortion, including the simplification of administrative procedures. The following comments by one abortion provider are representative of those of several other providers I interviewed:

> Nobody ever tells us they are having an abortion because of the sex of their foetus. We have no real proof that they are having sex-selective abortions. If we refuse to provide abortions for them, they may have unsafe abortions in private clinics. If the administrative procedure is too complicated, they can also find abortion services in private clinics. Private clinics with abortion services are available everywhere. Previously, we required an identity card and family record as part of the pre-abortion procedure; however, these requirements

> caused inconvenience to customers. So, we decided to leave off these requirements. If pregnant women want to have an abortion, they will try to do it by any means. (Abortion provider in a public hospital, 57 years old)

Most abortion providers denied taking part in or preventing sex-selective abortion. Some expressed sympathy for women seeking a sex-selective abortion and some arguments were also advanced in favour of sex selection, supporting the freedom and autonomy of patients to make their own reproductive decisions and the family planning aspect of avoiding unwanted births.

Many sonographers believed parents had the right to know the sex of their foetus:

> It is not a problem at all to tell mothers about the sex of their foetus as long as they do not have a sex-selective abortion. Wanting to know the sex of their baby is a parental need. Our customers are not satisfied if we do not tell them the sex of their baby. (Male, 54 years old)

One sonographer told me: 'A number of doctors became rich by performing illegal sex diagnoses or sex-selective abortions' (Female, 42 years old). In fact, responsibility is shifted between sonographers and abortion providers, with each blaming the other.

As we saw in Chapter 2, ineffective government management of new reproductive technologies and the private health sector is a major contributor to the prevalence of sex selection. Many other factors influence sex selection, but the popularity of ultrasonography in antenatal care and the boom in private clinics are two of the most important in Việt Nam. Clearly, in the context of reproductive health care in Việt Nam today, doctors and clinic managers have played an active role in the diffusion of sex-selection technology. Health workers and doctors at various levels have thus been the key enablers of sex-selective abortion.

Social organisations' responses

In Việt Nam, international agencies have conducted reproductive health and safe abortion advocacy programs on various scales. For example, WHO and IPAS, a global nonprofit organisation, provide technical support for safe abortion in Việt Nam, while Pathfinder International,

Marie Stopes International and Việt Nam Family Planning Association design and implement reproductive health projects. The UNFPA is an international development agency that assists Việt Nam to collect and analyse population data to better understand demographic trends and plan for future needs. Its activities are aimed at women's empowerment and equality, by supporting intervention projects and improving reproductive health and rights through the promotion of high-quality family planning services. As mentioned earlier, the first scientific evidence of the imbalance in Việt Nam's SRB came from the population surveys supported by the UNFPA.

At a press conference for World Population Day on 2 July 2010, Urmila Singh (2010), the UNFPA's deputy representative, said:

> The unusually rapid increase in the sex ratio at birth is a big challenge for Việt Nam … Though the Government of Việt Nam has clearly … [decreed] that sex determination of a foetus and abortion for sex selection are illegal, efforts need to be dedicated towards changing couples' traditional preference for male children, as well as towards empowering women's position in the family and society as a whole.

Over the past 20 years, the UNFPA has been engaged in bringing attention to sex selection—starting in China and India, but now also in other countries—and is working with sister agencies such as WHO, the UN International Children's Emergency Fund (UNICEF), the Office of the High Commissioner for Human Rights and the UN Development Fund for Women to address this problem. It is clear from the literature that combatting sex selection is more effective if there is a link between agencies coordinated by an independent governing agency and if a number of different interventions are employed. The lessons learned from South Korea, China and India are valuable for Việt Nam; some of these are outlined below.

At the beginning of 2006, China began national implementation of its 'Care for Girls' campaign, aimed at changing the ideology of son preference and related behaviour by publicising the relevant regulations and providing information on parenthood and reproductive health as well as various incentives. The project has contributed to a reduction in the SRB in China, which stopped increasing in 2006 (Li 2007).

Experiences from India indicate that the most important tool for change is improving the status of women through education and increasing their self-sufficiency. Education measures include a focus at the primary school level on women's rights and building girls' self-esteem, increased literacy and job training programs, improving women's access to higher education and public education campaigns about women's issues. It is believed these are the only ways to begin to effect true reform. In addition to education programs, promotion of credit and loan programs for women is an effective way to increase their self-sufficiency. Such programs provide small loans for the purchase of items such as sewing machines or looms, allowing women to use their skills to contribute to household income and improve their status within the family and community (Patel et al. 2006). The success of these activities in India owes much to the participation of the country's women's union. A 'community vigil' is a popular Indian method for educating community members about the negative consequences of a skewed SRB and placing responsibility on all members of the community to report incidents of sex-selective screening and abortion.

South Korea has also used an awareness campaign, employing young volunteers. Its experience is one that other countries could adopt as an approach to reducing son preference, by focusing on interventions that seek to alter social norms and accelerate the diffusion of new values (Chung and Das Gupta 2007).

Adopting experiences from other countries in the region, Việt Nam's Intervention Project for Reduction of the Sex Ratio at Birth, run in 18 provinces in 2009–10 by the GOPFP, aimed to include social organisations in its activities, such as the creation of associations for women who have only daughters and promise not to have a third child (*Câu lạc bộ phụ nữ sinh con một bề gái không sinh con thứ ba*). The rationale behind this proposal was that these women would help one another develop their household economy. Regrettably, the project's effectiveness has not yet been evaluated.

Việt Nam is building a social support system to counter the increasing imbalance in the SRB and looking for solutions to deal with the problem. One of the lessons from the successful control of population growth in Việt Nam is the necessity for cooperation between government and a multitude of agencies and the involvement of social organisations such as the women's union and youth union. At this stage, social organisations lack information and are therefore considered outsiders when it comes to responding to the imbalances in the SRB and sex selection. A leader of the local women's union in Thai Binh province told me in 2009:

> There may be more boys than girls recently. This phenomenon will have impacts upon marriage and the family. However, the upper levels of the women's union have not provided any official information about this matter.

Mass media responses

The mass media can help enrich the debate among the general public, various stakeholders, the medical community, health authorities and policymakers about sex selection and its potential impacts. In Việt Nam, however, a lack of coordination between researchers and the mass media means research results are not being disseminated. So far, few qualitative research projects have been conducted to gain a better understanding of the social and cultural factors underlying sex-selective abortion. Furthermore, there has been no research on the media's response to the issue of sex selection. From the beginning of 2008 to the end of 2010, I accessed the websites of popular newspapers such as *Lao Động* (*Labour*), *Gia Đình và Xã Hội* (*Family and Society*), *Đời Sống và Pháp luật* (*Life and Law*), *Phụ Nữ* (*Women*) and *Thanh Niên* (*Youth*) weekly and collected 71 articles related to sex selection. The number and content of these articles tell us something about trends in the media's coverage of the issue. Interestingly, the focus of reporting changed over time. Stories relating to the SRB and son preference were prevalent in 2008 and 2009, while articles about sex-determination methods and policies dominated in 2010. Over three years, these articles focused on six topics: the imbalance in the SRB in Việt Nam, son preference, sex-selection methods, sex-determination methods, Vietnamese policies and regulations on sex selection and sex-selective abortion.

Sex ratio at birth

The newspaper articles related to the SRB were based on results of recent population surveys. The emphasis of these articles changed following the release of statistical data on the imbalance in the SRB in Việt Nam. The titles of articles before the National Population Survey in

2009 often vaguely or sensationally warned about the imbalance in the SRB—for instance, 'Dangers of an imbalance in the sex ratio at birth' (*Nguy cơ mất cân bằng giới tính*) (A.T. 2009). After the survey, article titles pointed to more concrete information, such as 'The sex ratio at birth in Viet Nam is being seriously imbalanced' (*Mất cân bằng giới tính ở Việt Nam đã ở mức nghiêm trọng*) (Hạnh Thư, 2012) and 'The sex ratio at birth is increasing' (*Chênh lệch giới tính khi sinh tiếp tục gia tăng*) (T.H. 2017). These later articles maintained the previous sense of alarm, while providing more information to validate that stance.

Son preference

When providing explanations for son preference and sex-selective abortion, the newspapers tended to emphasise simplistic reasons such as the country's heritage of Confucianism or feudalism. One article, entitled 'Having a son: Everyone's "thirst"?' (*Con trai ai cũng khát*), reported: 'One of the reasons leading to the skewed sex ratio is the "backward" conception influenced by Confucianism, and the disregard of women's roles in their families and in the society' (Trịnh Trung Hòa 2008). Other explanations—such as those related to contemporary economic and social conditions and the effects of public policy—have not been explored.

Methods of sex-selection

In 2008, a number of newspaper and website articles about methods of sex selection were published, containing instructions for couples on how to conceive a baby of the desired sex; from 2009 to 2010, others expanded this discussion. An article entitled 'Herbal medicine for giving birth to a son' (*Bốc thuốc để con trai*) described how herbal medicines for conceiving a son could be easily obtained from healers, while the local authorities did not know about such sex-selection practices and were embarrassed about dealing with this phenomenon (Hà Thu and Lan Phương 2009). Another article, with the title 'Hunt high and low to find out ovulatory date' (*Ngược xuôi soi trứng*), also described preconception sex-selection methods, including the recent trend of using ultrasonography. The article concluded:

A number of women have a thirst for having a son from the perspective of valuing men above women. This perspective is considered to be outdated, but it still influences many families' happiness today. (Hương Thu 2008)

Sex-determination methods

Several articles considered sex determination, with titles such as 'Too easy to know the sex of the foetus' (*Quá dễ để biết giới tính thai nhi*) (Hải Hà 2007), 'Foetal sex diagnosis: Doctors and pregnant women in collusion' (*Chẩn đoán giới tính thai nhi: Bác sĩ 'bắt tay' với sản phụ*) (Ngọc Bảo 2012) and 'Sex determination: Prohibited but still practised' (*Xác định giới tính thai nhi: Cấm vẫn cứ làm*) (Thiên Nga and Nguyễn Cẩm 2008). The last article quoted a doctor in a private clinic: 'We answer our customers' inquiries. If we do not meet their demands, they will find other clinics. To keep a pregnancy or to have an abortion is a parent's right.'

Policies and regulations on sex selection

Policies and regulations on sex selection have been disseminated by the mass media in newspaper articles such as 'Violating regulations on sex selection will be dealt with by the law' (*Vi phạm về lựa chọn giới tính sẽ xử lý theo pháp luật*) (Thủy Hà 2017) and 'Work permits will be revoked if doctors perform sex determinations without permission' (*Rút giấy phép hành nghề nếu bác sĩ để lộ giới tính thai nhi*) (VTC News 2009). The articles quoted several regulations relating to sex selection but did not mention their effectiveness or people's perspectives of them.

Sex-selective abortion

On the whole, media reports reflected the perspectives and knowledge of government officials on sex-selective abortion, while information about women's and health providers' motivations for and experiences of such procedures was absent. The press coverage conveys an attitude of disapproval towards this practice, but without providing explanation or analysis. The media's lack of engagement with women's stories points to the fact that public debate about sex-selective abortion in Việt Nam is almost never about the reality of women's experiences. This perhaps reflects the fact that most women do not want to be involved in that debate because of the stigma around abortion and sex-selective abortion in particular. Furthermore, this is a 'sensitive' issue, so it is not easy for journalists to write or publish penetrating investigative reports on this subject. I still remember being contacted by a journalist who wanted— but was unable—to write an article about sex-selective abortion:

> I certainly went to the hospitals to interview pregnant women who were going to undergo an abortion. But, sadly, the interviewees told me that they would abort for reasons other than because they had female foetuses. (Journalist with *Thanh Niên* online)

Meanwhile, books on traditional and modern methods for preconception and prenatal sex selection were being sold in many bookshops, including that of the obstetrics and gynaecology hospital where I did this research. Some common books are *Sinh con theo ý muốn* (*Having Babies of Desired Gender*) (Đỗ Kính Tùng 2002); *Bí quyết sinh con theo ý muốn* (*The Secret of Having a Baby of the Desired Sex*) (Mai Liên 2008); *Sinh con, nuôi con cần biết: Sinh con theo ý muốn* (*Essential Knowledge about Giving Birth and Raising a Child: Having a Baby of the Desired Sex*) (Minh Quân 2009); *Phương pháp sinh con theo ý muốn* (*How to Conceive a Baby of the Desired Sex*) (Ngọc Lan 2004). These books provided information about what dietary regime to follow, how to calculate the day of ovulation and even ways to weaken the X sperm. In 2009, the government destroyed more than 30,000 copies of such books—27 titles in all—and closed seven websites instructing couples on how to conceive a baby of their desired sex.

Radio and television are immensely popular platforms in Việt Nam and are often more influential with viewers than other mass media. A study of the power of the media to reduce the incidence of sex selection in India indicates that television is the preferred platform for campaigners on this issue. Fictional drama and daily soap operas are the most popular genres among the core target audience (young women), providing a platform from which to focus on issues of gender equality (Naqvi 2006). Việt Nam has not yet taken advantage of radio and television to transmit messages aimed at reducing sex selection and promoting gender equality. A variety of formats could be considered for such communication, including short and full-length feature films, public service advertisements on radio and television and TV drama.

As yet, there has been no research evaluating the impact of mass media messaging on behavioural change in relation to sex selection in Việt Nam. This is also beyond the frame of this study. However, on the basis of comments made by communication experts and others engaged in interventions in this area, some shortcomings of the existing messaging on sex selection are that it tends to be targeted to women—ignoring the fact that sex-selection decisions are not made by women alone—and can have the unintended side effect of promoting misinformation and inducing fear in women seeking abortion services (Naqvi 2006).

Examples of successful messaging elsewhere include China's 'Care for Girls' campaign, which was aimed at changing behaviour around sex selection and which received vigorous support from citizens and social organisations. Meanwhile, India developed a slogan, 'Daughters are not for slaughter'. China's message encourages people to improve the environment for girls' survival and restore the natural SRB. India's slogan seems to imply that sex selection is a sin. At present, the GOPFP is seeking to develop its own messaging around sex selection. Such campaigns must be carefully developed so as not to present as an antiabortion campaign, drive practices further underground, promote simplistic stereotypes, accentuate stigmatisation or further silence and alienate those engaged in these practices. As we have seen in previous chapters, sex selection involves not only women, but also their families and society as a whole. It is necessary for any potential media campaign to consider the multiple layers and participants in the practice of sex selection. An information strategy seeking to change behaviour around sex selection should target a wider audience than just women of reproductive age. Furthermore, to be effective, it should be based on reliable data about the nature of sex-selective abortion in Việt Nam, particularly the circumstances, motivations and experiences of those engaged in the practice.

Conclusion

The debate about sex-selective abortion and the consequences of changes in the SRB in Việt Nam has been driven chiefly by international organisations and feminist researchers, who use India, China and South Korea as comparisons. This debate draws on recent data on macrosocial trends in Việt Nam, such as the SRB, on the experiences of other countries and on perspectives about ideal social wellbeing. To date, however, the debate has not been based on evidence of the circumstances of Vietnamese women and the contexts in which they make decisions about abortion. The extent to which sex-selective abortion is enabled or encouraged by Việt Nam's specific mix of population and health-sector reform policies has yet to be adequately explored. Furthermore, the debate is entirely lacking information about the motives and experiences of those who undergo sex-selective abortion in Việt Nam, increasing the risk of misunderstanding who engages in it, why they do so and how it is experienced.

At present, the prohibition against sex determination and sex-selective abortion in Việt Nam would appear to be unenforceable. There is a gap between government regulations and the current reality of sex selection. Efforts at prohibition have been ineffective for a number of reasons. First, both the state officials and the healthcare workers whom I interviewed generally shared the opinion held by many Vietnamese women and their families that sons are more important than daughters. This tends to diminish the political will to take any serious action against sex selection. Second, despite the fact the Vietnamese Government has enacted regulations against nonmedical foetal sex identification and sex-selective abortion, those who harbour a strong son preference continue to use illegal channels to access such services. Legislation is designed to deal with the proximate drivers of the rise in the SRB, but it cannot eliminate the fundamental causes of son preference. 'Legislation in these matters does not pay dividends unless accompanied by action/ interventions at the community level to bring about a change in attitude', according to Uday Shankar Mishra, associate professor at the Centre for Development Studies in Trivandrum, southern India (cited in Chatterjee 2009: 1410). Third, the responsibilities of sonographers, doctors and nurses, who are the gatekeepers in sex selection, have not been adequately addressed. Fourth, while there are many challenging social, ethical and political issues surrounding sex-selective abortion, there has so far been a lack of involvement of social organisations and a lack of research into and public debate about these issues.

At this stage, international organisations are bringing sex selection to the public's attention, while Vietnamese social organisations are latecomers or outsiders when it comes to responding to this emerging social phenomenon. Although the media conveys information about phenomena such as the imbalance in the SRB and sex-selection trends in society, the reports lack informed and critical analyses of sex-selective abortion or engagement with the stories of those who undertake the practices. Components crucial for the success of policy responses are further research on sex-selective abortion, dissemination of that research, education, mass communication and public debate. A comprehensive communications strategy to encourage behavioural change is of value, but its success will rely on advances in these policy components. Such a strategy must give voice to and illuminate the circumstances of the central participants in sex-selective abortion in a manner that does not further marginalise, stigmatise or silence them, but rather seeks understanding and allows them to contribute to the public debate.

Conclusion

As mentioned in the introduction, one of the reasons for conducting this project is that women's experiences of sex-selective abortion are still largely missing from dialogues about reproductive rights and health. My research has explored the motivations, circumstances and experiences of women in Việt Nam who make use of new reproductive technologies to determine the sex of their foetus and undertake a sex-selective abortion. The analysis is based on specific cases of women who have undergone sex-selective abortion, tracing their passage through the sex determination and abortion decision-making phases, and investigating their experiences during and after the abortion. The research has explored the women's interactions with the range of social actors and health institutions implicated in the process of sex selection, as well as examining social responses to sex-selective abortion. The crucial themes of this book are the notions of women's choice, health and suffering, and the moral and ethical dilemmas of sex-selective abortion.

Women's choice

Rosalind Petchesky emphasises two dimensions of reproductive decision-making: the individual and the social. The emphasis of the first is on the individual's control over their own body in accordance with a general principle of the 'right to bodily self-determination' (Petchesky 1980: 691). In this perspective, women should be allowed to make decisions about their own bodies and reproductive capacities. The second dimension emphasises the social construction of women's reproductive experiences. Women's social context influences (directly or indirectly) the choices they make. 'Women's reproductive situation is never the result of biology alone, but of biology mediated by social and cultural organisation' (Petchesky 1980: 667). My research sheds light on the sociocultural contexts in which women decide to proceed with a sex-selective abortion. As we have seen, the decision to have a sex-selective abortion is structured according to socioeconomic, cultural and political conditions. In the Vietnamese context, various factors influence this decision-making.

First, this research shows that son preference persists in Việt Nam for a number of mutually reinforcing reasons, and differs according to a woman's social position. Rural women are usually pressured by their family and kin to provide a male heir, while parents lacking access to state-provided aged care value sons as future providers for their old age. But urban women—especially professional women—are also influenced by social norms and ideologies that structure women's position within their family and society. Women who are more 'empowered' have greater opportunities to access information about sex-selection and related services. As Elizabeth Croll (2000) argues, gender equality among adults does not necessarily lead to gender equality among children. In the current era of low fertility, son preference puts more pressure on couples—and especially on women—to do what is necessary to produce a son. This research confirms that cadres and government workers are under simultaneous pressures to have at least one son and to stick to the one-or-two–child policy. Thus, the desire for sons continues to drive the family-building process in Việt Nam today.

Second, while women are victims of oppressive systems, they are also social actors who use resources (reproductive technology, in this case) to challenge or resist the patriarchal social system. Women are often pressured by others to seek foetal sex determination and sex-selective abortion, but many are also interested in knowing the sex of their unborn child and themselves initiate a sex-selective abortion. Having a son may improve the wellbeing of a woman's family and can be empowering for individual women. Therefore, women themselves find ways to improve or guarantee their status within their family and community. Rather than challenging and changing the dominant cultural stereotype, Vietnamese women accept and tend to perpetuate the existing social and moral orders. Women both suffer from and resist patriarchal expectations, and both passively endure and actively shape their reproductive destiny. These phenomena have been observed in the application of reproductive technologies for contraception (Gammeltoft 1999) and in circumstances where abortion is illegal and considered sinful (Whittaker 2004).

Third, rapid socioeconomic transformation and the global circulation of new reproductive technologies have influenced women's abortion choices. Not long after it was introduced to Việt Nam, ultrasound technology was being used in a range of prenatal health services. Its use today is booming and escaping legal controls. It is interesting that the increasing use of ultrasonography for sex selection coincides with a revival of traditional sex-selection methods, rather than replacing them, as we might have expected according to standard scenarios of modernisation and technology transfer. The practice of sex selection in Việt Nam is an aspect of the complex and dynamic market for reproductive health services and demonstrates that women's traditional desire to influence their reproductive destiny remains particularly strong. The failure to regulate the private health sector and the lack of government response to the spread of new sex-determination practices have allowed sex-selective abortions to occur relatively unchecked.

Son preference has been reinforced by the advances in the new reproductive technology. The global circulation of ultrasound technology has permitted couples to reliably produce offspring of the desired sex through prenatal sex diagnosis, thus changing gendered relations at local sites such as Việt Nam. These developments pose major challenges for the management of reproductive health services that are part of a globalised market. The responses of women to new reproductive technologies are attributable not just to 'tradition' and local hegemonies, but also to the effects of globally circulating knowledge and practices on their lives. New reproductive technologies suggest possibilities for increased freedom and innovative change, but they also frequently open the door to new forms of domination or neocolonial expansion.

Fourth, women's reproductive choices are made against official policies limiting the number of children per family and prohibiting sex-selective abortion. There are a number of studies suggesting the link between the government's efforts to control population growth and sex-selective abortion. This research provides evidence of the policy implications of sex-selective abortion. The case of Việt Nam indicates that state intervention in relation to abortion—legalising abortion and prohibiting sex-selective abortion—represents a complex and sometimes contradictory policy. State policies on sex selection and population control are attempts not only to contain women's abortion practices, but also to control the size and composition of the population. In other words, in the politics of fertility control, the practice of sex-selective abortion represents a fusion of control.

In short, women negotiate various contradictory forces within which their lives and their reproductive agency are embedded. Considering women's position in reproductive decision-making, this study shows that significant pressure is placed on women to have a son. Women often have to choose a sex-selective abortion because of the pressure of social norms and official policies. Although this research challenges the portrayal of women as passive victims of patriarchal institutions that grant them little choice, it nonetheless observes that the reproductive agency they display is significantly constrained. As Petchesky (1980: 675) argues:

> [W]omen make their own reproductive choices, but they do not make them under conditions which they themselves create but under social conditions and constraints which they, as mere individuals, are powerless to change.

Women's health

Sex-selective abortion is usually conducted in the second trimester of pregnancy. While the WHO is trying to decrease the proportion of abortions in the population, especially those in the second trimester of pregnancy, the popularity of sex-selective abortion is a crucial factor impeding the realisation of this aim. Safe techniques for second-trimester abortion were introduced in Việt Nam in the early 2000s at the same time that the introduction of new reproductive technologies was leading to an increase in sex-selective abortions. A newly introduced abortion technique—dilation and evacuation—has allowed women to terminate their second-trimester pregnancies more safely and easily compared with the older method of saline distillation. Advances in new reproductive technologies and obstetrics techniques that hold such promise for improving women's health have been used for non-medical purposes and, because of insufficient management and supervision, have contributed to the rapid increase in sex-selective abortions in the country. As in other developing countries, in Việt Nam, health regulators have been unable to keep up with the development and utilisation of new reproductive technologies.

In Việt Nam, the difficulty in restricting abortions for sex selection is that the ultrasonography and abortion procedures may be undertaken at separate clinics. Women sometimes use public clinics for an abortion after having a sex-detection scan at a private hospital. Abortion services are inexpensive and widely available, provided by public as well as private health services (Gammeltoft 2002). The ease with which determined people can evade the ban on sex-selective abortion by drawing selectively on specialists and services in different sites poses a major challenge for public health regulators. The strong demand for and supply of sex-selection technologies, the multitude of private service providers and the plurality of pathways that those seeking sex-selective abortion can take to achieve their aim combine to make these practices particularly difficult to regulate.

Counsellors and abortion providers in the hospital where I conducted most of my research were confident they could identify a case of sex-selective abortion according to the number and sex of children of the woman seeking an abortion. The majority of abortion providers were aware of the ban on sex-selective abortion; however, they conducted such procedures—for a number of reasons. They sympathised with sonless women in a patriarchal society. Doctors worried about the effects on women's health if they were unable to access a safe abortion. And second-trimester abortions are also profitable for abortion providers. More importantly, health staff cannot refuse an abortion request since, in Việt Nam, abortion is a woman's right. It should be remembered that sex-selective abortion-seekers often conceal the real reason they are seeking an abortion, claiming that they already have enough children or they face difficult economic circumstances. Sex-selective abortion can therefore be easily hidden from the relevant authorities. Some policymakers blame the accessibility of abortion in Việt Nam for sex-selective abortion and propose tightening regulations on abortion and restricting access. However, regulations regarding sex-selective abortion are tied up with other laws on reproductive health. We should remember that restricting access to abortion can have adverse consequences on women's health.

Clearly, counselling can play an important role in the abortion process, especially sex-selective abortion. The quality of counselling in cases of sex-selective abortion in Việt Nam is affected not only by the poor clinical conditions (lack of staff, overworked staff, untrained counsellors), but also by the perceptions of counsellors, influenced by larger sociocultural and political circumstances. As a consequence of inadequate counselling, women face a multitude of anxieties and psychological issues and are not given adequate opportunities to reflect on their decision. Although women may present to a hospital intending to have a sex-selective abortion, not all will decide to proceed. The provision of more effective counselling at this critical stage could sway more of those who are ambivalent.

This study demonstrates that women having a sex-selective abortion experience a great number of conflicting emotions before, during and after the procedure. Emotional attachment to the foetus, lack of social support and moral attitudes towards abortion increase the likelihood of women experiencing negative feelings post abortion. To reduce poor post-abortion outcomes for women, women's mental health should receive more attention from families and healthcare providers.

In relation to illegal sex-selective abortion, the physical complications can be more dangerous than the psychological ones for women, and the burden may not rest solely with the individual women, but also with medical institutions and society as a whole. Most of the abortion providers I met believed illegal abortions could lead to serious medical complications, and they expressed concern for women's health if they did not access safe abortion services. Therefore, bans on abortion alone cannot resolve this issue. Counselling together with legislative and social action aimed at promoting gender equality and women's human rights are needed to reduce the cultural, emotional and psychological pressures driving the demand for sex-selective abortion.

Women's suffering

The high prevalence of abortion in Việt Nam does not mean there are no emotional or ethical concerns about the procedure. In this research, I discovered that sex-selective abortions are traumatic for women in a number of ways. Women who had a sex-selective abortion experienced anxiety, depression, grief, guilt, sorrow and shame. A number of women experienced nightmares. Despite this, some women also experienced relief, believing abortion was the best option in the circumstances. All women in this study who had a sex-selective abortion left the remains of their foetus at the hospital. The main reason for this was a desire to keep their abortion a secret. However, many women were deeply concerned that the remains of the foetus be disposed of with proper dignity. Information about the deceased foetus is very important to women's psychological state after abortion and this should be addressed in counselling.

The generally poor quality of medical care, social understanding and public health policy regarding post-abortion care contribute to a high risk of complications for women. Women who have a sex-selective abortion are also at high risk of negative outcomes because of the stigma of abortion in society and the legislation prohibiting sex-selective abortion. Women who experienced physical pain and anxiety post abortion were often reluctant to seek follow-up medical care because of the illicit nature of the procedure and fear of being criticised for committing an immoral act. They also were unable to share their experiences and alleviate their anxiety by discussing their experiences with family, friends or others in their social network, instead preferring to keep their experiences secret. This silence also makes understanding the incidence and effects of sex-selective abortion particularly difficult for researchers and health professionals.

When women do not have psychological support from their family and institutional organisations, rituals such as making offerings, prayer and requiems for the souls of the aborted foetuses form part of the healing process. This research indicates that rituals not only help women resolve their complex feelings towards the child they lost, as Tine Gammeltoft (2010) observes; they are also a way of obtaining personal relief and healing for their suffering. The trauma, guilt and other forms of psychological suffering women experience can be expressed and recognised during such rituals. Rituals, therefore, help women seek moral forgiveness and understanding. By undertaking rituals, often in conjunction with others, women transform from passively suffering to actively healing their psychological wounds after an abortion.

The policy challenge

Statistics for SRB are not always available at the national level. Therefore, addressing the phenomenon of an imbalanced SRB is a key opportunity for the government to examine its current legislative framework and the extent to which laws and policies are in line with ideals of gender equality. The data on the SRB should be collected and disseminated to the wider public. Further analysis based on more complete and better-quality data is urgently needed to aid our understanding of this phenomenon and its trends. The government should also fully support the development of innovative activities that stimulate discussion of sex-selection issues.

One of the most contentious debates around sex-selective abortion is whether it should be prohibited. On the one hand, an official ban on prenatal sex selection has value because the knowledge that they are breaking the law may provide people scope to reflect on the pros and cons of having an abortion. On the other hand, one could argue that sex-selective abortion is a logical extension of existing state policies, including family planning and the insistence on small families; public health policies that make abortions safe and readily accessible; the state's emphasis on the maintenance of traditional Vietnamese cultural identity in the context of globalisation; the support of the state for market-based mechanisms in all aspects of healthcare provision; and the devolution to individual families of the rights and responsibilities of making their own reproductive decisions. Women undergo sex-selective abortion to comply with state regulations and/or because of bullying from their family, while at the same time being encouraged to utilise market-based health services and take responsibility for their own wellbeing. Sex-selective abortion therefore raises challenging questions about the regulation of legal abortion and illegal sex-selective abortion.

Ineffective attempts to regulate ultrasonography and ban sex-selective abortion indicate that bans alone will not stop sex determination and sex-selective abortion. Sex selection must be tackled at more fundamental and comprehensive social, economic, political and legal levels. Better regulation of private clinics that offer sex determination and the enhancement of abortion counselling services are among the interventions in the public health field that, according to my findings, might make a difference. The creation of professional bodies supporting responsible practices among doctors and nurses, including education and the review of credentials, is another aspect of what must be a multifaceted strategy of dealing with sex-selective abortion. Rather than simply banning sex-selective abortion, Việt Nam should also address the root causes of son preference and gender inequality. For example, solutions could include improving social security and financial support for elderly people, especially those without sons, providing better education and more employment opportunities for women and creating space for the evolution of alternative traditions and cultural conceptions that confer recognition and status on women irrespective of whether they have a son.

The challenges for women's reproductive health

In this research, women were situated at the centre of reproductive behaviour within their families, their communities and the wider society. The research builds a profile of sex-selective abortion in Việt Nam, as a resource to enable governments, professionals and social organisations to establish social policies, interventions and support services. It has to be said that there are no immediately identifiable or simple solutions to the problem of sex-selective abortion. Moreover, in working on reproductive health rights in Việt Nam, the government and international and local organisations should be aware and respectful of women's individual rights. A need also exists to understand the terrible dilemmas and the silent suffering experienced by women who undertake such abortions. So far, women have remained marginal to most national and international debates about and policies on sex selection. We should bring women's needs, interests and experiences into these debates and make their wellbeing the focus of policies aimed at tackling sex-selective abortion. The silence surrounding sex-selective abortion remains a major challenge for individuals and society. Ending this silence would help women who undergo sex-selective abortion and involve the whole society in forging positive responses to this phenomenon.

Bibliography

Legislation

Ministry of Health Official Document (2009), 3121/BYT-BMTE, 21 May 2009, Hà Nội.

National Assembly of Vietnam (2003). Pháp lệnh của Ủy ban thường vụ Quốc hội số 06/2003/PL-UBTVQH11 ngày 9 tháng 1 năm 2003 về dân số [Ordinance on Population of the Standing Committee of the National Assembly, No. 06/2003/PL-UBTVQH11 on population], 9 January 2003, Hà Nội.

National Assembly of Vietnam (2009). Pháp lệnh sửa đổi Điều 10 của Pháp lệnh dân số của Ủy ban thường vụ Quốc hội, 15/2008/PL-UBTVQH12 [Ordinance to revise Article 10 of the Ordinance on Population of the Standing Committee of the National Assembly, No. 15/2008/PL-UBTVQH12], 27 December 2008, Hà Nội.

National Assembly of Vietnam (2013). *The Constitution of the Socialist Republic of Viet Nam*, amended in 2013, approved by the National Assembly of the Socialist Republic of Viet Nam, term XIII, at its sixth session on 28 November 2013, Hà Nội.

Vietnamese Government (2006). Nghị định 114/2006/ND-CP về xử phạt vi phạm hành chính về dân số và trẻ em [Decree 114/2006/ND-CP defining the sanction of administrative violations on population and children], October 2006, Hà Nội.

Books, articles, chapters, other media

Adler, Nancy E., Henry P. David, Brenda N. Major, Susan H. Roth, Nancy F. Russo and Gail E. Wyatt (1990). 'Psychological responses after abortion'. *Science* 248(4951): 41–44. doi.org/10.1126/science.2181664.

Alfirevic, Zarko, Faris Mujezinovic and Karin Sundberg (2017 [2003]). 'Amniocentesis and chorionic villus sampling for prenatal diagnosis (Review)'. *Cochrane Database of Systematic Reviews* 9(CD003252). doi.org/10.1002/14651858.CD003252.pub2.

Andrews, Janet L. and Joyceen S. Boyle (2003). 'African American adolescents' experiences with unplanned pregnancy and elective abortion'. *Health Care for Women International* 24(5): 414–33. doi.org/10.1080/07399330390212199.

Angelo, Joanne (1994). 'The negative impact of abortion on women and families: The many faces of abortion grief'. In *Post-Abortion Aftermath*, edited by Michael T. Mannion, pp. 44–105, Kansas City: Sheed & Ward.

Armsworth, Mary W. (1991). 'Psychological response to abortion'. *Journal of Counseling and Development* 69(4): 377–79. doi.org/10.1002/j.1556-6676.1991.tb01527.x.

Arnold, Fred (1975). *The Value of Children: A Cross-National Study. Introduction and Comparative Analysis*. Honolulu: East-West Population Institute, East-West Center.

Arnold, Fred (1997). 'Gender preferences for children: Findings from the demographic and health surveys'. Presented to 23rd General Population Conference of the International Union for the Scientific Study of Population, Beijing, 11–17 October.

Asher, John D. (1972). 'Abortion counseling'. *American Journal of Public Health* 62(5): 686–88. doi.org/10.2105/AJPH.62.5.686.

Ashton, J. R. (1980). 'The psychosocial outcome of induced abortion'. *British Journal of Obstetrics & Gynaecology* 87(12): 1115–122. doi.org/10.1111/j.1471-0528.1980.tb04483.x.

A.T. (2009). 'Nguy cơ mất cân bằng giới tính' ['Dangers of an imbalance in the sex ratio at birth']. *Quảng Nam Online*, 28 December. Online: nguoiquangxaque.com/xa-hoi/y-te/200912/nguy-co-mat-can-bang-gioi-tinh-68130 (accessed 30 November 2010).

Bang Nguyen Pham, Wayne Hall, Peter Hill and Chalapati Rao (2008). 'Analysis of socio-political and health practices influencing sex ratio at birth in Viet Nam'. *Reproductive Health Matters* 16(32): 176–84. doi.org/10.1016/S0968-8080(08)32412-4.

Barnard, Catherine Anne (1990). *The Long-Term Psychosocial Effects of Abortion*. Portsmouth, NH: Institute for Pregnancy Loss.

Barrett, Jennifer and Cynthia Buckley (2007). 'Constrained contraceptive choice: IUD prevalence in Uzbekistan'. *International Family Planning Perspectives* 33(2): 50–57. doi.org/10.1363/3305007.

Becker, Stan, Eva Bazant and Carole Meyers (2008). 'Couples counseling at an abortion clinic: A pilot study'. *Contraception* 78(5): 424–31. doi.org/10.1016/j.contraception.2008.06.011.

Beenhakker, Britta, Stan Becker, Stephanie Hires, Nell Molano Di Targiana, Paul Blumethal and George Huggins (2004). 'Are partners available for post-abortion contraceptive counseling? A pilot study in a Baltimore city clinic'. *Contraception* 69(5): 419–23. doi.org/10.1016/j.contraception.2003.12.013.

Bélanger, Danièle (2002). 'Son preference in a rural village in North Vietnam'. *Studies in Family Planning* 33(4): 321–34. doi.org/10.1111/j.1728-4465.2002.00321.x.

Bélanger, Danièle and Khuat Thi Hai Oanh (2009). 'Second-trimester abortions and sex-selection of children in Hanoi, Vietnam'. *Population Studies* 63(2): 163–71. doi.org/10.1080/00324720902859380.

Bélanger, Danièle and Khuat Thu Hong (1998). 'Young single women using abortion in Hanoi, Vietnam'. *Asia-Pacific Population Journal* 13(2): 3–26.

Bélanger, Danièle and Khuat Thu Hong (1999). 'Single women's experiences of sexual relationships and abortion in Hanoi, Vietnam'. *Reproductive Health Matters* 7(14): 71–82. doi.org/10.1016/S0968-8080(99)90008-3.

Bélanger, Danièle, Khuat Thi Hai Oanh, Liu Jianye, Le Thanh Thuy and Pham Viet Thanh (2003). 'Are sex ratios increasing in Vietnam?'. *Population* 58(2): 231–50. doi.org/10.3917/pope.302.0231 and doi.org/10.2307/3246604.

Benagiano, Giuseppe and Paola Bianchi (1999). 'Sex pre-selection: An aid to couples or a threat to humanity?'. *Human Reproduction* 14(4): 868–70. doi.org/10.1093/humrep/14.4.868.

Berer, Marge (2008). 'A critical appraisal of laws on second trimester abortion'. *Reproductive Health Matters* 16(S31): 3–13. doi.org/10.1016/S0968-8080(08)31395-0.

Berlin, Isaiah (1969). 'Two concepts of liberty'. In *Four Essays on Liberty: Part 2*, pp. 118–72. London: Oxford University Press.

Blakely, Mary Kay (1984). 'Morality and personhood: A feminist perspective'. In *Abortion and Women's Choice: The State, Sexuality and Reproductive Freedom*, edited by Rosalind Pollack Petchesky, pp. 330–67. New York: Longman Inc.

Boyle, Mary and Jane McEvoy (1998). 'Putting abortion in its social context: Northern Irish women's experiences of abortion in England'. *Health* 2(3): 283–304. doi.org/10.1177/136345939800200302.

Bradshaw, Zoë and Pauline Slade (2003). 'The effects of induced abortion on emotional experiences and relationships: A critical review of the literature'. *Clinical Psychology Review* 23(7): 929–58. doi.org/10.1016/j.cpr. 2003.09.001.

Burgess, Robin and Juzhong Zhuang (2002). *Modernization and son preference in People's Republic of China*. Manila: ERD Working Paper Series, Asian Development Bank.

Burnell, George M. and Mary A. Norfleet (1987). 'Women's self-reported responses to abortion'. *Journal of Psychology* 121(1): 71–76. doi.org/10.10 80/00223980.1987.9712645.

Burr, Rachel (2014). 'The complexity of morality: Being a "good child" in Vietnam'. *Journal of Moral Education* 43(2): 156–68. doi.org/10.1080/030 57240.2014.893421.

Byrne, Peter (2000). 'Stigma of mental illness and ways of diminishing it'. *Advances in Psychiatric Treatment* 6(1): 65–72. doi.org/10.1192/apt.6.1.65.

Cain, Mead (1993). 'Patriarchal structure and demographic change'. In *Women's Position and Demographic Change*, edited by Nora Federici, Karen Oppenheim Mason and Sølvi Sogner, pp. 43–60. Oxford: Clarendon Press.

Central Population and Housing Census Steering Committee (2010). *The 2009 Vietnam Population and Housing Census: Major Findings*. Hà Nội: General Statistics Office of Vietnam.

Charmaz, Kathy (2000). 'Grounded theory: Objectivist and constructivist method'. In *Handbook of Qualitative Research*, edited by Norman K. Denzin and Yvonna S. Lincoln, pp. 509–35. Thousand Oaks, CA: Sage Publications.

Chatterjee, Patralekha (2009). 'Sex ratio imbalance worsens in Vietnam'. *The Lancet* 374(9699): 1410. doi.org/10.1016/S0140-6736(09)61847-X.

Chung, Woojin and Monica Das Gupta (2007). 'The decline of son preference in South Korea: The roles of development and public policy'. *Population and Development Review* 33(4): 757–83. doi.org/10.1111/j.1728-4457.2007. 00196.x.

Clow, W. M. and A. C. Crompton (1973). 'The wounded uterus: Pregnancy after hysterotomy'. *British Medical Journal* 1: 321–23. doi.org/10.1136/ bmj.1.5849.321.

Cohen, Larry and Susan Roth (1984). 'Coping with abortion'. *Journal of Human Stress* 10(3): 140–45. doi.org/10.1080/0097840X.1984.9934968.

Comendant, Rodica and Marge Berer (2008). 'Second trimester abortion: Women's health and public policy'. *Reproductive Health Matters* 16(S31): 1–2. doi.org/10.1016/S0968-8080(08)31390-1.

Coovadia, Hoosen, Rachel Jewkes, Peter Barron, David Sanders and Diane McIntyre (2009). 'The health and health system of South Africa: Historical roots of current public health challenges'. *The Lancet* 374: 817–34. doi.org/10.1016/S0140-6736(09)60951-X.

Cougle, Jeese R., David C. Reardon and Priscilla K. Coleman (2005). 'Generalized anxiety associated with unintended pregnancy: A cohort study of the 1995 National Survey of Family Growth'. *Journal of Anxiety Disorders* 19(1): 137–42. doi.org/10.1016/j.janxdis.2003.12.003.

Cozzarelli, Catherine, Nebi Sumer and Brenda Major (1998). 'Mental models of attachment and coping with abortion'. *Journal of Personality and Social Psychology* 74(2): 453–67. doi.org/10.1037/0022-3514.74.2.453.

Croll, Elizabeth (2000). *Endangered Daughters: Discrimination and Development in Asia*. London: Routledge.

Dahl, Edgar (2003). 'Procreative liberty: The case for preconception sex selection'. *Reproductive BioMedicine Online* 7(4): 380–84. doi.org/10.1016/S1472-6483(10)61880-9.

Dalvie, Suchitra S. (2008). 'Second trimester abortions in India'. *Reproductive Health Matters* 16(S31): 37–45. doi.org/10.1016/S0968-8080(08)31384-6.

Daly, Kerry (2000). *Qualitative Methods of Family Studies and Human Development*. London: Sage Publications.

Đặng Nghiêm Vạn (2003). *Lý Luận Về Tôn Giáo và Tình Hình Tôn Giáo ở Việt Nam* [*Theory of Religions and Religious Situations in Vietnam*]. Hà Nội: National Political Publishing House.

Das, Veena (2007). *Life and Words: Violence and the Descent into the Ordinary*. Berkeley, CA: University of California Press.

Das Gupta, Monica (1987). 'Selective discrimination against female children in rural Punjab, India'. *Population Development Review* 13(1): 77–100. doi.org/10.2307/1972121.

Das Gupta, Monica and Mari Bhat (1997). 'Fertility decline and increased manifestation of sex bias in India'. *Population Studies* 51(3): 307–15. doi.or g/10.1080/0032472031000150076.

David, Henry P. (1992). 'Abortion in Europe, 1920–1991: A public health perspective'. *Studies in Family Planning* 23(1): 1–22. doi.org/10.2307/ 1966824.

Denzin, Norman K. and Yvonna S. Lincoln (eds) (1994). *Handbook of Qualitative Research*. Thousand Oaks, CA: Sage Publications.

Dickson-Swift, Virginia, Erica Lyn James and Pranee Liamputtong (2008). *Undertaking Sensitive Research in the Health and Social Sciences: Managing Boundaries, Emotions, and Risks*. New York: Cambridge University Press. doi.org/10.1017/CBO9780511545481.

Đỗ Kính Tùng (2002). *Sinh con theo ý muốn* [*Having Babies of Desired Gender*]. Hà Nội: Medical Publishing House.

Dương Quốc Trọng (2012). 'Giảm thiểu mất cân bằng giới tính khi sinh ở Việt Nam: Ba giải pháp, bốn kiến nghị' [To reduce the imbalance of SRB in Viet Nam: Three solutions, four recommendations], *Gia Đình và Xã Hội Online*, 20 December. Online: www.giadinh.net.vn/dan-so/giam-thieu- mat-can-bang-gioi-tinh-khi-sinh-o-viet-nam-ba-giai-phap-bon-kien- nghi-201212200314488.htm (accessed 15 November 2018).

Efrat, Z., O. O. Akinfenwa and K. H. Nicolaides (1999). 'First-trimester determination of fetal gender by ultrasound'. *Ultrasound in Obstetrics & Gynecology* 13(5): 305–307. doi.org/10.1046/j.1469-0705.1999.13050305.x.

El Dawla, Aida Seif, Amal Abdel Hadi and Nadia Abdel Wahab (1998). 'Women's wit over men's: Trade-offs and strategic accommodations in Egyptian women's reproductive lives'. In *Negotiating Reproductive Rights*, edited by Rosalind Petchesky and Karen Judd, pp. 68–107. London: Zed Books.

Evans-Pritchard, Edward Evan (1976). *Witchcraft, Oracles and Magic among the Azande*. Oxford: Clarendon Press.

Federici, Nora, Karen Oppenheim Mason and Sølvi Sogner (eds) (1993). *Women's Position and Demographic Change*. Oxford: Clarendon Press.

Feldman, Kenneth and David Smith (1975). 'Fetal phallic growth and penile standards for newborn male infants'. *Journal of Pediatrics* 86(3): 395–98. doi.org/10.1016/S0022-3476(75)80969-3.

Fletcher, Ruth (1995). 'Silences: Irish women and abortion'. *Feminist Review* 50: 44–66. doi.org/10.2307/1395490 and doi.org/10.1057/fr.1995.21.

Franklin, Sarah (1993). Life itself. Paper delivered at the Centre for Cultural Values, Lancaster University, Lancaster, 13 June.

Gallo, Maria and Nguyen C. Nghia (2007). 'Real life is different: A qualitative study of why women delay abortion until the second trimester in Vietnam'. *Social Science and Medicine* 64(9): 1812–822. doi.org/10.1016/j.socscimed.2007.02.005.

Gammeltoft, Tine (1999). *Women's Bodies, Women's Worries*. Richmond, UK: Curzon Press.

Gammeltoft, Tine (2002). 'Between "science" and "superstition": Moral perceptions of induced abortion among urban youth in Vietnam'. *Culture, Medicine and Psychiatry* 26(3): 313–38. doi.org/10.1023/A:1021210405417.

Gammeltoft, Tine (2003). 'The ritualisation of abortion in contemporary Vietnam'. *The Australian Journal of Anthropology* 14(2): 129–43. doi.org/10.1111/j.1835-9310.2003.tb00226.x.

Gammeltoft, Tine (2008). 'Figures of transversality: State power and prenatal screening in contemporary Vietnam'. *American Ethnologist* 35(4): 570–87. doi.org/10.1111/j.1548-1425.2008.00099.x

Gammeltoft, Tine (2010). 'Between remembering and forgetting: Maintaining moral motherhood after late-term abortion'. In *Abortion in Asia: Local Dilemmas, Global Politics*, edited by Andrea Whittaker, pp. 56–77. New York: Berghahn Books.

Gammeltoft, Tine (2014). *Haunting Images: A Cultural Account of Selective Reproduction in Vietnam*. Berkeley, CA: University of California Press. doi.org/10.1525/california/9780520278424.001.0001.

Gammeltoft, Tine and Hạnh Thị Thuý Nguyễn (2007). 'The commodification of obstetric ultrasound scanning in Hanoi, Viet Nam'. *Reproductive Health Matters* 15(29): 163–71. doi.org/10.1016/S0968-8080(06)29280-2.

Gammeltoft, Tine, Trần Minh Hằng, Nguyễn Thị Hiệp and Nguyễn Thị Thúy Hạnh (2008). 'Late-term abortion for fetal anomaly: Vietnamese women's experiences'. *Reproductive Health Matters* 16(3): 46–56. doi.org/10.1016/S0968-8080(08)31373-1.

Ganatra, Bela, Siddhi Hirve and V. N. Rao (2001). 'Sex-selective abortion: Evidence from a community-based study in western India'. *Asia-Pacific Population Journal* 16(2): 109–124.

General Statistics Office of Vietnam (2000). *Vietnam Living Standard Survey 1997–1998*. Hà Nội: Statistical Publishing House.

Gilles, Kate and Charlotte Feldman-Jacobs (2012). *When technology and tradition collide: From gender bias to sex selection*. Policy Brief. Washington, DC: Population Reference Bureau. Online: pdfs.semanticscholar.org/e782/285e6c852b7b3df46e80681b114b4bf18df9.pdf (accessed 6 June 2018).

Goffman, Erving (1963). *Stigma: Notes on the Management of Spoiled Identity*. Englewood Cliffs, NJ: Prentice-Hall.

Goodkind, Daniel (1994). 'Abortion in Vietnam: Measurements, puzzles, and concerns'. *Studies in Family Planning* 25(6): 342–52. doi.org/10.2307/2137878.

Goodkind, Daniel (1999a). 'Do parents prefer sons in North Korea?'. *Studies in Family Planning* 30(3): 212–18. doi.org/10.1111/j.1728-4465.1999.00212.x.

Goodkind, Daniel (1999b). 'Should prenatal sex selection be restricted? Ethical questions and their implications for research and policy'. *Population Studies* 53(1): 49–61. doi.org/10.1080/00324720308069.

Goodwin, Phillippa and Jane Ogden (2007). 'Women's reflections upon their past abortions: An exploration of how and why emotional reactions change over time'. *Psychology and Health* 22(2): 231–48. doi.org/10.1080/14768320600682384.

Grabich, Carol (2007). *Qualitative Data Analysis: An Introduction*. London: Sage Publications.

Gray, Ronald (1991). 'Natural family planning and sex selection: Fact or fiction?'. *American Journal of Obstetrics and Gynecology* 165(6[2]): 1982–984. doi.org/10.1016/S0002-9378(11)90558-4.

Gray, Ronald H., Joe L. Simpson, Adenike C. Bitto, John T. Queenan, Chuanjun Li, Robert. T. Kambic, Alfredo Perez, Patricio Mena, Maurizio Barbato, W. Stevenson and V. Jennings (1998). 'Sex ratio associated with timing of insemination and length of the follicular phase in planned and unplanned pregnancies during use of natural family planning'. *Human Reproduction* 13(5): 1397–400. doi.org/10.1093/humrep/13.5.1397.

Griffin, Susan (1978). *Women and Nature: The Roaring Inside Her*. New York: Harper Row.

Gross, Michael (1999). 'After feticide: Coping with late-term abortion in Israel, Western Europe, and the United States'. *Cambridge Quarterly of Healthcare Ethics* 8(4): 449–62. doi.org/10.1017/S096318019980406X.

Gu, Baochang and Krishna Roy (1995). 'Sex ratio at birth in China with reference to other areas of East Asia: What we know'. *Asia-Pacific Population Journal* 10(3): 17–42. Online: www.ncbi.nlm.nih.gov/pubmed/12290692 (accessed 15 May 2018).

Guba, Egon and Yvonna Lincoln (1994). 'Competing paradigms in qualitative research'. In *Handbook of Qualitative Research*, edited by Norman K. Denzin and Yvonna S. Lincoln, pp. 105–116. Thousand Oaks, CA: Sage Publications.

Guilmoto, Christophe Z. (2007a). 'Causes and policy issues of sex ratio at birth in Asia and Vietnam'. Presented to Workshop on Imbalance of Sex Ratio at Birth in Asia Region and Vietnam, National Press Conference Centre, Hà Nội, 20 December.

Guilmoto, Christophe Z. (2007b). 'Characteristics of sex-ratio imbalance of India and future scenarios'. Presented to 4th Asia and Pacific Conference on Reproductive and Sexual Health and Rights, Hyderabad, India, 29–31 October.

Guilmoto, Christophe Z. (2008). *Recent Increase in Sex Ratio at Birth in Vietnam: A Review of Evidence.* Hà Nội: United Nations Population Fund.

Guilmoto, Christophe Z. (2009). 'The sex ratio transition in Asia'. *Population and Development Review* 35(3): 519–49. doi.org/10.1111/j.1728-4457.2009. 00295.x.

Guilmoto, Christophe Z., Xuyên Hoàng and Toàn Ngô Văn (2009). 'Recent increase in sex ratio at birth in Viet Nam'. *PloS ONE* 4(2): 1–7. doi.org/ 10.1371/journal.pone.0004624.

Gupta, Jyotsna Agnihotri (1996). 'New freedom, new dependency: New reproductive technologies, women's health and autonomy'. PhD dissertation. Leiden: Leiden University.

Gustafsson, Mai Lan (2009). *War and Shadows: The Haunting of Vietnam.* Ithaca, NY: Cornell University Press.

Hadley, Janet (1996). *Abortion: Between Freedom and Necessity.* Philadelphia: Temple University Press.

Hải Hà (2007). 'Quá dễ để biết giới tính thai nhi' [Too easy to know the sex of the foetus]. *VnExpress*, 28 December. Online: giadinh.vnexpress.net/ tin-tuc/to-am/qua-de-dang-de-biet-gioi-tinh-thai-nhi-2267260.html (accessed 17 June 2018).

Handwerker, Lisa (2002). 'The politics of making modern babies in China: Reproductive technologies and the "new" eugenics'. In *Infertility around the Globe: New Thinking on Childlessness, Gender, and Reproductive Technologies*, edited by Marcia C. Inhorn and Frank van Balen, pp. 298–314. Berkeley, CA: University of California Press.

Hạnh Thư (2012). 'Mất cân bằng giới tính ở Việt Nam đã ở mức nghiêm trọng' ['The sex ratio at birth in Viet Nam is being seriously imbalanced']. *Thời báo Kinhtế Sàigòn Online*, 4 November. Online: https://www.thesaigontimes.vn/86429/Mat-can-bang-gioi-tinh-da-o-muc-nghiem-trong.html (accessed 25 May 2017).

Harding, Sandra (1986). *The Science Question in Feminism*. Milton Keynes, UK: Open University Press.

Harris, Amy A. (2004). 'Supportive counseling before and after elective pregnancy termination'. *Journal of Midwifery and Women's Health* 49(2): 105–12. doi.org/10.1016/j.jmwh.2003.11.008 and doi.org/10.1016/S1526-9523(03)00494-X.

Hà Thu and Lan Phương (2009). 'Bốc thuốc đẻ con trai' [Herbal medicine for giving birth to a son]. *Gia Đình* [*Family*], 5 May.

Haughton, Jonathan (1997). 'Falling fertility in Vietnam'. *Population Studies* 51(2): 203–11. doi.org/10.1080/0032472031000149916.

Haughton, Jonathan and Dominique Haughton (1995). 'Son preference in Vietnam'. *Studies in Family Planning* 26(6): 325–37. doi.org/10.2307/2138098.

Henry, David (1992). 'Abortion in Europe, 1920–91: A public health perspective'. *Studies in Family Planning* 23(1): 1–22. doi.org/10.2307/1966824.

Hess, Rosanna (2004). 'Dimensions of women's long-term post-abortion experience'. *Maternal Child Nursing* 29(3): 193–98. doi.org/10.1097/0000 5721-200405000-00011.

Hiebert, Paul (1985). *Anthropological Insights for Missionaries*. Grand Rapids, MI: Baker Book House.

Hoàng, Tuyết, Thùy Phan and Trang Huỳnh (2008). 'Second trimester abortion in Viet Nam: Changing to recommended methods and improving service delivery'. *Reproductive Health Matters* 16(S31): 145–51. doi.org/10.1016/S0968-8080(08)31393-7.

Hull, Terry (1990). 'Recent trends in sex ratios at birth in China'. *Population and Development Review* 16(1): 63–83. doi.org/10.2307/1972529.

Hunfeld, J. A. M., J. W. Wladimiroff and J. Passchier (1994). 'Pregnancy termination, perceived control, and perinatal grief'. *Psychological Reports* 74(1): 217–18. doi.org/10.2466/pr0.1994.74.1.217.

Hương Thu (2008). 'Hunt high and low to find out ovulatory date' [Ngược xuôi soi trứng]. *Phụ Nữ* [Women], 24 July.

Hvistendahl, Mara (2011). *Unnatural Selection: Choosing Boys over Girls, and the Consequences of a World Full of Men*. New York: Public Affairs.

Inchani, Lisa and Dejian Lai (2008). 'Association of educational level and child sex ratio in rural and urban India'. *Social Indicators Research* 86(1): 69–81. doi.org/10.1007/s11205-007-9098-2.

Inhorn, Marcia C. and Frank van Balen (2002). *Infertility around the Globe: New Thinking on Childlessness, Gender, and Reproductive Technologies*. Berkeley, CA: University of California Press.

Institute for Social Development Studies (2007). 'New "common sense": Family planning policy and sex ratio in Viet Nam—Findings from a qualitative study in Bac Ninh, Ha Tay and Binh Dinh'. Hà Nội: UNFPA. Online: www.unfpa.org/sites/default/files/resource-pdf/vietnam. pdf (accessed 15 May 2018).

Jing-Bao, Nie (2005). *Behind the Silence: Chinese Voices on Abortion*. Lanham, MD: Rowman & Littlefield.

Jing-Bao, Nie (2010). 'Limits of state intervention in sex-selective abortion: The case of China'. *Culture, Health & Sexuality* 12(2): 205–19. doi.org/ 10.1080/13691050903108431.

Jing-Bao, Nie (2011). 'Non-medical sex-selective abortion in China: Ethical and public policy issues in the context of 40 million missing females'. *British Medical Bulletin* 98(1): 7–20. doi.org/10.1093/bmb/ldr015.

Johansson, Annika, Le Thi Nham Tuyet, Nguyen The Lap and Kajsa Sundstrom (1996). 'Abortion in context: Women's experience in two villages in Thai Binh province, Vietnam'. *International Family Planning Perspectives* 22(3): 103–107. doi.org/10.2307/2950750.

Johansson, Annika, Nguyen The Lap, Hoang Thi, Hoa Vinod K and Bo Diwan Eriksson (1998). 'Population policy, son preference and the use of IUDs in North Vietnam'. *Reproductive Health Matters* 6(11): 66–76. doi.org/ 10.1016/S0968-8080(98)90083-0.

Johansson, Annika, Nguyen Thu Nga, Tran Quang Huy, Doan Du Dat and Kristina Holmgren (1998). 'Husbands' involvement in abortion in Vietnam'. *Studies in Family Planning* 29(4): 400–13. doi.org/10.2307/172252.

Johansson, Sten and Ola Nygren (1991). 'The missing girls of China: A new demographic account'. *Population Development Review* 17(1): 35–51. doi.org/10.2307/1972351.

Kessler, Ronald, Katherine McGonagle, Shanyang Zhao, Christopher Nelson, Michael Hughes, Suzann Eshleman, Hans-Ulrich Wittchen and Kenneth Kendler (1994). 'Lifetime and 12-month prevalence of DSM-III-R psychiatric disorders in the United States: Results from the National Comorbidity Study'. *Archives of General Psychiatry* 51(1): 8–19. doi.org/10.1001/archpsyc.1994.03950010008002.

Kleinman, Arthur and Joan Kleinman (1997). 'About suffering: Voice, genre, and moral community'. In *Social Suffering*, edited by Arthur Kleinman, Veena Das and Margaret Lock, pp. 25–46. Berkeley, CA: University of California Press.

Kumar, Anuradha, Leila Hessinia and Ellen M. H. Mitchell (2009). 'Conceptualising abortion stigma'. *Culture, Health & Sexuality* 11(6): 625–39. doi.org/10.1080/13691050902842741.

Kwon, Heonik (2006). *After the Massacre: Commemoration and Consolation in My Lai and Ha My*. Berkeley, CA: University of California Press. doi.org/10.1525/california/9780520247963.001.0001.

Kwon, Heonik (2008). *Ghosts of War in Vietnam*. Cambridge: Cambridge University Press. doi.org/10.1017/CBO9780511807596.

LaFleur, William R. (1992). *Liquid Life: Abortion and Buddhism in Japan*. Princeton, NJ: Princeton University Press.

Larsen, Ulla, Woojin Chung and Monica Das Gupta (1998). 'Fertility and son preference in Korea'. *Population Studies* 52(3): 317–25. doi.org/10.1080/0032472031000150496.

Lee, Raymond (1993). *Doing Research on Sensitive Topics*. Newbury Park, CA: Sage Publications.

Lee, Raymond and Claire Renzetti (1993). 'The problem of researching sensitive topics'. In *Doing Research on Sensitive Topics*, edited by Claire M. Renzetti and Raymond M. Lee, pp. 3–9. Newbury Park, CA: Sage Publications.

Li, Shuzhuo (2007). 'Imbalanced sex ratio at birth and comprehensive intervention in China'. Presented to 4th Asia Pacific Conference on Reproductive and Sexual Health and Rights, Hyderabad, India, 29–31 October.

Li, Yongping (1994). 'Sex ratios of infants and relations with some socioeconomic variables: Results of China's 1990 census and implications'. In *The 1990 Population Census of China—Proceedings of International Seminar*, edited by National Bureau of Statistics of China, pp. 348–65. Beijing: China Statistics Press.

Liên Châu (2017). 'Báo động về mất cân bằng giới tính ở Việt Nam' [Alarm at the imbalance in the sex ratio at birth]. *Thanh Niên Online*, 29 June. Online: thanhnien.vn/doi-song/bao-dong-mat-can-bang-gioi-tinh-o-viet-nam-850206.html (accessed 17 June 2018).

Lincoln, Yvonna and Egon Guba (1985). *Naturalistic Inquiry*. Beverly Hills, CA: Sage Publications.

Lithur, Nana Oye (2004). 'Destigmatizing abortion: Expanding community awareness of abortion as a reproductive health issue in Ghana'. *African Journal of Reproductive Health* 8(1): 70–74. doi.org/10.2307/3583308.

Lock, Margaret and Patricia Alice Kaufert (1998). *Pragmatic Women and Body Politics*. Cambridge: Cambridge University Press.

Lock, Margaret and Vinh-Kim Nguyen (2010). *An Anthropology of Biomedicine*. Malden, MA: Wiley-Blackwell.

Löfstedt, Petra, Luo Shusheng and Annika Johansson (2004). 'Abortion patterns and reported sex ratios at birth in rural Yunnan, China'. *Reproductive Health Matters* 12(24): 86–95. doi.org/10.1016/S0968-8080(04)24147-7.

Luong, Van Hy (1984). '"Brother" and "uncle": An analysis of rules, structural contradictions, and meaning in Vietnamese kinship'. *Anthropologist* 86(2) (NS): 290–315. doi.org/10.1525/aa.1984.86.2.02a00050.

Luong, Van Hy (2003). 'Wealth, power, and inequality: Global market, the state, and local socio-cultural dynamics'. In *Postwar Vietnam: Dynamics of a Transforming Society*, edited by Van Hy Luong, pp. 81–106. Singapore: Rowman & Littlefield.

Luong, Van Hy (ed.) (2003). *Postwar Vietnam: Dynamics of a Transforming Society*. Singapore: Rowman & Littlefield.

McIntyre, Marjorie, Beverly Anderson and Carol McDonald (2001). 'The intersection of relational and cultural narratives: Women's abortion experiences'. *Canadian Journal of Nursing Research* 33(3): 47–62.

Mahmood, Saba (2001). 'Feminist theory, embodiment, and the docile agent: Some reflections on the Egyptian Islamic revival'. *Cultural Anthropology* 16(2): 202–36. doi.org/10.1525/can.2001.16.2.202.

Mai Huy Bích (1993). *Đặc Điểm Gia Đình Đồng Bằng Sông Hồng [Family Features in the Red River Delta]*. Hà Nội: Culture Publishers.

Mai Liên (2008). *Bí quyết sinh con theo ý muốn [The Secret of Having a Baby of the Desired Sex]*. Hà Nội: Information Publisher.

Major, Brenda and Richard Gramzow (1999). 'Abortion as stigma: Cognitive and emotional implications of concealment'. *Journal of Personality and Social Psychology* 77(4): 735–45. doi.org/10.1037/0022-3514.77.4.735.

Malarney, Shaun Kingsley (2002). *Culture, Ritual, and Revolution in Vietnam*. Honolulu: University of Hawai'i Press.

Malarney, Shaun K. (2003). 'Return to the past? The dynamics of contemporary religious and ritual transformation'. In *Postwar Vietnam: Dynamics of a Transforming Society*, edited by Hy Van Luong, pp. 225–56. Singapore: Institute of Southeast Asian Studies.

Malinowski, Bronisław (2004 [1948]). *Magic, Science and Religion and Other Essays 1948*. Whitefish, MT: Kessinger Publishing.

Mannion, M. T. (ed.) (1994). *Post-Abortion Aftermath*. Kansas City: Sheed & Ward.

Marinac-Dabic, Danica, Cara Krulewitch and Roscoe Moore (2002). 'The safety of prenatal ultrasound exposure in human studies'. *Epidemiology* 13(3): S19–S22. doi.org/10.1097/00001648-200205001-00004.

Mies, Maria (1989). 'Self-determination: The end of a utopia?'. *Resources for Feminist Research* 18(3): 51–56.

Minh Quân (2009). *Sinh con, nuôi con cần biết [Essential Knowledge about Giving Birth and Raising a Child: Having a Baby of the Desired Sex]*. Thanh Hóa: Thanh Hóa Publishing.

Ministry of Health (MOH) (2002). *Causes of Maternal Mortality in Vietnam*. Hà Nội: Reproductive Health Department.

Ministry of Health (MOH) (2003). *National Standards and Guidelines for Reproductive Health Care Services*. Hà Nội: MOH.

Ministry of Health (MOH) (2005). *Health Statistics Yearbook*. Hà Nội: MOH.

Ministry of Health (MOH) (2006). *Health Statistics Yearbook*. Hà Nội: MOH.

Ministry of Health (MOH) (2009). *Reducing the Sex Ratio at Birth Project*. Documents of the Conference on Sex Ratio at Birth, Hà Nội, Vietnam, 8 July.

Ministry of Health (MOH) (2010). *Health Statistics Yearbook*. Hà Nội: MOH.

Mitchell, Lisa M. (2001). *Baby's First Picture: Ultrasound and the Politics of Fetal Subjects*. Toronto: University of Toronto Press. doi.org/10.3138/9781442671140.

Moskowitz, Marc (2001). *The Haunting Fetus: Abortion, Sexuality, and the Spirit World in Taiwan*. Honolulu: University of Hawai'i Press.

Mueller, Pallas and Brenda Major (1989). 'Self-blame, self-efficacy, and adjustment to abortion'. *Journal of Personality and Social Psychology* 57(6): 1059–1068. doi.org/10.1037/0022-3514.57.6.1059.

Mutharayappa, Rangamuthia, Kim Minja Choe, Fred Arnold and T. K. Roy (1997). *Son Preference and Its Effect on Fertility in India*. Mumbai: National Family Health Survey, International Institute for Population Sciences.

Naqvi, Farah (2006). *Images and Icons: Harnessing the Power of Mass Media to Promote Gender Equality and Reduce Practices of Sex Selection*. New Delhi: BBC World Service Trust.

Ngọc Bảo (2012). 'Chẩn đoán giới tính thai nhi: Bác sĩ "bắt tay" với sản phụ' [Foetal sex diagnosis: Doctors and pregnant women in collusion]. *An Ninh Thủ Đô Online*, 30 September. Online: anninhthudo.vn/doi-song/chan-doan-gioi-tinh-thai-nhi-bac-si-bat-tay-voi-san-phu/457872.antd (accessed 17 June 2018).

Ngọc Lan (2004). *Phương pháp sinh con theo ý muốn* [*How to Conceive a Baby of the Desired Sex*]. Hồ Chí Minh City: Cà Mau Publishing.

Nguyễn Đức Hinh and Nguyễn Thị Thu Hoài (2009). 'Tình Hình Phá Thai Tự Nguyện Quý I ở Bệnh Viện Phụ Sản Trung Ương Năm 2005' [First trimester termination of pregnancy in the National Hospital for Obstetrics and Gynaecology in 2005]. *Obstetrics and Gynecology Journal* 1(2009): 41–44.

Nguyễn Thị Thúy Hạnh, Nguyễn Huy Bạo and Tine Gammeltoft (2005). 'Siêu âm chuẩn đoán thai sớm tại thành thị Việt Nam: Liệu dịch vụ này có bị lạm dụng không' [Ultrasound scanning in urban Vietnam: Is it being over-used?], *Tạp chí Y học thực hành* [*Practical Medical Journal*] 530(11): 34–37.

Nguyen Vo Thu Huong (2008). *The Ironies of Freedom: Sex, Culture, and Neoliberal Governance in Vietnam*. Berkeley, CA: University of California Press.

Như Phú (2009). 'Hối Lỗi Với Thai Nhi' [Bringing remorse to the foetuses]. *Người Lao Động* (*Labour Newspaper*), 1 October. Online: nld.com.vn/200909 30114616840P0C1002/hoi-loi-voi-thai-nhi.htm (accessed 15 March 2011).

Oosterhoff, Pauline, Thu Anh Nguyen, Thuy Hanh Ngo, Ngoc Yen Pham, Pamela Wright and Annita Hardon (2008). 'Holding the line: Family responses to pregnancy and the desire for a child in the context of HIV in Vietnam'. *Culture, Health & Sexuality* 10(4): 403–16. doi.org/10.1080/13691050801915192.

Ortner, Sherry B. and Harriet Whitehead (1981). *Sexual Meanings: The Cultural Construction of Gender and Sexuality*. New York: Cambridge University Press.

Pachankis, John (2007). 'The psychological implications of concealing a stigma: A cognitive-affective-behavioral model'. *Psychological Bulletin* 133(2): 328–45. doi.org/10.1037/0033-2909.133.2.328.

Patel, Rita (1996). *The Practice of Sex Selective Abortion in India: May You be the Mother of a Hundred Sons*. Chapel Hill, NC: University Center for International Studies, University of North Carolina.

Patel, Tulsi (2007). 'Introduction: Gender relations, NRTs, and female foeticide.' In *Sex-Selective Abortion in India: Gender, Society and New Reproductive Technologies*, edited by Tulsi Patel, pp. 27–55. New Delhi: Sage Publications. doi.org/10.4135/9788178299587.

Patel, Vibhuti (2005). 'Sex selection & pre-birth elimination of girl child'. Presented to United Nations Convention to Review Status of Women at UN Headquarters, New York, 28 February – 11 March.

Patel, Vikram, Betty Kirkwood and Sulochana Pednekar (2006). 'Gender disadvantage and reproductive health risk factors for common mental disorders in women'. *Archives of General Psychiatry* 63: 404–13. doi.org/10.1001/archpsyc.63.4.404.

Peng, Peiyun (1997). *Zhongguo Jiefa Shengyu Quanshu* [*Complete Book of Family Planning in China*]. Beijing: China Population Press.

Petchesky, Rosalind Pollack (1980). 'Reproductive freedom: Beyond a woman's right to choose'. *Journal of Women in Culture and Society* 5(4): 661–85. doi.org/10.1086/493757.

Petchesky, Rosalind Pollack (ed.) (1984). *Abortion and Women's Choice: The State, Sexuality and Reproductive Freedom*. New York: Longman.

Petchesky, Rosalind Pollack (1987). 'Fetal images: The power of visual culture in the politics of reproduction'. *Feminist Studies* 13(2): 263–92. doi.org/10.2307/3177802.

Petchesky, Rosalind and Karen Judd (eds) (1990). *Negotiating Reproductive Rights: Women's Perspectives Across Countries and Cultures*. London: Zed Books.

Peterman, Jean P. (1996). *Telling their Stories: Puerto Rican Women and Abortion*. Boulder, CO: Westview Press.

Phạm Văn Bích (1999). *The Vietnamese Family in Change: The Case of the Red River Delta*. Richmond, UK: Curzon Press.

Postel-Coster, Els (1991). 'Gender, health, and population policy'. *Women and Autonomy Journal* 3(2): 4–7.

Quisenberry, J. H. and S. V. Chandiramani (1940). 'An experimental attempt to modify the sex ratio in rats and rabbits'. *Journal of Heredity* 31(12): 503–505. doi.org/10.1093/oxfordjournals.jhered.a104826.

Rapp, Rayna (2000). *Testing Women, Testing the Fetus*. New York: Routledge.

Renzetti, Claire M. and Raymond M. Lee (eds) (1993). *Researching Sensitive Topics*. Newbury Park, CA: Sage Publications.

Reproductive Health Department (2002). *Causes of Maternal Mortality in Vietnam*. Hà Nội: Ministry of Health.

Respondek, Andrea, Thanh Hao Tran and Hoang Nhu Nguyet Nguyen (2010). *Vietnam: Legal Aspects of the Health Care System*. Hồ Chí Minh City: Respondek & Fan.

Retherford, Robert D. and T. K. Roy (2002). 'Factors affecting sex-selective abortion in India'. Presented to 20th Population Census Conference, Ulaanbaatar, Mongolia, 19–21 June.

Rice, Pranee Liamputtong (ed.) (1999). *Asian Mothers, Western Birth: Pregnancy, Childbirth, and Childrearing—The Asian Experience in an English-Speaking Country*. Melbourne: Ausmed Publications.

Rorvik, David M. and Landrum B. Shettles (1980 [1971]). *Your Baby's Sex: Now You Can Choose*. New York: Bantam Books.

Royal College of Obstetricians and Gynaecologists (RCOG) (2004). *The Care of Women Requesting Induced Abortion: Evidence-Based Clinical Guideline Number 7*. London: RCOG Press.

Sakkar, N. N. (2008). 'The impact of intimate partner violence on women's reproductive health and pregnancy outcomes'. *Journal of Obstetrics & Gynaecology* 28(3): 266–71. doi.org/10.1080/01443610802042415.

Savulescu, Julian (1999). 'Sex selection: The case for'. *Medical Journal of Australia* 171(7): 373–75.

Scott, Joan W. and Debra Keates (eds) (2001). *Schools of Thought: Twenty-Five Years of Interpretive Social Science*. Princeton, NJ: Princeton University Press.

Sedlenieks, Klavs (1999). 'Towards assisted gender relations'. MPhil degree essay, Department of Social Anthropology, University of Cambridge.

Segen, J. C. (2002). *Concise Dictionary of Modern Medicine*. New York: McGraw-Hill.

Sen, Amartya (1990). 'More than 100 million women are missing'. *New York Review of Books* 37(20): 61–66.

Shils, Edward A. and Edward A. Finch (eds and trans) (1949). *Max Weber on the Methodology of the Social Sciences*. Glencoe, IL: Free Press.

Shiva, Vandana (1988). *Staying Alive: Women, Ecology and Survival in India*. New Delhi: Kali for Women.

Singh, Urmila (2010). 'Speech by Ms Urmila Singh, UNFPA Deputy Representative on behalf of the United Nations Country Team'. World Population Day 2010 Press Conference, United Nations Vietnam, 2 July. Online: www.un.org.vn/en/unfpa-speeches/1413-speech-by-by-ms-urmila-singh-unfpa-deputy-representative-on-behalf-of-the-united-nations-country-team.html (accessed 17 June 2018).

Smith, Gene M., Phillip G. Stubblefield, Linda Chirchirillo and M. J. McCarthy (1979). 'Pain of first-trimester abortion: Its quantification and relations with other variables'. *American Journal of Obstetrics and Gynecology* 133(5): 489–98. doi.org/10.1016/0002-9378(79)90282-5.

Stanworth, Michelle (1987). 'Reproductive technologies and the deconstruction of motherhood'. In *Reproductive Technologies: Gender, Motherhood, and Medicine*, edited by Michelle Stanworth, pp. 10–35. Minneapolis: University of Minnesota Press.

Stanworth, Michelle (ed.) (1987). *Reproductive Technologies: Gender, Motherhood, and Medicine*. Minneapolis: University of Minnesota Press.

Sureau, Claude (1999). 'Gender selection: A crime against humanity or the exercise of a fundamental right?'. *Human Reproduction* 14(4): 867–68. doi.org/10.1093/humrep/14.4.867.

Taft, Angela J. and Lyndsey F. Watson (2007). 'Termination of pregnancy: Associations with partner violence and other factors in a national cohort of young Australian women'. *Australian and New Zealand Journal of Public Health* 31(2): 135–42. doi.org/10.1111/j.1753-6405.2007.00031.x.

Taylor, Charles (2001). 'Modernity and identity'. In *Schools of Thought: Twenty-Five Years of Interpretive Social Science*, edited by Joan W. Scott and Debra Keates, pp. 139–53. Princeton, NJ: Princeton University Press.

Taylor, Philip (ed.) (2004). *Social Inequality in Vietnam and the Challenges to Reform*. Singapore: Institute of Southeast Asian Studies.

Taylor, Philip (2007). 'Modernity and re-enchantment in post-revolutionary Vietnam'. In *Modernity and Re-Enchantment: Religion in Post-Revolutionary Vietnam*, edited by Philip Taylor, pp. 1–56. Singapore: Institute of Southeast Asian Studies.

Teichman, Yona, Shlomo Shenhar and Shmuel Segal (1993). 'Emotional distress in Israeli women before and after abortion'. *American Journal of Orthopsychiatry* 63(2): 277–88. doi.org/10.1037/h0079435.

T. H. (2017). 'Chênh lệch giới tính khi sinh tiếp tục gia tăng' [The sex ratio at birth is increasing]. *Đại Đoàn Kết Online*, 27 June. Online: daidoanket.vn/suc-khoe/chenh-lech-gioi-tinh-khi-sinh-tiep-tuc-gia-tang-tintuc370845 (accessed 17 June 2018).

Thiên Nga and Nguyễn Cẩm (2008). 'Xác định giới tính thai nhi: Cấm vẫn cứ làm' [Sex determination: Prohibited but still practised]. *Family Online*, October. Online: afamily.vn/xac-dinh-gioi-tinh-thai-nhi-cam-cu-cam-lam-van-lam-20090106024849734.chn (accessed 17 June 2018).

Thompson, Jennifer Merrill (2004). *Chasing the Gender Dream*. Imperial Beach, CA: Aventine Press.

Thu Mai (2010). 'Đại Lễ Cầu Siêu Cho 8000 Vong Nhi' [A great ceremony for 8,000 fetal souls]. *VTV VN*. Online: vtv.vn/article/get/dai-le-cau-sieu-cho-8000-vong-nhi-----7533489a23.html (accessed 20 April 2011).

Thủy Hà (2017). 'Vi phạm về lựa chọn giới tính sẽ xử lý theo pháp luật' [Violating regulations on sex selection will be dealt with by the law]. *Ấp bắc*, 9 November. Online: baoapbac.vn/suc-khoe-y-te/201711/lua-chon-gioi-tinh-thai-nhi-la-vi-pham-phap-luat-766059/ (accessed 17 June 2018).

Tipping, Gill, Viet Dung Truong, Thanh Tam Nguyen and Malcolm Segall (1994). *Quality of public health services and household health care decisions in rural communes of Vietnam*. Research Report No. 27. Brighton, UK: Institute of Development Studies.

Törnbom, Marie and Anders Moller (1999). 'Repeat abortion: A qualitative study'. *Journal of Psychosomatic Obstetrics & Gynaecology* 20(1): 21–30. doi.org/10.3109/01674829909075573.

Tran, Ha (1999). 'Antenatal and postnatal maternity care for Vietnamese women'. In *Asian Mothers, Western Birth: Pregnancy, Childbirth, and Childrearing—The Asian Experience in an English-Speaking Country*, edited by Pranee Liamputtong Rice, pp. 61–76. Melbourne: Ausmed Publications.

Trần Minh Hằng (2005). 'Ultrasound scanning for fetal malformation in Hanoi Obstetrics and Gynecology Hospital, Vietnam: Women's reproductive decision-making'. Masters thesis, University of Copenhagen, Denmark.

Trịnh Trung Hòa (2008). 'Con trai ai cũng khát?' [Having a son: Everyone's "thirst"?]. *Gia đình và Xã hội (Family and Society)*, 5 May.

Trybulski, JoAnn (2005). 'The long-term phenomena of women's post-abortion experiences'. *Western Journal of Nursing Research* 27(5): 559–76. doi.org/10.1177/0193945905275936.

Turner, Victor (1995 [1969]). *The Ritual Process: Structure and Anti-Structure*. Chicago: Aldine.

Tylor, Edward Burnett (1971). *Primitive Culture: Researches into the Development of Mythology, Philosophy, Religion, Art, and Custom*. London: John Murray.

Underwood, Meredith (1999). 'Strategies of survival: Women, abortion, and popular religion in contemporary Japan'. *Journal of American Academic Religion* 67(4): 739–68. doi.org/10.1093/jaarel/67.4.739.

United Nations (UN) (1995). Beijing Platform for Action 1995, Fourth World Conference on Women, United Nations, Beijing.

United Nations (UN) (2013). 'World population policies 2013'. *Report of the Population Division*. New York: UN.

United Nations Population Fund (UNFPA) (1994). *Programme of Action Adopted at the International Conference on Population and Development, 5–13 September 1994*. New York: UNFPA.

United Nations Population Fund (UNFPA) (2004). *Saving Mothers' Lives: The Challenge Continues*. New York: UNFPA.

United Nations Population Fund (UNFPA) (2005). *Viet Nam's Population Growth: What Does the Data Tell Us?* Hà Nội: UNFPA.

United Nations Population Fund (UNFPA) (2006). *Viet Nam's Population Growth: What the Latest Data Tell Us*. Hà Nội: UNFPA.

United Nations Population Fund (UNFPA) (2007). *Population Growth in Viet Nam: What Does the Data from 2006 Tell Us?* Hà Nội: UNFPA.

United Nations Population Fund (UNFPA) (2009a). *Recent Change in the Sex Ratio at Birth in Viet Nam: A Review of Evidence*. Hà Nội: UNFPA.

United Nations Population Fund (UNFPA) (2009b). *UNFPA Guidance Note on Prenatal Sex Selection*. Hà Nội: UNFPA.

United Nations Population Fund (UNFPA) (2010). *Sex Ratio at Birth Imbalances in Viet Nam: Evidence from the 2009 Census*. Hà Nội: UNFPA.

United Nations Population Fund (UNFPA) (2012). *Sex Imbalances at Birth: Trends, Differentials and Policy Implications*. Bangkok: UNFPA.

United Nations Population Fund (UNFPA) (2015). *Sex Ratio at Birth in Viet Nam: New Evidence from the Intercensal Population and Housing Survey in 2014*. Hà Nội: UNFPA.

van Balen, Frank and Marcia C. Inhorn (2003). 'Son preference, sex selection, and the "new" new reproductive technologies'. *International Health Services Journal* 33(2): 235–352. doi.org/10.2190/PP5X-V039-3QGK-YQJB.

Van-Gennep, Arnold (1960). *Rites of Passage*, translated by Monica B. Vizedom and Gabrielle L. Caffee. London: Routledge & Kegan Paul.

van Praag, Bernard, Paul Frijtersvan and Ada Ferrer-i-Carbonell (2003). 'The anatomy of subjective well-being'. *Journal of Economic Behaviour and Organization* 51(1): 29–49. doi.org/10.1016/S0167-2681(02)00140-3.

Visaria, Leela (2007). 'Deficit of girls in India: Can it be attributed to female selective abortion?'. In *Sex-Selective Abortion in India: Gender, Society and New Reproductive Technologies*, edited by Tulsi Patel, pp. 61–79. New Delhi: Sage Publications. doi.org/10.4135/9788178299587.n2.

VTC News (2009). 'Rút giấy phép hành nghề nếu bác sĩ để lộ giới tính thai nhi' [Work permits will be revoked if doctors perform sex determinations without permission]. *Nông Nghiệp Việt Nam Online*, 9 July. Online: https://m.nongnghiep.vn/rut-giay-hanh-nghe-voi-bs-de-lo-gioi-tinh-thai-nhi-post35968.html (accessed 17 June 2018).

Vũ Quý Nhân (1992). 'Family planning program in Vietnam'. *Vietnam Social Sciences* 39: 3–20.

Vương Xuân Tình (1994). 'The need for sons: Problems and solutions'. *Social Sciences* 1(39): 25–28.

Warren, Mary Anne (1985). *Gendercide: The Implications of Sex-Selection*. Totowa, NJ: Rowman & Allanheld.

Wasielewski, Patricia L. (1992). 'Post-abortion syndrome: Emotional battles over interaction and ideology'. *Humboldt Journal of Social Relations* 18(2): 101–29.

Wei Chen (2007). 'Induced abortion and its demographic consequences'. In *Transition and Challenge: China's Population at the Beginning of the 21st Century*, edited by Zhongwei Zhao and Fei Guo, pp. 87–107. New York: Oxford University Press. doi.org/10.1093/acprof:oso/9780199299294.003.0006.

Weinberg, C. R., D. D. Baird and A. J. Wilcox (1995). 'Endocrinology: The sex of the baby may be related to the length of the follicular phase in the conception cycle'. *Human Reproduction* 10(2): 304–307. doi.org/10.1093/oxfordjournals.humrep.a135932.

Werner, Jayne Susan (2002). 'Gender, household, and state: Renovation as social process in Vietnam'. In *Gender, Household, State: Đổi Mới in Vietnam*, edited by Jayne Susan Werner and Danièle Bélanger, pp. 29–47. Ithaca, NY: Cornell Southeast Asia Program Publications.

Werner, Jayne Susan and Danièle Bélanger (eds) (2002). *Gender, Household, State: Đổi Mới in Vietnam*. Ithaca, NY: Cornell Southeast Asia Program Publications.

Werner, Jayne Susan and Danièle Bélanger (2002). 'Introduction: Gender and Vietnam studies'. In *Gender, Household, State: Đổi Mới in Vietnam*, edited by Jayne Susan Wener and Danièle Bélanger, pp. 1–28. Ithaca, NY: Cornell Southeast Asia Program Publications.

Whittaker, Andrea (2002). 'Eliciting qualitative information about induced abortion: Lessons from north-east Thailand'. *Health Care for Women International* 23(6–7): 631–41.

Whittaker, Andrea (2004). *Abortion, Sin and the State in Thailand*. New York: Routledge Curzon. doi.org/10.4324/9780203429440.

Whittaker, Andrea (ed.) (2010). *Abortion in Asia: Local Dilemmas, Global Politics*. New York: Berghahn Books.

Williamson, Nancy E. (1976). *Sons or Daughters: A Cross-Cultural Survey of Parental Preferences*. Beverly Hills, CA: Sage Publications.

Woodcock, Scott (2011). 'Abortion counselling and the informed consent dilemma'. *Bioethics (Online)* 25(9): 495–504. doi.org/10.1111/j.1467-8519.2009.01798.x.

World Health Organization (WHO) (1999). *Abortion in Vietnam: An Assessment of Policy, Program and Research Issues*. Geneva: WHO.

World Health Organization (WHO) (2002). *Assessment of Trade in Health Services and GATS: Background Note for WHO International Consultation*. Geneva: WHO.

World Health Organization (WHO) (2003a). *Safe Abortion: Technical and Policy Guidance for Health Systems*. Geneva: WHO.

World Health Organization (WHO) (2003b). *Unsafe Abortion: Global and Regional Estimates of the Incidence of Unsafe Abortion and Associated Mortality in 2003*. Fifth edition. Geneva: WHO.

World Health Organization (WHO) (2011). *Preventing Gender-Biased Sex Selection*. Geneva: WHO.

World Health Organization (WHO) in Vietnam (2009). *Health Financing*. Hà Nội: WHO Representative Office in Vietnam.

Yoon, Yong J. (2006). 'Gender imbalance: The male/female sex ratio determination'. *Journal of Bioeconomics* 8(3): 253–68. doi.org/10.1007/s10818-006-9006-x.

Zabin, Laurie Schwab, Marilyn B. Hirsch and Mark Emerson (1989). 'When urban adolescents choose abortion: Effects on education, psychological status and subsequent pregnancy'. *Family Planning Perspectives* 21(6): 248–55. doi.org/10.2307/2135377.

Zapka, Jane G., Stephenie Lemon, Laura E. Peterson, Heather Palmer and Marlene B. Goldman (2001). 'The silent consumer: Women's reports and ratings of abortion services'. *Medical Care* 39(1): 50–60. doi.org/10.1097/00005650-200101000-00007.

Zhao, Zhongwei and Fei Guo (eds) (2007). *Transition and Challenge: China's Population at the Beginning of the 21st Century*. New York: Oxford University Press. doi.org/10.1093/acprof:oso/9780199299294.001.0001.

Zhu, Chuzhu, Shuzhou Li, Changrong Qiu, Hiu Ping and Jin Anrong (1997). *The Dual Effects of the Family Planning Programme on Chinese Women*. Bilingual Chinese and English version. Xi'an: Xi'an Jiaotong University Press.

www.ingramcontent.com/pod-product-compliance
Lightning Source LLC
Chambersburg PA
CBHW050810270326
41926CB00040B/4640